# QUIET
# NO MORE

# QUIET NO MORE

## NEW POLITICAL ACTIVISM IN CANADA AND AROUND THE GLOBE

## JOEL D. HARDEN

JAMES LORIMER & COMPANY LTD., PUBLISHERS
TORONTO

James Lorimer & Company Ltd., Publishers acknowledges the support of the Ontario Arts Council. We acknowledge the financial support of the Government of Canada through the Canada Book Fund for our publishing activities. We acknowledge the support of the Canada Council for the Arts which last year invested $24.3 million in writing and publishing throughout Canada. We acknowledge the Government of Ontario through the Ontario Media Development Corporation's Ontario Book Initiative.

Cover design: Tyler Cleroux
Cover image: Ben Powless

Library and Archives Canada Cataloguing in Publication

Harden, Joel D., author
    Quiet no more : new political activism in Canada and around the globe / Joel D. Harden.

Includes bibliographical references and index.
Issued also in electronic format.
ISBN 978-1-4594-0507-3 (pbk.).—ISBN 978-1-4594-0508-0 (epub)

    1. Protest movements--Canada.  2. Protest movements.
3. Political participation--Canada.  4. Political participation.
5. Political activists--Canada.  6. Political activists.  I. Title.

JC328.3.H37 2013   322.40971   C2013-904167-2   C2013-904168-0

James Lorimer & Company Ltd., Publishers
317 Adelaide Street West, Suite 1002
Toronto, ON, Canada
M5V 1P9
www.lorimer.ca

Printed and bound in Canada.

*To Clarita, who helped me climb this mountain*
*To Erma Davison, my grandmother and writing muse*
*To Adele and Emery, whose generation inherits*
*our successes, mistakes, and uncertain future*

# CONTENTS

# PREFACE:

# WHY WRITE THIS BOOK?

*Writing a book is a long, exhaustive struggle, like a long bout of some painful illness. One would never undertake such a thing if one were not driven by some demon whom one can neither resist nor understand.*

*For all one knows that demon is simply the same instinct that makes a baby squall for attention. And yet it is also true that one can write nothing readable unless one constantly struggles to efface one's own personality. Good prose is like a windowpane. I cannot say with certainty which of my motives are the strongest, but I know which of them deserve to be followed.*

*And looking back through my work, I see that it is invariably where I lacked a POLITICAL purpose that I wrote lifeless books and was betrayed into purple passages, sentences without meaning, decorative adjectives and humbug generally.*

*— George Orwell*[1]

*You have a right to express what you see, what you feel, and what you think. To be bold. To be as bold with your vision as you can possibly be. Our salvation, to the extent that we have one, will come out of people realizing the crisis of our species and of the planet and offering their deepest dream of what's possible.*

— *Alice Walker*[2]

I wrote this book to make sense of my experience as an activist, both in theoretical and practical terms. To a great extent, that experience has been driven by sentiments expressed in the above quotations, both of which come from writers I deeply respect. At its core, this book is about the recognition of injustice, the curiosity to imagine alternatives, and the desire to seek change. At a formative moment in my education, that is the path I chose: I realized something was wrong with the world and decided my life must be devoted to changing it. That realization inspired me, haunted me, nurtured me, and willed me through challenging times. Nevertheless, once I understood the power of grassroots activism, of campaigns based on the ideas, talents, and dreams of everyday people, I was hooked; I needed to do more, know more, and experience more. As my intellectual capacities developed, that understanding morphed into a desire to write about what I've seen, heard, and done first-hand. What follows is a brief sense of that journey, and why it motivated me to write this book. I hope it gives readers a better sense of where I'm coming from, and why talking about activism is as important as doing it first-hand.

Since my first days in Canada's student movement, I've learned countless lessons about movement-building, conflict, and effective activism. It was during this early period, in 1995, that I first appreciated the power of grassroots activism when a conservative government in Ontario cut social assistance benefits (or "welfare") for the poor by 21.6 per cent. I remember being in graduate school and seething at the poor-bashing on regular display in the mainstream media, which shrieked about "welfare cheats," among other pejoratives.

My formative years came from a family headed by a single mother that relied on social assistance at certain moments to survive. The thought that our family, or any low-income family, for that matter, was a social burden infuriated me. When I was very young, after a tough divorce, my family was down on its luck and needed social supports to get back on track (which, thankfully for us, did happen). But the idea that society would be better off with fewer groceries on our shelves was appalling, as was the notion that we reaped generous benefits afforded by hard-done "taxpayers." I snapped, asked a friend to accompany me to Ontario's provincial legislature, and waited for an opportune moment to catcall Ontario Premier Mike Harris from the visitor's gallery. When I did it (and was arrested for it), I was shocked at the degree of support that came. After being detained for a short while, I walked out to a battery of cameras and reporters who asked why I had disrupted the premier. "I had no choice," was my answer, "when this premier disrupts the lives of poor families. Beating up on the poor has become a sport lately, and I've frankly had enough of it."

Three years later, I found myself in tense conversations with fellow student activists, and once again appreciated the power of grassroots activism. By 1998, I had immersed myself in campus organizing and earned an elected position in the Canadian Federation of Students. But when planning began for our yearly rally against tuition fee increases, I was surprised at the divergence of views. Some advocated a rally, as usual, outside Ontario's legislature, featuring speeches from politicians about visions for post-secondary education. Others (like me) wanted to put the emphasis elsewhere, and hold our Toronto rally at Bay and King Streets, right in the heart of Canada's financial district. Politicians, we insisted, were merely distractions from a larger agenda — it was the big banks, after all, that benefited from a growing mountain of student debt.

Our arguments prevailed, and the January 28, 1998 rally was a watershed moment in Canada's activist scene. Thousands attended, while hundreds later occupied the offices of the Toronto-Dominion Bank overnight to protest the rising costs of post-secondary education. Passers-by brought us food and slapped us with high-fives. Even media coverage was generally positive. As Occupy Wall Street did in 2011, we were sticking it to Canada's powerful, and most were pleased to see it happen.

Three years later, after going back to finish my graduate studies in political science, I was once again embroiled in a major conflict as a university worker, and reminded of the power of grassroots activism. York University's negotiators, under significant pressure from the government of Ontario, served notice that they wanted "tuition indexation," among other things, taken out of my union's collective agreement. That may seem like a technical, insignificant demand, yet it was anything but — tuition indexation (which by 2001 only existed for graduate students at York) meant our employer could not raise tuition fees to take back wage increases. Instead, when tuition increased, as it did every year, our wages would be indexed to the higher cost, and we therefore lost no ground. Our employer didn't like that, and appealed to undergrads and others to side with it.

Given our activism, however, this strategy backfired. My colleagues worked hard to mobilize union members and communicate to undergrads and the wider campus community that York management was going to make the cost of graduate school unaffordable. We documented the rise in executive salaries (York's president at the time had a personal staff of five, complete with a luxury car and driver), and asked whether "cupboard is bare" claims could be believed. We held mass meetings that propelled an eventual strike lasting seventy-eight days through the winter and drew on the creativity, passion, and talent of research assistants, teaching assistants, and contract faculty (who by then did 40 per cent of teaching on campus). We faced a hostile mainstream media, university officials who engaged in petty attacks, and even dissension from our own ranks as the strike wore on. But despite all that, the power of our union changed the context of university life. Until then, graduate school was a largely atomizing experience where we separately toiled to please our academic masters. During the strike, we came together, supported each other, and ultimately took the tuition indexation clawback (and other things) off the table. We won a decent settlement at a time when many unions stood still. I was never more proud to be a union member, a student of political science, and a believer in people-driven politics.

I spent several years after that engaged in movements for peace and global justice, and managed, thankfully, to finish my academic work in these very areas. As I was wrapping up my dissertation, some Toronto activists were inspired to help conscientious objectors (or "war resisters") in the US military who had fled to Canada to avoid service in the Iraq or Afghanistan wars. Soon a movement emerged, known as the War Resisters Support Campaign (WRSC), to do precisely this, built largely on the experience of war resisters during the Vietnam era. In 2005, I became a WRSC activist in the Ottawa-Gatineau region where my partner and I had moved to pursue new jobs, and this deepened my understanding about activism in our highly militaristic era. This campaign achieved several gains, not the least of which was some reprieve for soldiers who would otherwise be subject to flawed military tribunals. On a more profound level, however, our campaign contributed to policy shifts in the US military itself, a remarkable outcome for a grassroots effort with few resources. I will cite the experience of two war resisters in Ottawa to support this point.

The first, James Burmeister, used our campaign to challenge atrocities being committed by sniper teams he witnessed in downtown Baghdad during the initial years of the Iraq War. These teams, according to Burmeister, placed street-level cameras on tripods with signs reading "Property of the US Government" in English and Arabic. When civilians approached these cameras, snipers were ordered to open fire, a practice

Burmeister was told would meet "kill targets" established by Central Command. After arriving in Ottawa in 2005, Burmeister drew public attention to the role of "small kill teams." Within weeks, former military comrades informed Burmeister that the "small kill teams" had been disbanded in his unit. And so, with a modest grassroots effort, the streets of Baghdad were made safer for war-torn Iraqis.

Bethany Smith, another soldier we helped, challenged the persecution and harassment of gay/lesbian/bisexual/transgendered (GLBT) soldiers in the US military. Smith, like many GLBT soldiers, endured constant abuse in basic training when her sexual orientation became known. She faced months of threats, assaults, and taunts from fellow soldiers and higher-ranking officials. Smith knew her base (Fort Campbell, Kentucky) had a reputation for anti-gay brutality. In 1999, a gay soldier named Barry Winchell had been beaten to death in his own bunk. Following a death threat posted in her dorm room, Smith fled Fort Campbell with another soldier. She sought refugee status in Ottawa and spoke out against the US military's "Don't ask, don't tell" policy. Sources from inside the US military have said this contributed to pressure that encouraged the review of "Don't ask, don't tell" under the Obama administration, which led to a partial repeal of the policy. Like Burmeister's case, Smith's also confirmed the value of community organizing and reinforced my own interest in grassroots activism.

The experiences I describe in this preface are the backdrop to what follows, and my primary motivation for writing this book. They have led me to believe in the enduring value of bottom-up change, where grassroots activists are quiet no more: The most effective campaigns allow people to take politics into their own hands and shape it themselves. That is a theme I saw in the other cases documented here, and it has a profound resonance. I invite you to read on, debate what you read, and apply it to your own work as an activist or concerned citizen.

# INTRODUCTION:

## THE LEFT, NEOLIBERALISM, AND GRASSROOTS ACTIVISM

*So what is to be done? Voting for someone different at the next election seems a pathetically inadequate response — and it is. In Manhattan's Zucotti Park, where the Occupy Wall Street protesters have been centred, few have demanded different politicians or new laws.*

*Instead, the protesters have shown, by the nature of their movement, a new way: debates and decisions that include everyone, a culture of collaboration and sharing, and a belief that there are many changes, not one, necessary to make a better world. No one claims the right to lead this movement: There are many voices that want to be heard.*

*But although Occupy Wall Street is a sharp cry of anger echoed by many across the U.S., and indeed more widely around the world, the protest alone will not be enough. What is needed instead is a much more fundamental, wholly new method of doing things.*

*No longer should we look for change to emerge from untrusted politicians, arguing in distant chambers. As turkeys will not vote for Thanksgiving and Christmas, these institutions will not reform themselves.*

*We have to accept the painful reality that we can no longer rely on government policy to solve our most deep-seated and intractable problems, from climate change to social alienation. Instead, we need to look to ourselves for the necessary action.*

*— Carne Ross, former senior British Diplomat who resigned before the 2003 Iraq War*[1]

This book is about emerging forms of progressive, social-justice-inspired activism and its impact on the world around us. It is, as Carne Ross has written, about the activist "method of doing things" I described from my own experience in this book's preface. It is about emerging forms of activism that reject the fend-for-yourself doctrine of neoliberalism,[2] the dominant philosophy of global capitalism, and seek grassroots campaigns for social change. New political movements like Occupy Wall Street, Idle No More, and the Arab Spring illustrate this trend; in all of these examples, activists are defying the top-down trend common to progressive campaigning in earlier eras. They are not waiting for charismatic leaders to point the way forward, or detailed manifestos debating the finer points of activist ideologies. They are *actors* in the fight for a better world, and expect to use their own thoughts, voices, and hands. They are *thinkers* who see beyond the assumptions of mainstream politics and the limited horizons of progressive groups and thinkers. They are *organizers* who make strategic choices, build institutions, and create opportunities for activist projects. They are no one's stage army, awaiting moments to be summoned and later dismissed. They are outspoken, outlandish, and pushing the margins of received wisdom. They are, to paraphrase today's bold Aboriginal warriors, quiet no more.

My shorthand for this phenomenon is "grassroots activism," and it is something changing societies the world over. As I explain in this book, activists espousing bottom-up campaigns have challenged our neoliberal era, suggesting pathways to a more co-operative and sustainable future. Their impact has been felt in established political institutions — like governments, political parties, and even many social justice groups — where experts or top officials make most decisions. While these institutions remain dominant in our world, they are increasingly less attractive to those seeking to change it.

But why, some might say, should we care? Why does it matter if grassroots activism shifts larger progressive groups, or nudges the political establishment? How is that novel or newsworthy? The simple response is that grassroots movements, of all progressive forces, *are* having an impact on the public conversation on a host of subjects, evoking scorn or praise, and bringing about change in the order of things. Skeptics should consider recent history. Why would Mitt Romney, a voice for the 1 per cent if there ever was one, use Occupy Wall Street rhetoric in a bid for the US presidency? How have Quebec students, Chicago teachers, or Greek citizens blunted the impact of austerity agendas? How have climate justice activists stalled the pipeline dreams of the world's most profitable corporations? How did Syriza, a Greek political party including avowed revolutionaries, nearly form a minority government in 2012? Why have independent news programs like *Democracy Now!* gained vast audiences and influenced the direction of the mainstream media? How did peoples' movements topple decades-old dictatorships in the Arab world?

These are glimpses into powerful, compelling forms of grassroots activism that have made gains in tough times, often in the face of significant pressure. They emerge from the severity of the challenges facing our world and the impatience of those who want to change it. This book is about them and for them, and it seeks a conversation with them and their supporters. It is also for those wanting to appreciate what's special about grassroots activism, and why it is, has been, and will continue to be a important part of modern democracies. It is written by a grassroots activist, comes from appreciation of grassroots principles, and is premised on the theme of quiet no more: that people of conscience must speak out, take democracy back from its elite-worn mould, and change it from the bottom up.

Unfortunately, the existing literature on activism doesn't offer much to grasp today's grassroots movements. Academic studies — through the canon of Social Movement Theory and related work[3] — offer a sea of terminology to categorize forms of activism, discussing "opportunity structures," "identity claims" at issue, or "resources" and "constraints" of participants. Most popular books on activism avoid or limit discussion of philosophy or history, and are therefore themselves limited by the details of the subject at hand. Such works have created partial insights but no broader perspective to explain why grassroots activism is popular today, what it holds in common with its historical predecessors, and what its prospects for success are. This book aims to fill this gap in the literature and invite debate about how today's grassroots movements are making their mark. In doing so, it proposes a new approach that appreciates key features of grassroots activism: its place (where it happens), its ideas (why it happens), and its organization (how it happens).

Of course, some might dismiss this book as fashionable or of little use. Despite notable achievements, grassroots activism today is quickly contained, appearing in a flash only to be marginalized later by more powerful forces. This holds true for peoples' movements in the Middle East, students or teachers facing intransigent governments, or protesters occupying city parks. In this midst of such limitations, activists are posing tough questions, many of which get to the heart of issues raised in this book. What sustains and nurtures grassroots activism? Can large progressive groups work constructively with grassroots movements and avoid dominating (or absorbing) them? When does grassroots activism risk creating its own "tyranny of the structureless," where strong personalities foster elitism despite a commitment to direct democracy? And, most importantly, given their rise and fall, are grassroots movements ultimately effective? And if they are, how can this form of activism bring lasting results?

To answer these questions, one needs a ground-level appreciation of grassroots movements, and a historical sense of their significance — both of which I offer here. Aided by first-hand access to grassroots movements and activists, I examine the influence of bottom-up politics in political parties, unions, and social movements. In all these places, grassroots activists have espoused ideas, built institutions, mobilized supporters, and targeted adversaries in a long-running tradition of seekers after direct democracy. Their efforts have shifted the political establishment and enlivened work in established progressive groups. In doing so, they also offer clues about how decades of neoliberal dominance in our politics and culture can be changed. These are the useful, meaningful, and subversive contributions I review here.

## CHAPTER OUTLINE

This book is divided into six chapters. Following this introduction, chapter one surveys grassroots activism largely within the territorial boundaries of Mexico, Canada, and the United States (what Aboriginal activists call "Turtle Island"). Chapter two analyzes the role of grassroots movements in recent years and their common role as cogs that turn larger wheels (e.g., large progressive groups and institutions of mainstream politics). To this end, I review a "powershift" in green activism, the re-emergence of Aboriginal militancy through the Idle No More movement, and grassroots campaigns to assist long-suffering Palestinians. Chapter three then studies the impact of grassroots activism in trade unions. Following a review of the debate on the "crisis" in working class politics, I bring in examples to illustrate how grassroots movements have emerged in recent years, most notably where workplace battles have championed community organizing and union-member-driven campaigns. These, I think, reveal the potential for grassroots activism in unions today; they also recall earlier union traditions and suggest the necessity to rebuild rank and file networks to shift the fortunes of organized labour. Chapter four surveys the relationship between progressive political parties and grassroots activism; a case is made that a grassroots influence in electoral politics is emerging, but one vulnerable to disruption by larger forces. An important choice that will bear upon the fortunes of each of the instances I discuss is the emphasis Left parties place on movement-inspired practices.

Chapter five then identifies the strengths and weakness of the existing literature on progressive activism, and proposes a new approach that grasps the place, ideas, and organization of progressive grassroots activism. My intent, unlike much "objective" social science, is to offer "movement-relevant" theory that acknowledges the unique contributions of activists and others who are seeking to understand them. Chapter six provides this book with the conclusion that brings together the insights of previous chapters. Above all, I argue that activists are faced with two important tasks: first, to embrace the anti-systemic ideas of recent grassroots activism; and second, to champion the bottom-up forms of political organization that have characterized dissent in recent years. In the process, activists can avoid alliances with projects involving "lesser evils" and expand on the exciting forms of activism documented in this book. There are, as I explain, historical lessons that offer clues about how grassroots activism can be nurtured and broadened in the places, ideas, and organizations of today's effective protest movements. The key dilemma, and it is one that is open to interpretation, is whether grassroots activism will remain possible in the years and decades ahead. For the sake of the planet and our children's future, I hold out hope, despite many dire warnings, that it will.

# 1
# GRASSROOTS ACTIVISM:
## A RECENT HISTORY

*We learned a long time ago that we should never subject ourselves to the schedules of the powerful. We had to follow our own calendar, and impose it on those above.*

*— EZLN Subcomandante Marcos*[1]

To readers, this will seem odd — but there is an actual day I remember grasping the power of grassroots activism. The day was January 1, 1994, and an armed uprising happened in San Cristóbal de las Casas, a town in the Chiapas region of Mexico. The uprising was facilitated by the Zapatista National Liberation Army ("Zapatistas", "Zapatismo", or "EZLN" for short), and it challenged, among several things, the introduction of the North American Free Trade Agreement (NAFTA). NAFTA's trade specialists expected a coronation of neoliberal principles in the mainstream media, but the message from Chiapas was entirely different.

At the time, I was a third-year university student with little appreciation of protest as a form of political expression. Like most people, I was accustomed to elected leaders dominating political conversations; politics as I understood it was captured in struggles between Brian Mulroney and Elijah Harper, Margaret Thatcher and Tony Benn, or George H.W. Bush and Bill Clinton. The Zapatistas, for me, heralded something quite different — this was a peoples' movement that challenged neoliberal economic assumptions most politicians assumed were immutable. They held out indigenous traditions against the incursions of Western corporations, arguing instead for forms of local democracy and sovereign control over natural resources. I was awestruck by their audacious spirit, and would remain glued to news documenting this upstart political force. The EZLN, as I would understand in the two decades that followed, would inspire a resurgence in grassroots activism and challenge the ideological dominance of neoliberalism. In this chapter I review those decades, and discuss how they shaped the context for emerging protest movements.

## ¡YA BASTA!: ZAPATISMO ANNOUNCES A GRASSROOTS REVOLUTION

As the EZLN made their mark in local and global politics, their immediate relevance to progressives worldwide was increasingly clear. In April 2004, I attended an activist "potluck/fundraiser" at Queen's University (in Kingston, Ontario), the proceeds of which were to finance a solidarity convoy to Chiapas (travelling, naturally, in an old VW camper van). This local example was hardly unique — the Zapatista rebellion touched off a wave of global solidarity campaigns in support of the over thirty indigenous groups involved. At issue was elimination of Article 27 from the Mexican Constitution, legislation that dealt with the right of indigenous and peasant groups to petition for disused land (held either privately or through the state). Article 27 was first won through the tumultuous Mexican Revolution of 1910–19, where a mass movement emerged calling for *Tierra y Libertad* (Land and Liberty). The specialists behind the NAFTA process made it clear that Article 27 was incompatible with a neoliberal framework of continental trade. Curiously enough, the decision to forge ahead with repealing Article 27 set the context for a re-emergence of grassroots politics worldwide.

The defiant cry of *¡Ya Basta!* (Enough!) was the response to NAFTA by the Zapatistas, who regarded the repeal of Article 27 as the last straw in over five hundred years of colonial repression. Despite living in one of the most resource-rich areas in all of Mexico, the people of Chiapas were (and remain) beset by grinding poverty. Chiapas produces (among other things) over half of Mexico's hydroelectricity, but 39 per cent of the population (at the time of the 1994 uprising) earned less than the minimum wage, and over 50 per cent lived in homes without running water. The Zapatistas' decision to oppose NAFTA came first from these terrible lived realities, but the effect of their courage made an impact well beyond Mexico's borders.

Often hailed as the first "online revolution," the Zapatista movement used the Internet repeatedly to communicate its messages and issue appeals for support. The Zapatistas' unique, poetic style was often expressed through the words of Subcomandante Marcos — a spokesperson many likened to a "one-man Web." Naomi Klein, an outspoken supporter of Zapatismo, describes the lasting impact of these untraditional methods:

> *For years I have watched the Zapatistas' ideas spread though*
> *activist circles, passed along second- and third-hand: a*
> *phrase, a way to run a meeting, a metaphor that twists your*
> *brain around. Unlike classic revolutionaries who preach*
> *through bullhorns and from pulpits, Marcos has spread the*
> *Zapatista word through riddles and long, pregnant silences.*
> *Revolutionaries who don't want power. People who must*
> *hide their faces to be seen. A world with many worlds in it.*
> *A movement of one no and many yeses. These phrases seem*

*simple at first, but don't be fooled. They have a way of bur-*
*rowing into the consciousness, cropping up in strange places,*
*being repeated until they take on the quality of truth—but*
*not absolute truth: a truth, as the Zapatistas might say, with*
*many truths in it.*[2]

In these slogans — which, Klein was quite right, were quickly taken up by progressive movements — two themes are clear. The first is an unabashed solidarity with those "on the margins" resisting neoliberalism around the world. Those engaged in the immediate needs of the Zapatista struggle have never made a distinction between themselves and their international support elsewhere; "we are all Zapatistas" is a refrain commonly voiced in EZLN-inspired activists. In a famous statement to a reporter who (like many others) asked after his real identity, Marcos offered the following reply:

*Marcos is gay in San Francisco, a black in South Africa, Asian*
*in Europe, a Chicano in San Isidro, an anarchist in Spain,*
*a Palestinian in Israel, an indigenous person in the streets*
*of San Cristóbal … a woman alone in a Metro station at 10*
*p.m., a retired person standing around in the Zocalo, a peas-*
*ant without land, an underground editor, an unemployed*
*worker, a doctor with no office, a non-conformist student,*
*a dissident against neoliberalism, a writer without books or*
*readers, and a Zapatista in the Mexican southeast. In other*
*words, Marcos is a human being in this world. Marcos is*
*every untolerated, oppressed, exploited minority that is re-*
*sisting and saying "Enough!"*[3]

As I continued my graduate studies at York University, I remember this quotation making the rounds with campus activists. It captured something many of us were groping toward in our studies of power, alienation, and patterns of resistance. As we studied various doctrines in political theory, a wide gap was apparent between mainstream political actors and movements engaged in community activism. In this context, Zapatismo became an international symbol for defying neoliberalism and challenging the limited framework of established political discourse. A second constant theme that would prove equally popular, however, was the insistence Zapatismo placed on grassroots activism and the need for participatory models of activist work. As Marcos would emphasize much later: "We are not those who, foolishly, hope that from above will come the justice that can only come from below, the freedom that can only be won with all, the democracy which is struggled for at all levels and all the time."[4] Paul Kingsnorth, a British admirer of Zapatismo, would add that "the Zapatistas translated struggle into a language that the world can feel, and invited us all to read ourselves into the story, not as supporters but as participants."[5]

In announcing a politics of grassroots internationalism, Zapatismo struck a chord with those grown weary with top-down progressive organizations and exultant neoliberal reforms. Soon after their 1994 uprising, the Zapatistas hosted meetings (*ecuentros*) and national referenda (*consultas*) to mobilize support for their cause. (Supporters in Kingston, Ontario, among many others, wanted to see these for themselves.) These efforts would inspire wider networks of activists who were organizing elsewhere, something Marcos (with characteristic modesty) could already sense in 1998:

> *Don't give too much weight to the EZLN; it's nothing but a symptom of something more. Years from now, whether or not the EZLN is still around, there is going to be protest and social ferment in many places. I know this because when we rose up against the government, we began to receive displays of solidarity and sympathy not only from Mexicans, but from people in Chile, Argentina, Canada, the United States, and*

*Central America. They told us that the uprising represents*
*something that they wanted to say, each in his or her respect-*
*ive country. I believe the fallacious notion of the end of history*
*has finally been destroyed.[6]*

What Marcos and the Zapatistas saw emerging was a global wave of anti-neoliberal movements gaining wider attention by the mid to late 1990s. David McNally has chronicled the key moments of this period, beginning with Zapatismo and moving on to other protest events. In December 1995, millions in France struck against the neoliberal reforms proposed by government of Alain Juppé, and ultimately the reforms were rescinded. As the economies of East Asia were mired in crisis from 1997 to 1998, throngs of people led militant strikes in South Korea, while upstart Indonesian protests deposed the hated Suharto regime. To McNally's list other events should be added: the derailing of the planned Multilateral Agreement on Investment (MAI) in 1998 (elaborated upon below), eleven city-wide strikes in Ontario against a neoliberal government, and the protests that greeted meetings of the Asia Pacific Economic Community (APEC) in the Philippines and Canada from 1996 to 1997. In each of these cases, the aggressive agenda of establishing property rights for international investment triggered a groundswell of activist responses.

I remember feeling the infectious spirit of this protest era during a Semi-Annual General Meeting of the Canadian Federation of Students (CFS) in March 1998. I was there as a representative of the York University Graduate Students Association, and the CFS had invited Democracy Street, a Vancouver-based activist group, to talk about their experience protesting the APEC meetings held in Vancouver that year. Garth Mullins, a well-known Vancouver activist, led the presentation, detailing the repression meted out against activists daring to protest in sight of world leaders. Mullins talked about how the University of British Columbia (UBC) had been transformed into a vast security zone to ensure the safety of visiting dignitaries. This group had included Indonesia's Suharto who had ruled for two decades, overseen the slaughter of progressive groups, and facilitated the brutal occupation of neighbouring East Timor. UBC students and others were appalled at the red carpet treatment given to such monsters and the neoliberal policies of APEC that widened gaps between rich and poor. On November 25, 1997, over fifteen hundred engaged in civil disobedience at the APEC security perimeter, an act that drew loud applause from activists and movements the world over. Like many others who saw the presentation, I was hooked right away; I bought a Democracy Street T-shirt and immersed myself in similar mobilizations against the Ontario government.

By this point, two actors were prominent in the anti-neoliberal events of the mid to late 1990s. The first were progressive non-governmental organizations (NGOs), most notably those groups affiliated to the International Forum on Globalization (IFG). While most left-wing political parties had accepted neoliberal ideas (particularly those in power), IFG-affiliated groups would revive the Keynesian tradition and call for fairer trade regimes that respected human rights and environmental standards. In some instances, this involved supporting the wholesale rejection of existing trade deals or institutions; in other cases, it meant advocating adding progressive clauses to existing agreements. Mass international conferences of thousands were held against "corporate rule" in Berkeley and Toronto by 1996, and both pledged to highlight the often hidden efforts of multinational business. (The Toronto event was the largest activist conference I had seen to date.)

The international campaign against the proposed Multilateral Agreement on Investment (MAI) would provide the first obvious moment when NGOs demonstrated their potential as a source of resistance. In 1996, the Council of Canadians — a prominent NGO with a membership base of over a hundred thousand — began questioning trade officials about an international document promoting the deregulation of Canada's national investment rules. Roy McGregor, Canada's Minister for International Trade at the time, denied the document existed, but this later proved false once the Council of Canadians obtained a copy of the draft MAI in March 1997. Further inquiry revealed that the Canadian government had been meeting with business lobbyists on the matter for over four years, as Maude Barlow told me. The Council immediately took its campaign against the MAI into the public domain (networked globally through the IFG), enlivening an international audience to resist an agenda Maude Barlow described in these terms:

> The MAI has become a metaphor for the debate on economic globalization . . . and people are tired of being told they have no alternative. Suddenly something comes along that is so outrageous, so egregious, so off the wall, over the top un-acceptable, that it becomes a way for us to talk about the rest of it . . . the MAI's purpose is to remove the nation state's abil-ity to control global capital, mobile capital. It takes away all levels of government's right to dictate the terms under which investment comes in and out of a country. The single most important role for us now, in 1998, as we approach the mil-lennium, as citizens of the world, is to bring the rule of law to global capital . . . If we don't do that we will not be able to fight the other battles . . . and we have to do that together.[7]

When the French government rejected the MAI in February 1998, the Organisation for Economic Co-operation and Development (OECD) shelved the proposal two months later. In an age of neo-liberal dominance, globally networked NGOs had scored a decisive victory, which even the *Financial Times* acknowledged: "They have condemned the [MAI] as a secret conspiracy to ensure global dom-ination by multinational companies, and mobilized an international movement of grassroots resistance. The NGOs have tasted blood. They'll be back for more."[8]

The second actor that gained prominence in this period was youth networks and campus-based organizations with Zapatista-like politics. These groups were knit together through People's Global Action (PGA), an international network first begun through the 1996 International Encounter for Humanity and Against Neoliberalism hosted by the Zapatistas in La Realidad, Mexico. Activists who first met in La Realidad later formed the PGA at a meeting hosted in Geneva in 1998. There they agreed on a statement of their shared concerns, voiced in one moment by Olivier de Marcellus, an organizer of the Geneva proceedings: "We have to start aiming at the head; we have been militants fighting against nuclear power, against homelessness, sexism — different tentacles of the monster. You are never going to really do it that way, you really have to aim at the head."[9] The "head" identified after 1998 was the World Trade Organization (WTO), which had planned its 1999 Ministerial in Seattle for November 30 to December 2, 1999. The PGA issued a call from its Geneva conference for international protests against the WTO during its 1999 Ministerial. It is in this chain of events that we can grasp what took place in Seattle at the end of the twentieth century.

## AFTER SEATTLE: ANOTHER GENERATION NAMES THE SYSTEM (1999–2001)

While earlier anti-neoliberal demonstrations had been equally defiant, protest against the World Trade Organization's 1999 Ministerial in Seattle distinguished itself by four major traits, all of which would affect events to come. The first was its heralding of an international anti-neoliberal movement, one where participants got a sense of their global support. Many of the protesters in Seattle demonstrated this internationalism in practice. Jeffrey St. Clair recalls "a robust internationalist contingent ... French farmers, Korean greens, Canadian wheat growers, Mexican environmentalists, Chinese dissidents, Ecuadorian anti-dam organizers, U'wa tribespeople from the Colombian rainforest and British campaigners against genetically modified foods."[10] Mark Lichbach explains that Seattle was only the largest component of a global protest against the WTO: The fifty thousand protesters in Seattle (not to mention those in other US cities) were matched by demonstrations elsewhere that brought out over a hundred thousand people in anti-WTO events worldwide. Eleven cities in India saw demonstrations in the thousands. In the Philippines, thousands of anti-WTO protesters crowded the streets of Manila on November 30, 1999, and later stormed the US Embassy on December 3, 1999, decrying the police brutality activists in Seattle faced. It was such global solidarity in protest, an exciting corollary to the ever-expanding reach of global capitalism, that transformed isolated activists in the West and inspired those in the South who had fought neoliberalism for decades.

By this point, I was deeply immersed in Toronto's Mobilization for Global Justice — an activist network that celebrated anti-WTO protests and facilitated further mass movement organizing. At the time, we said the global justice movement had "started in Seattle." This was not because anti-WTO protest had finally emerged on US soil, though this was certainly important. The claim was far more significant: Activists were inspired by the emergence of a global anti-neoliberal movement conscious of itself, and reveling in its reach and resonance. Our movement remained weak compared to well-heeled adversaries, but it created a framework for global solidarity that emboldened grassroots activism.

The second noticeable trait of the anti-WTO protests was the forms of protest it encouraged. John Sellers, a key organizer of the Ruckus Society (an offshoot itself of Greenpeace and EarthFirst!), facilitated well-attended direct action camps in the lead-up to Seattle that trained activists in an array of obstructive tactics. "Lock-box" devices were created to join activists sitting down in street intersections, and protesters trained to prepare for prison conditions and police intimidation tactics. Three months before the anti-WTO demonstrations, a Direct Action Network (DAN) formed in the Seattle area that repeated (and in some cases expanded on) the work conducted by the Ruckus Society, and found itself swamped with participants. Starhawk, a prominent US-based direct action trainer, oversaw workshops for thousands through the DAN prior to the events of November 30 to December 2, 1999.

Also of interest were the guidelines for the DAN's work, and the participatory organizing in Seattle that featured the decentralized modes of affinity groups, clusters, and "spokescouncils." Those interested in taking part were asked to agree to common guidelines established by the DAN. These included refraining from violence (physical or verbal), carrying weapons, using drugs or alcohol, and property destruction. (Not everyone adhered to these guidelines, but most would.) Participants were then asked to form affinity groups, and each group decided its preferred role for the demonstration, keeping in mind the larger objective of blockading the WTO conference site. Each affinity group elected a spokesperson for a larger spokescouncil where affinity group representatives would regularly meet and plan their efforts before the start of the demonstration. For the most part, decisions taken at the spokescouncil were conducted on a consensus basis, and rarely resorted to a majority vote. Once the council had heard from all participating affinity groups, its representatives would organize the demonstration site into various geographic "clusters," ensuring a minimum of duplication and conflicting tactics. The security forces in Seattle would be completely overwhelmed by this decentralized approach, while activists seized on the confusion to consolidate certain blockades.

A third important trait of the WTO protests were alliances formed between unions and other social movements, though this outcome was, in large measure, an unexpected surprise. Jaggi Singh, a prominent anarchist, told me that Seattle was a moment when different activists "found each other," when social movements joined with unions against a target of common scorn. "Teamsters and Turtles, together at last" was the slogan many recall from dissent in Seattle, given that thousands of trade unionists destined for an AFL-CIO march away from direct action blockades at the WTO meeting site had second thoughts about just ambling along. Three workers described to John Charlton, a British independent journalist, a prevalent mood in the march: "In a decision we considered a betrayal … the AFL-CIO organizers detoured the march route … a group of marshals stood in front of a street to block our path towards the direct action protesters. We decided to join the direct action group and continued straight through the line of marshals. We found ourselves in a war zone."[11] Charlie Kimber, another British independent journalist who witnessed the breakaway march, recalls the moment poignantly:

> *"We're going to the convention," shouted one crane operator. "I'm going to help those turtle kids," said another docker, referring to the environmental protesters on the receiving end of police brutality a few streets away. For a minute the line of marshals held and then, slowly, it began to part. Chanting, cheering, the trade unionists swept straight on. The two groups, the workers and the young protesters, met. "Union!" screamed the trade unionists. "Power!" replied the students and youth. "Solidarity! Solidarity!" they chanted together.*[12]

As many have pointed out since, the decision of some union activists to break from the official march was not spontaneous. The largest union contingents were from Seattle and the US Northwest, many of who had been working on joint campaigns with other social movements for some time. A notable case was the campaign organized by the Steelworkers and the environmental group EarthFirst! against Kaiser Corporation, which had locked out its workers and hired replacement workers to break the union. EarthFirst! organizers, in conjunction with their Steelworker counterparts, made a series of appeals to loggers organized as replacement workers, pointing out the environmental and human costs of their company's practices. The result was a campaign for support that ultimately beat Kaiser by seeking out the support of replacement workers; as green and labour activists worked on this joint effort, they created new relationships of solidarity. Green activists had long avoided any co-operative work with labour, but small relationships of trust emerged over the course of these days through practical experience. This example would be repeated elsewhere in the American Northwest through unions like the Teamsters and Longshoreworkers, both of which had long-established networks with other activist groups. In the heat of Seattle, when union activists saw social movement allies under attack while engaging in non-violent civil disobedience, they broke ranks. The spectacle of this alliance was an outcome that shocked both the defenders and critics of the WTO.

As I heard first-hand reports from Seattle veterans, it confirmed my belief that something profound was taking place. Almost immediately, the landscape of political ideas was expanding, for, inspired by this period, there was a tendency to move from particular concerns to more fundamental questions, which had a profound effect on popular debate. Sam Gindin explained the resulting new "terrain of social justice" in these terms:

> *If social justice could no longer be discussed without addressing globalization, Seattle declared that globalization could no longer be addressed without addressing capitalism. And so, in the course of their resistance, a new generation of protesters dared to name the system that hath no name. By naming the previously unspoken social system behind globalization, globalization was being politicized.*
>
> *Where "globalization" had become a weapon brandished by business, politicians, and the media to explain what we couldn't do, placing capitalism itself up for discussion and criticism was part of insisting that the limits we faced were socially constructed, and could therefore be challenged, stretched, and one day overcome. The protesters raised the stakes because enough of them didn't want in, but demanded*

*something different. The term "anti-capitalism" arrived on the public agenda.*[13]

These developments were important for activists, but they also made their mark in established politics. Multilateral trade institutions felt compelled to explain how their efforts "helped the poor." Politicians and think tanks often responded in similar terms, making clear that protesters were shaping debate. As even *The Economist* was loath to acknowledge:

> *the protesters are right that the most pressing moral, political and economic issue of our time is Third World poverty. And they are right that the tide of "globalisation", powerful as the engines driving it may be, can be turned back. The fact that both these things are true is what makes the protesters – and, crucially, the strand of popular opinion that sympathises with them – so terribly dangerous.*[14]

A report issued earlier by the Canadian Security Intelligence Service (CSIS) also acknowledged the growing popularity and scope of the movement:

> *the philosophy of capitalism is also under attack, facing charges that it is ignoring the social welfare of individuals, and destroying cultures and the ecology in the quest for growth and profit. As prominent corporate names come under fire, making for good publicity and media attention, groups such as animal-rights activists and environmental protection advocates vie for an opportunity to share the spotlight, many making similar claims about exploitation.*[15]

These responses demonstrated the impact of today's grassroots activists. At the same time, the Seattle moment harboured its own contradictions and faced an array of challenges once events spread elsewhere. Indeed, the Seattle example would never be re-enacted completely; bold internationalism, bottom-up organizing, and bold ideas would remain, but the diversity and coherence of the activism suffered under the pressure of raging debates. The first of these concerned issues around protest tactics and the planning of movement events.

I witnessed the first open rupture among activists on this question during protests against the Free Trade Area of the Americas (FTAA) meeting in Quebec City in April 2001. Lisa Fithian, a well-known Seattle veteran and DAN activist, circulated a critical letter during a pre-protest "Consulta" held January 27 and 28, 2001; the letter was openly critical of the Convergence des Luttes Anticapitalistes (CLAC). CLAC — an anarchist group and long-standing People's Global Action affiliate — was among the groups hosting the protests, but had insisted successfully on a "diversity of tactics" platform that allowed for an array of activist practices during the demonstration (up to and including property destruction and physical clashes with police). Fithian's letter voiced the concerns of activist groups committed to non-violent civil disobedience, and warned against provoking the police into unnecessary conflicts. Philippe Duhamel of Opération SalAMI was among the most prominent of Quebec-based activists to debate CLAC on this question, but neither Fithian or Duhamel persuaded CLAC or the Consulta to change course. The protests against the FTAA in Quebec City went ahead with "diversity of tactics" as their guiding basis of unity.

While many hailed the over eighty thousand who protested in Quebec as a victory, debates over tactics continued as protests drew to a close. CLAC and other anarchist groups assailed union leaders who took activists away from battles at the security perimeter; at the largest protest march, this amounted to a four-kilometre "march to nowhere" in a parking lot far away from protest events. Others insisted that tear gas and police repression did not respect the preordained "green/yellow/red" zones designated for various tactics, and criticized CLAC and others defending a "diversity of tactics" approach. These debates in Quebec City were soon repeated in Toronto and other centres of activist politics. The shootings of activists at subsequent protests in Sweden, Papua New Guinea, and Italy left many fearful and concerned with confrontational approaches to police repression. Some insisted such tactics would do little to change the diversity (including, importantly, racial diversity) of the activist events, and urged different proposals to build solidarity among equity-seeking groups through community-based organizing.

By 2001, however, the most pitched debates were over interpretations of what emerging forms of grassroots activism had accomplished, and where they might be going. Some, like Naomi Klein, Michael Hardt, and Antonio Negri, offered anarchist imaginaries describing resistance as a diffuse, horizontal, leaderless form of dissent. A different view came from social democratic thinkers, some of whom favoured the restructuring of trade regimes, or more decentralized models with overarching rules. Still others felt activists needed a coherent vision and strategy for political power. Could spokescouncils and affinity groups, they asked, be sustained after demonstrations, or fused with existing progressive groups? To those who held this line, Klein's reply was harsh:

> When critics say that the protesters lack vision, what they are really saying is that they lack an overarching revolutionary philosophy — like Marxism, deep ecology or social anarchy — on which they all agree. That is absolutely true, and for this we should be extraordinarily thankful ...
>
> It is to this young movement's credit that it has as yet fended off all of these agendas and has rejected everyone's generously donated manifesto, holding out for an acceptably democratic, representative process to take its resistance to the next stage.
>
> Will it be a ten-point plan? A new political doctrine? Maybe not. Maybe out of the chaotic network of hubs and

*spokes, something else will emerge: not a blueprint for some utopian new world, but a plan to protect the possibility of many worlds — "a world", as the Zapatistas say, "with many worlds in it."*

*Maybe instead of meeting the proponents of neoliberalism head on, this movement of movements will surround them from all directions.*[16]

As someone deeply attuned to activist developments, Klein reflected the culture of movement organizing in the post-Seattle period. In the countless events and meetings I attended, there was a constant tendency toward inclusiveness (and away from fixed ideological positions); people were reluctant to foist predetermined agendas, and those who did were among the least influential. In this activist political culture, an array of ideas still jostled for attention, but an overall clarity of purpose was not forthcoming. As Susan George explained to a packed audience at the 2000 World Social Forum in Porto Alegre, Brazil: "I'm sorry to admit it, but I haven't the slightest idea what overthrowing capitalism means in the early twenty-first century."[17] Walden Bello, a Philipino movement thinker, wrote about the potential for "deglobalization," with regional and local development as its focus. Still others pushed for more immediate concerns, like solidarity with those detained in mass protests or with racialized communities under attack from immigration officials. The debates that raged around alternatives saw a flurry of responses. Soon enough, however, a twist in the road of global politics would throw open an entirely different set of circumstances.

## BLOWBACK AND ITS VICTIMS: GRASSROOTS ACTIVISM VS. AMERICAN EMPIRE

Almost two years after Seattle, as grassroots activism remained a force to be reckoned with, an event shocked the world. On September 11, 2001, the first large-scale attack on US soil in almost two centuries would facilitate a new era of American militarism. With thousands dead in New York City and Washington, DC (and many more later in Afghanistan and Iraq), the open-ended US "War on Terror" thrust grassroots activism into entirely different circumstances. Previous debates about "violent tactics" took on a whole new meaning; political dissent now operated in a climate of suspected terrorism. The Teamster-Turtle alliance seen in Seattle ruptured considerably. The Bush administration helped sever these ties through appeals to US workers to band together with "their government" and to protect the "American way of life."

For some odd reason, I woke early on the day America's 9/11 happened. Sergio, my Chilean roommate (and fellow graduate student) threw open my door and found me engrossed, ironically enough, in "security studies" reports about emerging forms of activism. "Follow me," he said, "we must turn on the news — you are not going to believe what's happening." Minutes later, we watched a second plane crash into Manhattan's World Trade Centre in shocked disbelief. Living as we did in downtown Toronto, our instinct was to seek out activist cafes and gathering spots. Within minutes, these places coursed with similar conversations; we grieved the loss of life, lamented what 9/11 meant for emerging forms of progressive activism and what US retaliation would mean for Muslims and the Arab world in general.

Soon enough, "we are all New Yorkers" became a slogan used to recapture the legitimacy of Democrats and Republicans, both of whom had spent decades paving the way for neoliberal reforms. Such myths were happily amplified by a mainstream press that rarely asked why the US government was reviled by millions (perhaps billions) the world over. No thought was given to the caustic irony my roommate Sergio and other Chileans knew from bitter experience: that Augusto Pinochet's murderous coup in Chile had been waged on another September 11, in 1973, with the active support of the US military. As William Blum explains, similar acts of US state-sponsored terror decorated the landscape of the last two centuries but were never raised through the "objective" channels of journalism. Instead it was Chalmers Johnson, an American academic unknown outside university circles, who offered this eerie description of "blowback" against the US Empire over a year before the events of 9/11:

> One [person's] terrorist is . . . another [person's] freedom
> fighter, and what U.S. officials denounce as unprovoked ter-
> rorist attacks on its innocent citizens are often meant as re-
> taliation for previous American imperial actions. Terrorists
> attack innocent and undefended American targets precisely
> because American soldiers and sailors firing cruise missiles
> from ships at sea or sitting in B-52 bombers at extremely high
> altitudes or supporting brutal and repressive regimes from
> Washington seem invulnerable.[18]

As activists organized in daunting conditions, they discovered Chalmers's work (and works by others like him) and read and used it widely. Still, "blowback" and upstart American militarism were not the only significant obstacles to progressive movements. America's 9/11 exposed a weakness in the wider activist community: Few understood the relationship between war and neoliberalism, and this became a profound weakness once political debate required this analysis. In 2000, I saw this first-hand at York University; the place was an atypical course — facilitated by Leo Panitch and Sam Gindin — entitled "Social Justice and Political Activists," and it included both graduate students and many prominent movement organizers. Dan Heap, a talented community activist and former NDP politician, repeatedly asked for "war" and "militarism" to be included in our discussions, but, time and again, those subjects were skirted. We focused instead on the turbulence of world markets, emerging socio-economic patterns, various forms of protest, and key readings in political theory. To me foreign policy concerns were distant, complex subjects. It was one thing to denounce the horrors of multinational corporations and call for a better world on that basis. It was rather different to review the record of the US Empire in the Middle East, the role of Islamic political movements in this context, and the relationship between these things and America's 9/11. An insightful set of interviews with key US activists acknowledged that these complicated circumstances "hit the "pause button" for many organizers."[19]

The most noticeable absence among the ranks of protesters after 9/11 was organized labour. While some labour leaders urged "sober thought" and openly worried about a "backlash" against recent immigrants (particularly of Arabic descent), many declared their solidarity with the US government. John Sweeny, the erstwhile left-leaning president of the AFL-CIO, declared workers were "fully behind the President and the leadership of our nation in this time of national crisis …We will fully support the appropriate American response."[20] Russ Davis, a prominent organizer with Massachusetts Jobs With Justice and strong supporter of grassroots activism, appealed against creating an anti-war movement given the support in working-class communities for retaliation after America's 9/11.

Some progressive groups were actually pleased with the ebb in protest and happily returned to negotiating boardrooms with "realistic" proposals. An instructive case was Oxfam, which released a report after 9/11 punctuated by the following statement: "History makes a mockery of the claim that trade cannot work for the poor … Since the mid-1970s, rapid growth in exports has contributed to a wider process of economic growth which has lifted more than four hundred million people out of poverty".[21] Kevin Watkins, the report's author and senior policy adviser for Oxfam, defended this position by arguing that "the extreme element of the anti-globalization movement is wrong … Trade can deliver much more [for poor countries] than aid or debt relief."[22]

Behind such remarks were serious political disagreements. Some in the movement were opposed to analyzing war as the new catalyst for those opposed to neoliberal capitalism. Though small peace vigils and marches emerged almost immediately, the Seattle momentum was noticeably altered; the most glaring difference, as Davis had predicted, was the relative absence of organized labour. Nevertheless, Howard Zinn, a celebrated historian of protest movements, provided a sober historical perspective that urged activists not to lose hope:

> *Things are starting earlier now than they did with the Vietnam War. In the spring of 1965, we had 100 people on the Boston Common. Just a week or so ago, we had 2,000 people at Copley Square. It's starting earlier, and I believe it will grow.*
>
> *Immediately after September 11, if you talked about American foreign policy as having anything to do with the problem, people were horrified. It was too close. People thought you were diminishing the tragedy. I think as time passes, it will be easier to think in more long-term ways.*[23]

History would vindicate these words — the emergence of peace activism happened faster than many imagined. As activists worked to regroup, protests in Europe and the Middle East shifted to a decisive anti-war footing. Huge demonstrations grew apace (most notably in Egypt, Syria, Australia, Britain, Italy, and Spain). Starhawk would claim that it was crucial for the movement to "stay in the streets;" during Canadian protests in Kananaskis against the G8, she urged activists to remain committed to social justice work at the "local and global level." "We fight on a thousand fronts," she insisted, and with

> *new wars on the horizon every day, ongoing violence in the Middle East and the far East, an invasion of Iraq on the Bush agenda, it's a vitally important moment to draw attention to the links between militarism and global corporate capitalism, to pry Canada away from backing the US drive for hegemony, to unite the movement for global justice with the movement for peace.*[24]

By mid 2002, these arguments were gaining steam, as tens of thousands took part in peace demonstrations held January 18, 2003, to oppose a looming war in Iraq. February 15, 2003, however, would set an unprecedented example of protest on a far wider scale; over thirty million marched in more than six hundred cities around the world, by far the largest co-ordinated protest in world history. I vividly remember being in Toronto, fortunately beside Faith Nolan, a celebrated musician and social activist, and feeling the power of eighty thousand people marching in common cause. We were part of a global voice against militarism, and a movement that even the *New York Times* called a "second world superpower." Sid Lacombe, then National Coordinator for the Canadian Peace Alliance, remembers February 15 as the moment when the world "revealed its like-mindedness on the streets, we stood and were counted, and voted with our feet."[25] Millions in the Middle East watched images of mass demonstrations in the West, expressing the same enthusiasm as earlier reactions to the spectacle of dissent in Seattle. International peace conferences that began that year in Cairo marked the first time in recent history that delegations of Western activists met their counterparts in the Arab world. The stirring example of grassroots activism leapt onto the world stage once again.

If the Seattle protest era politicized talk of globalization, peace activism did likewise for foreign policy discussions; it put age-old debates concerning imperialism back on the table. Arundhati Roy, the Indian writer and activist, exemplified this in her address to the 2003 World Social Forum, insisting the real name of "corporate globalization" was "imperialism." Debates about the prospects of the US Empire drew considerable interest. Organizers of the 2003 European Social Forum found this out first-hand, as thousands swamped facilities meant for a few hundred, for a debate between Antonio Negri and Alex Callinicos — two movement thinkers with sharply conflicting positions.

As the impact of war in in Iraq took hold, however, the momentum of progressive activism became noticeably different. Mass rallies continued, but not on the scale seen previously. In the activist circles I frequented, people questioned the effectiveness of demonstrations and moral appeals for governments to change course. While smaller campaigns persisted, some with more success than others, a general malaise presided. In the United States, this mood intensified after an unsuccessful bid to oust the George W. Bush administration in the 2004 election; the same was true in Canada with election of a Conservative federal government two years later. Even still, hundreds of thousands marched worldwide during the anniversary of the Iraq invasion on March 20, 2006, while over three hundred and fifty thousand marched April 29, 2006, in New York City to continue to proclaim US opposition to the Iraq war.

By 2008, however, the political terrain had shifted for other reasons. After revelations about dubious financial investments, neoliberal capitalism faced its worst crisis since the 1930s — the story and outcome of which are now broadly known. The world's capitals were quickly embroiled in efforts to save finance from itself, while Wall Street insiders (as we learned later) used this moment to enrich themselves, mostly with impunity, in spite of the fraud they committed. In the resulting economic slump, governments spent over $13 trillion in bailouts and economic "stimulus," followed by harsh austerity measures in the months and years to come.

Initially, two political actors rose to prominence in this period. The first was a mass movement to elect Barack Obama, an Illinois State Senator and former community organizer, to the office of US President. That movement (as I discuss in chapter four) would trumpet grassroots phrases ("Yes We Can") and inspire the anti-war majority that connected with world public opinion. The November 2008 presidential election saw Obama's historic election as the first African-American president, an outcome greeted with massive rallies and high hopes. For many, Obama symbolized a new kind of politics after the Bush/Cheney years. He claimed to be pro-union, angry at Wall Street, knowledgeable about climate change, committed to extend affordable health care, supportive of women's reproductive freedoms, and willing to draw back the US war machine. These were at least the perceptions that earned Obama millions in donations from often meagre bank accounts. They motivated a new generation into electoral politics who had never taken such work seriously before. But this movement was grassroots in rhetoric only. Legions of Obama campaigners were skilfully used as a stage army, and never given support to act independently.

This muzzling of the Obama movement would embolden right-wing populism, the second actor to emerge in the months after the 2008 economic crisis. Groups like the Tea Party accused Obama of being soft on Wall Street while at the same time dangerously ambitious in restoring the auto industry and extending health care coverage. A libertarian strand of US society coalesced around such claims, targeting the Obama administration as a "socialist regime" headed by a "nominally American" president (subtle or overt racism was common in Tea Party literature and slogans). Influential supporters — like the Wisconsin-based Koch Brothers — channelled money to broadcast these ideas, which were later amplified by largely uncritical, compliant, and corporate-owned mainstream media. The impact was serious for the 2010 US mid-term elections — the Obama administration lost its "super majority," and emboldened Republicans now dominated the political scene.

Inspiration for a new round of progressive activism would come from elsewhere, from a place, ironically enough, at the receiving end of the American Empire. That place was the Middle East, which, in a matter of months, established a new political context everywhere. In 2011, movement organizers were swept into a maelstrom of activity *Time* Magazine called the "year of the protester." The larger movement would be known as the Arab Spring, and its waves would wash up on the shores of North America. As the last segment in this chapter, I turn to that story next.

# THE IMPACT OF THE ARAB SPRING

*Blame the times and not me.*
*Maybe by setting myself on fire, life can change.*
— *Tarek al-Tayeb Mohammed Bouazizi*[26]

At first, I had a curious perspective on Arab Spring. My partner and I were on parental leave, both of us ensconced in the glow of our second child. I had warned fellow activists to expect delayed communications and limited contact via the Internet or phone. My objective was to close off the world as much as was possible, to focus on the momentous events in our family. Needless to say, that soon became impossible in the first days after 2011 began. Those aware of my research interests, particularly those with Middle Eastern roots, sought out my opinion on the cascade of events transpiring across the Arab world. On January 10, I opened my laptop for the first time in weeks, and set about discovering precisely what was going on. The chain of events I discovered shocked me.

On January 4, 2011, Tarek al-Tayeb Mohammed Bouazizi, a 26-year-old Tunisian street vendor, set himself ablaze in front of his local government office. The day before, he had borrowed the equivalent of US$200 to buy produce, and faced the precarious circumstance of repaying these funds on short notice. As always, he had to sell or face financial ruin, for Bouazizi had no available money to cover his debt otherwise. Like many young Tunisians, he had worked from an early age to provide for his family. He supported his mother, his disabled uncle, and his younger siblings, and he helped finance university fees for one of his sisters — all from a cart of fruit and vegetables. Close friends said that, despite his modest means, he even gave food to others less fortunate when possible.

These circumstances weren't helped on January 4, 2011, when government officials, as always, harassed Bouazizi for selling without a vendor's permit. Bouazizi had no money for potential bribes, or supplies to barter in exchange for leniency. After his cart was toppled and seized, officials took turns beating him, even spitting in his face (according to bystanders) as he writhed on the pavement. Bouazizi later stormed down to the local government offices, demanding his supplies back. When these appeals were ignored, he turned inward; Bouazizi chose suicide, and found the closest computer to enter his final thoughts in two Facebook messages, cited at the start of this section. The first, a note to his mother, was a gut-wrenching apology for having failed (in his view) as an economic provider. The second was an appeal to his wider network of friends, which suggests he wished his suicide to be seen as motivation to transform fear into action. That wish would be granted. Within a month, Tunisia's president resigned in the face of mass protests. Ferment quickly spread across the Arab world, but notably in Egypt, where the impact of activist mobilizations swamped Cairo's Tahrir Square.

As most mainstream accounts explain, an important actor in Egyptian mobilizations was the April 6 Youth Movement, a network that emerged three years previously to bolster union protest against the Hosni Mubarak regime. In reality, by 2011, the April 6 Youth Movement was relatively small, with no more than a few dozen active participants; it was an offshoot of youth activism that had grown steadily since Egyptians mobilized in conjunction with global anti-war demonstrations in 2003. (Over fifty thousand rallied in Cairo on February 15, 2003.) As James Clark, a Toronto-based activist who participated in the Cairo peace movement conferences, told me, these events were closely monitored by the Mubarak regime and largely seen as a means to deflect anger away from domestic politics. The regime didn't mind Egyptians rallying to protest the Iraq War, and it took the same attitude to mass rallies opposing Israel's oppression of Palestinians. This, as it turned out, was a tactical error; anti-war mobilizations created an activist infrastructure that later facilitated Mubarak's own political demise.

By 2006, as this infrastructure came together, confidence was building among Egyptians to challenge the Mubarak regime. International activists saw this first-hand at the annual peace conferences in Cairo. A recurring complaint was Egypt's massive and growing gap between rich and poor, which at this point was staggering. While the Mubarak family was purportedly worth over US$70 billion, 40 per cent of Egyptians subsisted on roughly US$2 a day. Egyptian workers had steadily opposed this trend, but their activism was rarely reported in the mainstream press. In the decade preceding the Arab Spring, over thirty-three hundred strikes, sit-ins and other forms of labour unrest took place, many of which extended well beyond single workplaces. These actions, it should be noted, happened largely outside the official Egypt Trade Union Federation, which for decades operated with close ties to the Mubarak regime. Workers instead formed independent unions or created strike committees that often split (or disrupted) official institutions. April 6, 2008, was the high point of this labour activism, when a general strike was called by twenty-two thousand textile workers in Mahalla al-Kubra, at a factory that remains Egypt's largest workplace. The workers aimed beyond their immediate needs, demanding an increase to the national minimum wage. The strike was repressed, but the workers drew mass mobilizations into the streets to protest against the high costs of living, notably the cost of subsidized bread.

The April 6 Youth Movement emerged then, but not as the engine of the Egyptian revolution to come. It was a small, bold voice that appealed to workers' movements and anti-regime activists who had been fighting for years. Its organizers dispersed across the nation, leafletting mosques, churches, and workplaces, some of which had not seen such political outreach in years. Online, Asmaa Mahfouz, an April 6 Youth Movement organizer, sounded a widely heard appeal through a YouTube video. On January 17, she called for a mass mobilization in Tahrir Square to protest the killing of Khalid Saeed (beaten to death by police the previous year) and calling on Egypt's interior minister to resign; the appeal drew only a few friends and dozens of security personnel. Undaunted, Mahfouz sat before her computer once more, taking aim at the male chauvinism that marked much of Egyptian society. Repeating a pitch that many had already made, she appealed for mass protests on January 25:

*If you think yourself a man, come with me on 25 January. Whoever says women shouldn't go to protests because they will get beaten, let him have some honor and manhood and come with me on 25 January. Whoever says it is not worth it because there will only be a handful of people, I want to tell him, "You are the reason behind this, and you are a traitor, just like the president or any security cop who beats us in the streets."*

*Your presence with us will make a difference, a big difference. Talk to your neighbors, your colleagues, friends and family, and tell them to come . . . Sitting at home and just following us on the news or Facebook leads to our humiliation, leads to my own humiliation. If you have honor and dignity as a man, come.*

*Come and protect me and other girls in the protest. If you stay at home, then you deserve all that is being done, and you will be guilty before your nation and your people. And you'll be responsible for what happens to us on the streets while you sit at home.*[27]

This message struck a chord and inspired protest organizing that spiralled beyond anyone's expectations. The January 25 mobilization was massive, and suffered horrendous attacks from regime forces (846 protesters were killed and over six thousand injured). That violence, however, only emboldened the movement, which opted to create a permanent encampment in Tahrir Square. Soon even doctors, lawyers, and university professors joined surging crowds in Tahrir, all of whom demanded the ouster of Mubarak and declaration of free elections. By February this protest movement had spread well inside the Egyptian workforce — Mahalla al-Kubra's textile workers struck again, and were joined this time by powerful unions from the Suez Canal. This, many agree, was the decisive force that crippled the regime, giving rise to

Mubarak's ouster and the declaration of the first elections in Egyptian history. A wave of similar events soon spread across the Arab world, leading to mass protests, resignations, and a new era of grassroots activism. It is a process that was still unfolding as I wrote this book.

Alex Hanna, a graduate student I spoke with at the University of Wisconsin-Madison, witnessed the Egyptian uprising first-hand. Hanna's Egyptian-born parents had raised him in Wisconsin, but he travelled to Tahrir Square to seek out, and participate in, the revolution. While overseas, however, he received a flurry of e-mails about political events at home. On February 11, 2011, Wisconsin's state government announced its intention to abolish union bargaining rights and force through an array of austerity measures (through "special budget legislation" entitled SB-11). This led to an outpouring of rage in a place otherwise known for its progressive history. As Co-President of the UW-Madison Teaching Assistants' Union, Hanna went straight from the airport to the union hall. Almost immediately, he was embroiled in a mass movement against the state's attack on decades-old victories. The upsurge of anti-neoliberal protest seen that year in Greece and Spain was about to emerge in the American Midwest.

The movement's first action was a stunt where students, university workers, and their allies dumped thousands of Valentine's Day cards on the desk of State Governor Scott Walker, imploring him to "have a heart." Quickly after, activists seized on a different opportunity; the government needed to hold open budget hearings (where any citizen could speak) before their legislation could be passed. Those hearings became a focal point for state-wide mobilizations, with protesters creating massive queues as each person demanded to be heard. After fourteen hours, the government moved to cancel the hearings; but when the politicians left, the protesters stayed. In a spectacle that resembled a mini Tahrir Square, the Capitol Rotunda was occupied by hundreds of demonstrators who held the space for seventeen days.

Inspired by the occupation, Wisconsin Democrats chose a

complementary strategy: they fled to deny the quorum required to pass the government's legislation. The state would ram through SB-11 later with technical manouevres, but not before drawing mass protests, often with Republican supporters switching sides. Police and firefighters (who had been exempted from the anti-union provisions) joined the protests, which at one point swelled to over a hundred thousand people — about half the population of Madison itself.

The Wisconsin uprising spread to other states where right-wing governments attempted similar measures, with some degree of success in mitigating the damage. Most importantly, after a long hiatus, the US labour movement was visible again, with union members feeling empowered against their adversaries. By June, after mass protests failed to stop the Wisconsin Republicans, the movement turned to an electoral strategy of recalling government supporters, and building a "Walkerville" tent city to keep resistance visible. At the same time, a similar (though smaller) movement erected "Bloombergville" on the sidewalk facing New York City Hall, a protest challenging Mayor Michael Bloomberg's austerity measures.[28] "Bloombergville" was also a vibrant democracy, with activists working together to plan and co-ordinate teach-ins and outreach to New York City and the wider world. "Bloombergville" subsided after the city's budget passed, but it earned broad media coverage and demonstrated an example of direct democracy in practice. A few months later, grassroots activism would return to Lower Manhattan, but this time on a far larger scale.

On September 17, 2011, three years after the 2008 economic crisis, a movement had emerged to challenge finance capital in its own backyard. The place was Zuccotti Park, a green patch huddled in the concrete jungle of Lower Manhattan's financial district. This movement was called "Occupy Wall Street," and its example spread quickly around the world. *Adbusters*, a magazine based in Vancouver, had put out the first appeal for an Occupy Wall Street mobilization with a simple message, one linked to an ongoing Twitter feed:

*WHAT IS OUR ONE DEMAND?*
*#OCCUPYWALLSTREET*
*SEPTEMBER 17*
*BRING A TENT*

This call would initially bring hundreds, and later thousands, to Zuccotti Park, later renamed "Liberty Square" by the Occupy movement. Initially, participants were prevented from erecting tents and slept overnight in sleeping bags under blankets. As numbers swelled, however, the ban became unworkable; a lively tent city soon filled Liberty Square, with movements in other cities soon following suit. Unions were visible in Occupy encampments (more as supporters than campers), recalling the earlier precedent in Seattle of Teamster-Turtle alliances. At its height, the Occupy movement was linked with 1,087 events in 87 countries, most of these being permanent encampments lasting weeks or months. As I discussed these developments with friends who, like me, donated to (or participated in) Occupy encampments on a regular basis, it was clear a new spirit of resistance had arrived in North America's progressive community.

The movement's rallying cry — "We are the 99 percent!" — highlighted, like the Arab Spring, the yawning gap between the super-rich and everyone else, and did so to great effect. By early October 2011, even *Bloomberg News* reported the top 1 per cent of US earners had netted 93 per cent of income growth in recent decades. Similar stories dotted the landscape of the mainstream press worldwide and shifted the political debate. The two previous years had witnessed the resurgence of right-wing populism despite the worst economic slump since the early 1930s. Now politicians and pundits faced a different reality: A new (largely young) generation, seizing on the example of the Arab Spring, were rejecting the stark inequalities and crass materialism of capitalist society. They saw no future for themselves, and no substance behind the "work hard, get ahead" neoliberal credo of capitalism's apologists.

Like others before them, they wanted a more participative, authentic democracy, one no longer suffocated by the greed of a global elite. They also sought new conceptions of a more just world, and were prepared through their encampments to show how it might work in practice. As Judy Rebick explains, there were important links between this activism and core principles of democratic theory:

> *Thomas Paine, a father of the American Revolution and an important democratic theorist, pointed out in his 1791 essay* Rights of Man *that "It appears to general observation, that revolutions create genius and talents; but those events do no more than bring them forward." The democracy that Paine imagined would bring forward the same genius of ordinary people every day. Of course, it didn't happen like that.*
>
> *In many ways the Occupy movement is creating the kind of democracy Paine imagined centuries ago. But more than that, the encampments also provide the sense of community that neoliberalism, the latest stage of capitalism, has destroyed. Margaret Thatcher famously said, "There is no such thing as society, there are individual men and women, and there are families," in her argument against the idea of collective responsibility for one another through government.[29]*

In a spectacle reminiscent of the Seattle era, Occupy activists challenged neoliberal assumptions, but this time through activism that did not involve travelling to elite trade summits. Occupy, while global, was also local; if capitalism stood for crass individualism and for taking away collective rights, Occupy's purpose meant restoring a collective sense of social justice through exciting forms of grassroots activism. As I saw first-hand in Ottawa (and friends reported from elsewhere), participants shared in the daily tasks of encampment life — making food, soliciting donations, caring for those injured or sick, facilitating an array of learning experiences. It was an example of what anthropologists call an "intentional community," where the marginalized create an empowering space against the prejudices of mainstream society.

It didn't take long for prominent movement thinkers to visit and participate in Occupy encampments, extolling the virtues of what they found there. In late September, filmmaker and activist Michael Moore visited Liberty Square and spoke about the movement's historical significance. He used Occupy's "people's mic," where participants repeated in unison a speaker's comments a few sentences at a time to undermine city bylaws against electric amplification:

> *I just got back to New York twelve hours ago and I wanted to come down here as soon as I could. I've spent over twenty years fighting Wall Street, Health Insurance Companies — the whole lot of them.*
>
> *A lot of that has been alone or just with a very few people. It warms my heart to see all of you here! I know that each and every one of you — each of you represents another thousand, another ten thousand — people across this country.*
>
> *Do not despair because there's only a few hundred here right now. All great movements start with just a few people . . . Everyone will remember, three months from now, six months from now, a hundred years from now . . . and we started this movement — thank you, all of you for everything you've done. It's an honor to be in your presence. Thank you very much.*[30]

Barely a month later, Asmaa Mahfouz appeared in Liberty Square echoing Moore's sentiments and noting the movement's common cause with what happened in the Arab Spring. "Many of US residents were in solidarity with us," she said. "So, we have to keep going all over the world, because another world is possible for all of us."[31]

Still, by the end of 2011, Occupy encampments faced enormous strain, given the movement's strategic choices. The most obvious was the decision to maintain permanent encampments; this led to intense exchanges with security forces, but also, at times, between movement participants. It was one thing to assail the 1 per cent, or neoliberal capitalism itself. It was another to resist police incursions, maintain the daily needs of occupiers, satisfy a commitment to horizontal, "consensus-driven" mass meetings, while also meeting the mental health needs of the homeless and others who frequented the encampments. In this sense, Occupy's inclusiveness was a challenge, but one participants felt was crucial to shoulder.

Other progressives lamented where Occupy fell short. A commitment to anti-oppression — to being mindful of (and challenging) racism, sexism, homophobia, and transphobia, among other things — was often championed in this movement, but that didn't prevent several instances where that objective was questioned. Some noted the lack of racial diversity in the movement, and even a lack of analytical depth in grasping the interplay of race and the movement's own identity. Brittany Robinson, an Occupy activist and African-American filmmaker from the Bronx, put it this way:

> *Why are people of color missing? There are a couple of easy answers to that. For one, it's socioeconomic advantages that some people have and they don't. For the most part, people of color have to work and can't take off five days of work and go protest. There's also not strong enough outreach from the Occupy Wall Street movement to these areas — let's say Brownsville, or the Bronx, or Queens — where these people of color are impacted directly by the issues that they are fighting for here.*[32]

In Ottawa and Toronto, when Aboriginal activists voiced their discomfort with white progressives donning an "Occupy" banner because the land, they insisted, was already being occupied by Canada, a colonial power, they were asked to rethink their arguments as "semantical concerns." Another frequent complaint was instances of sexual assault, which some encampments addressed better than others. These were real concerns that, at times, limited Occupy's outreach and challenged its internal cohesion.

Occupy's refusal to offer demands also drew outrage from the mainstream media, and even from some in progressive circles. As before with the Seattle protests, the movement was asked to present a manifesto others could rally behind. Faced with that challenge, organizers preferred a more open-ended terrain. It was enough, most felt, to alert public opinion to exploitation and oppression, and demonstrate forms of co-operative living in practice. Battling over the ideal plan would sap the movement's vitality and detract from the more important task of radical education. That argument offered a useful solution to a long-standing problem, but it also limited the potential for resistance and meant others could steal Occupy's rhetoric to suit their own needs. Mitt Romney and Barack Obama, for example, took turns presenting themselves as candidates for the 99 per cent as they battled for the US presidency. In that case and others, Occupy shaped popular discourse, but a coherent and consistent means to exercise resistance was yet to be discovered. After a few months, Occupy encampments were closed, leading some to conclude the movement had subsided.

In reality, however, Occupy veterans shifted to related concerns. In due course, a student strike in Quebec, mobilizations against oil pipelines, relief efforts for Hurricane Sandy, and support for indigenous political action gave activists plenty of work. The appeal of grassroots activism would remain, the spectacle of protest movements would continue, and the importance of participatory organizing would once again be understood. The rest of this book chronicles the evolution of these things in social movements, unions, and political parties. I firmly believe these developments, while contradictory, can renew and transform the political Left.

# 2

# GRASSROOTS MOVEMENTS:
## COGS THAT TURN LARGER WHEELS

*I attempted to rise, but was not able to stir: for as I happened to lie on my back, I found my arms and legs were strongly fastened on each side to the ground; and my hair, which was long and thick, tied down in the same manner.*

*I likewise felt several slender ligatures across my body, from my armpits to my thighs. I could only look upwards, the sun began to grow hot, and the light offended mine eyes. I heard a confused noise about me, but in the posture I lay, could see nothing except the sky.*

— *Jonathan Swift*, Gulliver's Travels[1]

*"Sometimes," said Pooh, "the smallest things take up the most room in your heart."*

— *A. A. Milne*, The House at Pooh Corner[2]

So far in this book, I've claimed a resurgence in activism requires fresh thinking about modern protest. Today's grassroots movements, I've argued, emerge from an important recent history, one first seen with the rise of Zapatismo, but continued in other waves of progressive dissent. Throughout, activists have blurred local/global distinctions, embraced bold ideas, and pioneered new forms of political organization. These are the hallmarks of today's bottom-up movements who often punch, as political actors, well above their weight.

This was something Jeremy Brecher, Tim Costello, and Brendan Smith observed over a decade ago in their insightful book *Globalization from Below*, and they invoked *Gulliver's Travels* to emphasize its potentials. The metaphor was accurate, and is even worth extending into the more familiar world of A. A. Milne's *Winnie-the-Pooh*. As I have seen from personal experience, grassroots movements, like Swift's Lilliputians, can tie up a corporate Gulliver with a thousand threads. And like Milne's warm, disarming Pooh, they can "occupy" the most room in our hearts.

But hold on, some might say, what do such pleasant generalities obscure? Today's activists and movements may offer important contributions, and at times even challenge neoliberal ideas. But capitalism's apologists remain entrenched in power positions, while a progressive establishment — unions, large NGOs, and foundations — drives most social justice work. In fact, many claim neoliberal ideas have seeped into established Left groups, shaping the contours of progressive campaigns in worrying directions. A growing literature documents this worrying trend and the thinking that sees "political legitimacy" as more important than training a new generation of troublemakers. Today the average Canadian NGO, one study claims, draws 50 per cent of its budget from government transfers, and that source is precarious at best. By 2009, the overall size of the US "non-profit industrial complex" was a staggering $1.3 trillion, or the seventh largest economy on earth, with much room taken by corporate fronts posing as movement friends. And unions, while outsiders in their early years, are now important brokers in mainstream politics, and often find themselves in conflict with other progressive groups.

These are uncomfortable realities, and those aware of them are unlikely to be pleased with grassroots blips on the wider progressive landscape. Vague references to "civil society" and "social movements" won't help either, given that these terms obscure disagreements and obstacles to restoring the power of progressive ideas. More important is analysis that questions the direction of progressive strategy, and the ideas and factors informing it. This chapter offers that very analysis, but seen through the contributions of grassroots movements who have, in key moments, shifted established Left groups and even the political mainstream. In the cases reviewed here, grassroots movements operate like a small cog that turns those larger wheels. This is the exciting process I highlight in activism for climate justice, indigenous sovereignty, and Palestinian human rights.

## POWERSHIFT? GRASSROOTS ACTIVISM IN MOVEMENTS FOR CLIMATE JUSTICE

*Mountaintop removal and climate change, and all the other injustices that we are experiencing, are not being driven solely by the coal industry, solely by lobbyists, or solely by the failure of our politicians. They are also happening because of the cowardice of the environmental movement.*

*We hold the power right here to create our vision of a healthy and just world, if we are willing to make the sacrifices to make it happen. And if we're not, if we don't have the will right now to end mountaintop removal this year, if we don't have that courage and that commitment, then when are we gonna get it?*

— *Tim DeChristopher, April 17, 2011*[3]

Tim DeChristopher, a green activist from West Virginia, spoke these words to a packed audience of ten thousand at "Powershift," an important conference of environmental youth activists. His speech reflected a widespread sentiment in green movements, one frustrated with slow progress on urgent problems. Since the publication of Rachel Carson's *Silent Spring* in 1962, North America's green movements have highlighted the negative impacts of human activity in the natural world and won reforms on issues like toxic chemicals, acid rain, and the treatment of municipal waste. "Mountaintop removal," the subject DeChristopher cites, is a telling recent example; it involves a surreal process where up to 250 metres of rock and soil is blasted from woodland heights to access coal seams. To facilitate this, forests are clear-cut, while massive draglines tear open mountaintops in short order. Other giant machines then dig up and cart away the coal, while the residue (aka: mountaintops) is dumped into nearby valleys. Meanwhile, ecosystems are destroyed, habitats are altered, and traditional mining communities are changed forever. This process, concentrated largely in the Appalachian mountain range of DeChristopher's home, has elicited a firestorm of protest, but it has not stopped the fossil fuels industry. Instead, as with tar sands development, or hydraulic fracturing ("fracking") for natural gas, "mountaintop removal" is touted as an "energy security" strategy to end our "reliance on foreign oil." In reality, these practices demonstrate the insatiable growth of fossil fuels extraction at the expense of a warming planet.

By the time of DeChristopher's speech, the green activists I knew were mired in an intense process of soul-searching. Despite eloquent appeals to politicians, adept consciousness-raising efforts, and a wealth of scientific evidence, neoliberal, market-driven ideas still dominated the climate change debate. On the one hand, industry lobbyists tried to frighten the public with the prospects of tougher greenhouse gas emissions targets and, in doing so, reinforced people's ambivalence: While many championed green initiatives (e.g., municipal recycling, public transportation, community gardens), the prospects of dramatic reforms, at least as the industry defined them, seemed daunting. On the other hand, most established green groups also did not look beyond market-driven alternatives (e.g., cap-and-trade systems for polluters and sustainable choices for consumers). Environmentalists were hamstrung by the reality that consumer-based solutions weren't enough, and they didn't challenge the power of the fossil fuels industry. Bill McKibben, a well-known green organizer, described the dilemma this way:

> We know a lot about what strategies don't work. Green groups, for instance, have spent a lot of time trying to change individual lifestyles: the iconic twisty light bulb has been installed by the millions, but so have a new generation of energy-sucking flatscreen TVs. Most of us are fundamentally ambivalent about going green: We like cheap flights to warm places, and we're certainly not going to give them up if everyone else is still taking them.
>
> Since all of us are in some way the beneficiaries of cheap fossil fuel, tackling climate change has been like trying to build a movement against yourself — it's as if the gay-rights movement had to be constructed entirely from evangelical preachers, or the abolition movement from slaveholders.
>
> People perceive — correctly — that their individual actions will not make a decisive difference in the atmospheric concentration of $CO_2$; by 2010, a poll found that "while recycling is widespread in America and 73 percent of those polled are paying bills online in order to save paper," only four percent had reduced their utility use and only three percent had purchased hybrid cars. Given a hundred years, you could conceivably change lifestyles enough to matter — but time is precisely what we lack.[4]

In these limited horizons, traditional green activism was floundering, and that impasse meant little progress in formal decision-making circles. The 2009 UN climate change conference in Copenhagen meandered for weeks before leaders brokered a compromise that pleased no one. The mandatory emissions targets in the 1997 Kyoto Protocol were replaced by less stringent voluntary measures. The American *Clean Energy and Security Act*, a singular obsession of many US green groups for months, was diluted beyond recognition to pass the House of Representatives on June 26, 2009. The following year, it was defeated in the US Senate.

US officials blamed the global financial crisis and pointed a finger at industrializing economies (like India and China) for being reluctant to entertain serious changes. Those concerns, of course, were distractions from the larger political context. By early 2011, green activism had not forced anyone's hand, and DeChristopher was not alone in bemoaning a lack of urgency among environmentalists themselves. The green activists I spoke with lamented the shortcomings of early Powershift conferences in 2007 and 2009 that, while providing an important place for organizing, often validated the top-down strategies common to large environmental groups. Emphasis was placed on articulate speakers, detailed research, and training aimed at convincing political leaders to champion green issues. The logic underlying this strategy was plain enough; greens believed the facts were clear and decision-makers would be moved to act on the basis of the facts. Who could ignore the impact of climate change after Hurricane Katrina and the horrifying spectacle of families left abandoned on rooftops? Who could refute the case made in Al Gore's *An Inconvenient Truth*, the first widely seen film on climate change in decades? Who could deny the earth's warming temperatures, rising oceans, and melting ice-caps? After decades of UN climate change conferences, the urgency to act was palpable, and many felt hope was around the corner. In November 2008, on the night of his election victory, Barack Obama promised action to "cool the ocean's waters, and allow the planet to heal." He appointed Van Jones, a prominent green organizer, to oversee the growth of green jobs. He pledged subsidies for renewable forms of energy production, and fuel efficiency limits on cars. As the Copenhagen UN conference approached, most greens expected leadership from the podium and urgency from those with political power.

What they got, of course, was quite different. The Copenhagen conference, as several activists told me, was an important turning point; it was a "powershift" of its own for green organizing and the strategies used to demand action on climate change. When top-down reform proved impossible, a revolt soon found its outraged voice. In Copenhagen, President Obama faced direct action protests from Western activists and a groundswell of anger from the global South. These voices came together on the streets — and, when possible, in conference sites — and were met by heavy-handed riot police. As the talks ended, a statement from Greenpeace International captured a widespread mood:

> The city of Copenhagen is a climate crime scene tonight, with the guilty men and women fleeing to the airport in shame. World leaders had a once in a generation chance to change the world for good, to avert catastrophic climate change. What we needed was a legally binding agreement that was fair to developing countries and ambitious when it came to emissions cuts and ending deforestation. In the end they produced a poor deal full of loopholes big enough to fly Air Force One through. We've seen a year of crises, but today it is clear that the biggest one facing humanity is a leadership crisis.[5]

After Copenhagen, the green organizers I knew (most of whom were young, campus-based activists) used grassroots activism to address the leadership crisis on climate change. Rather than turning to politicians, they turned to themselves and pursued bottom-up efforts to broaden education and urgency for green alternatives. For inspiration, many drew on principles of "environmental justice" first articulated by indigenous, African-American, and Latino-American activists in the early 1990s. At the 1991 People of Color Environmental Justice Leadership Summit in Washington, DC, these communities came together to expose the link between environmental degradation and racism (the term "environmental racism" — now widely used — was first heard there). At issue were state and corporate actors who for decades had used North America's communities of colour as dumping grounds for toxic waste, or places where green reforms such as removing lead municipal water pipes went undone. To chart a new course, activists produced the 1991 Principles of Environmental Justice, a document grounded in years of community organizing. The 1991 principles heralded a "grassroots national and international movement of peoples of color to fight the destruction and taking of our lands and communities." This movement, they declared, was one intent on the "political, economic, and environmental self-determination of all peoples."

In 2002, another statement of environmental justice principles emerged — but this time it came from the global South and was linked to the threat of climate change. A historic meeting in Indonesia produced the Bali Principles of Climate Justice; the meeting participants — representing an alliance of North and South progressive groups — resolved to "broaden the constituency providing leadership on climate change." The Bali Principles also marked the first widely read effort that opposed neoliberal solutions and affirmed those who bear the brunt of climate change: "small island states, women, youth, coastal peoples, local communities, indigenous peoples, fisherfolk, poor people and the elderly." Further still, the Bali Principles, taking a cue from abolitionist movements of the nineteenth century, called for "the recognition of a principle of ecological debt that industrialized governments and transnational corporations owe the rest of the world as a result of their appropriation of the planet's capacity to absorb greenhouse gases." The notion of climate justice, it went on to say, "protects the rights of victims of climate change and associated injustices to receive full compensation, restoration, and reparation for loss of land, livelihood, and other damages." These were incendiary words from those who stood to suffer most from a warming planet. And yet, by 2006, when Al Gore's *Inconvenient Truth* made headlines, these developments were largely unknown among the white, middle-class activists dominant in green groups. By the collapse of the Copenhagen talks, however, that was no longer the case; grassroots activism was making an impact, and it soon changed the nature of green organizing altogether.

The coming together of the influential group 350.org in 2007 (initially by Bill McKibben, and joined later by an array of respected activists) was a formative moment. In its name, 350.org underlined the "tipping point" limit of carbon dioxide emissions (350 parts per million of the earth's atmosphere), a figure corroborated by respected scientists and climatologists. In its activism, 350.org reprised the earlier call from 1991 and 2002 and announced an interest in building "a global grassroots movement to solve the climate crisis." 350.org leaders and activists developed relationships with First Nations and made new alliances with movements from the global South. They broadened their appeals to the inclusive framework of "climate justice," and they posed demands that challenged market-driven "cap-and-trade" alternatives. Bolder tactics were encouraged to draw wider attention, up to and including civil disobedience. Many influential green groups (like 1Sky and Tar Sands Action) affiliated to (or joined) 350.org as its impact registered in the political establishment. These developments were also evident in Powershift conferences, which by 2009 had explicit antineoliberal themes and held workshops to train effective community organizers. Cameron Fenton and Amira Possian, two organizers of the Canadian Powershift in 2009, saw the moment this way:

> The collapse of the Copenhagen talks was a body-blow to the mainstream climate movement. It represented the failure of nearly 20 years of work to build consensus and faith in the United Nations climate negotiation process. But faith without

*political will proved fatal. Thankfully, at the same time, the global climate justice movement was beginning to coalesce around the notion that the top-down model of the mainstream environmental movement is fundamentally flawed in its ability to address the systemic inequalities at the root of the climate crisis.*

*While the climate justice movement is diverse, there are a few central ideas. The movement views the climate crisis as one of many symptoms of a global economic model based on resource extraction and limitless growth on a finite planet. It rejects false market-based solutions, which perpetuate root causes while allowing polluters to continue profiting off the commodification of the earth.*

*By taking direction from those most impacted by climate change, the movement aims to operate within a collective rights and justice-based framework in order to alleviate the unequal burden created by the crisis. Fueled by the rebel energy of youth climate change activists, the climate justice movement could actually bring about the economic, political and social systemic change needed to redefine industrialized society's relationship with the planet.*[6]

With this in mind, it's worth returning to DeChristopher's 2011 speech that I cited at the top of this section. As his listeners knew well, DeChristopher's credibility in calling for more urgency was intact. In 2008, he had prevented an illegal auction of land (sought by natural gas drillers) in Utah. He had posed as an interested bidder and scuppered a process shown later to be deeply flawed. As a prominent activist in Peaceful Uprising, a direct action group based in Utah, DeChristopher went on to push for non-violent civil disobedience in other areas. For his actions, DeChristopher was levied a $10,000 fine and sentenced to two years in prison (by, it should be noted, the Obama administration), but not before emerging as a beacon for climate justice activism.

White activists like DeChristopher joined an earlier tradition of progressive campaigns, all of which were led by people of colour: environmental justice activism in the 1980s and 1990s, the US civil rights movement of the 1950s and 1960s, and even the nineteenth-century abolitionist movement that fought the evil of slavery. Climate justice activists had formed key alliances and were ready to target corporate power. They soon engaged in tactics that stopped polluters in their tracks. The urgency to act rose to a steady boil, something obvious in the closings words of DeChristopher's Powershift speech: "Let this be the last Powershift," he said, "where we leave without fighting back. Now is our time to take a stand. We're done making statements. Let this be the last time that we come together just to make statements. From now on, our movement needs to take a stand."[7]

Without question, the stand has been taken. All across North America, climate justice activists have engaged in bold activism and taken the fight to the polluters themselves. In the Appalachian Mountains, waves of civil disobedience have challenged coal producers, leading some to stop operations altogether. On the West Coast, deep community organizing has challenged the proposed Northern Gateway Pipeline for moving bitumen from the tar sands, a movement that has unified First Nations and mobilized over two hundred thousand supporters. Activists stalled government pipeline hearings, at times through civil disobedience, stymieing the plans of powerful corporations like Enbridge and Kinder Morgan. That sentiment then turned eastward to confront proposals to carry tar sands bitumen along the proposed Keystone XL pipeline or through existing pipeline capacity from Sarnia to Montreal. These proposals have also been met by outbursts of civil disobedience: In September 2011, over two hundred activists were arrested on Parliament Hill in Ottawa, and 1,253 in front of the White House. In November 2012, tree-sitters in Texas delayed pipeline construction for eighty-five days. First Nations pipeline blockades are commonplace and continuing.

Large green groups like the Sierra Club have lifted their historic aversion to civil disobedience; today it is common to see green celebrities arrested alongside others willing to put their bodies on the line.

Following the September 2011 protests, the US government announced it would delay consideration of Keystone XL, a decision heralded as a movement victory. Still, pipeline boosters remain ensconced within the halls of power and even in the ranks of some progressive groups. Notable are building trades unions (a development most expected, given the jobs at stake), but more surprising are recent statements by the AFL-CIO — the common voice for most US-based unions. On February 27, 2012, its executive board issued a call for more pipeline construction after a controversial US State Department report that, among other absurdities, argued Canada-US pipelines wouldn't facilitate tar sands expansion. The AFL-CIO did not explicitly endorse Keystone XL, but it also did not oppose massive expansion of tar sands operations. Richard Trumka, the AFL-CIO's president, justified the position this way: "We are all unanimous by saying we should build the pipeline, but we have to do it consistent with all environmental standards. I think we can work that out, I really do, and we are for that happening. We can do it [in an] environmental way and still create the jobs."[8]

For the climate justice activists, such reasoning flies in the face of climate change science and rears the ugly head of environmental racism once again. That may not be the AFL-CIO's intent, but it is the consequence of its position. When all humanity knows about climate change, it is unacceptable, even unconscionable, to think there is an "environmental way" to facilitate Keystone XL or other pipelines designed for tar sands bitumen. The Fort Chipewyan First Nation who live immediately downstream from the tar sands know this better and anyone. After four decades of development, they have seen heightened cancers, ruined ecosystems, and destroyed livelihoods. Allan Adam, their chief, had this response to arguments about Keystone XL being "non-consequential" in environmental terms:

*The fact that the Keystone XL pipeline is deemed as non-consequential simply paves the way for its approval and is directly connected to the unabated expansion of tar sands in my people's traditional lands ... and the Keystone is a vital pipeline for expansion.*

*Expansion of the tar sands means a death sentence for our way for life, destruction of eco-systems vital to the continuation of our inherent treaty rights and massive contributions to catastrophic global climate change, a fate we all share.*[9]

Marie Adam, a Fort Chipewyan elder, also speaks in lurid terms about what tar sands development has meant for her people. Lakes and rivers that once provided fresh drinking water are now fouled with daily leakages from tar sands tailings ponds — the oily residue left over from development. Pristine landscapes that once housed vast ecosystems are transformed into moonscapes, like nightmarish pictures from some dystopian movie. But above all, Adam's greatest concerns are for those who will inherit the toxic mess:

*I'm going to be 70, and I'm thinking about the children. Not just First Nations, I'm talking about everybody. The oil companies aren't thinking about how low the river is getting, how low this lake is getting. And that's very, very scary. All they see is this oil going by, you know, barrels and barrels; and money going up, up, up while our waters are doing down, down, down.*

*Fort Chip has so much cancer, so many people are sick ... how much more do they want to destroy? They are going over the limit, destroying Mother Earth, and destroying our water, our air, and those are the things we need. Without that, we will not exist.*

*I am so concerned about the water and the air for future generations. There's a saying that only when the last tree is chopped down, and only when the last fish is caught, and only when the last river is poisoned, only then will they know that money can't be eaten.*[10]

Ignoring appeals like these won't help North America's blue-green alliance. The climate justice organizers I know have a frank message for unions who support tar sands expansion: A few thousand jobs aren't worth the cost of a wrecked planet, the slow genocide of indigenous peoples, and damaged relationships between progressive movements. Some US unions understand this — the Transport Workers Union, Amalgamated Transit Union, and National Nurses United have all voiced their loud opposition. North of the forty-ninth parallel, the Communications, Energy, and Paperworkers Union (whose members include tar sands workers) have also opposed Keystone XL, claiming the risks far outweigh any minimal benefits. But these voices, as I wrote these words, were still in the minority. A majority of union leaders still seemed resigned to pipeline mega-projects and a massive expansion of tar sands development.

That impasse is unfortunate, but this much is certain: Whether or not organized labour's ambiguity shifts, green activism will not stop. Climate justice organizers will never accept that more tar sands extraction is a positive thing, even if it purports to enhance our "energy security." They will not cower when politicians call them "national security threats" or opponents of "job creation" — and the reasons for their stubbornness aren't hard to discover. As an old adage goes, there are no jobs on a dead planet; to avoid catastrophe, scientists claim 80 per cent of the planet's carbon reserves must stay in the ground. That is the objective climate justice activists I know intend to meet.

To inspire that outcome, 350.org has launched a "fossil free" campaign targeted at colleges and universities to urge pension fund divestment from holdings in the fossil fuels industry. On March 4, 2013, students from over seventy campuses gathered for an organizing conference in

Philadelphia, a development reminiscent of "students against sweat-shops" campaigns. North America's indigenous peoples — emboldened by the Idle No More movement discussed in this chapter's next section — are invoking treaty rights and pledging to challenge any further degradation of Mother Earth. Jackie Thomas, the influential chief of the Saik'uz First Nation (who has challenged Enbridge's proposed Northern Gateway pipeline), claims she has a wide mandate to block pipeline projects by any means necessary. At a fifty-thousand-strong climate justice rally in Washington, DC, she called out Enbridge specifically, noting its role in creating a stronger climate of resistance: "Never in my life have I ever seen white and Native together until now. Thank you, Enbridge, for doing this work for me."[11] This moment of green solidarity is historic, powerful, and not to be trifled with. Today's resurgence of grassroots activism, and its radicalization of green movements, has made it possible.

## IDLE NO MORE: THE RE-EMERGENCE AND RELEVANCE OF INDIGENOUS ACTIVISM

*Whether the Canadian citizens know it or not, Indigenous sovereignty and Treaties are the last stand protecting our lands and waters. It is our task and our duty to inform everyone that this is NOT about us and them. We must do this in a way that is peaceful and collectively done with all people.*

*— Sylvia McAdam, founder, Idle No More*[12]

For centuries, North America's indigenous peoples have been the object of interminable studies, reports, and well-meaning pledges, each of which yielded the same result. Now more than ever, they represent a Third World in First World conditions despite historic treaties meant to ensure indigenous sovereignty and cultural traditions. Poverty levels are obscene, and incarceration rates astoundingly high. These are, as many explain, the tell-tale signs of an oppressed people, the scars of which are all too plain on Indian land. The Cree of Attiwapiskat, whose remote northern community faces an acute housing crisis, offers a telling case in point.

Dubbed "Haiti at 40 below" by some, Attiwapiskat exemplifies the extent of Canada's colonial legacy. For three years, its chief, Theresa Spence, announced a housing crisis. As many as twenty-five residents huddle in one of the ramshackle bungalows, or survive in teepees without plumbing and running water. People wear nylon coats to meet arctic breezes, and families face soaring prices for staple items imported from elsewhere. To address these untenable conditions, a steady stream of largely white, male, and southern consultants have offered advice on "financial management," or tools to "maximize human capital." Lurking beneath this jargon is the ever-present reality of Indian and Norther Affairs Canada, whose policies — empowered by Canada's *Indian Act* — dictate most details of Attiwapiskat's daily existence. In this context, desperate attempts are made to spread resources across a yawning gap of need, but they always fall short in key areas such as housing. Without emergency appeals, Attiwapiskat's ongoing problems would be even worse, inconceivable as it sounds.

And yet, as indigenous activists told me, this dire situation for an indigenous people happens in a place where others earn great wealth. DeBeers, the South African mining giant, recently built a diamond mine ninety kilometres away from Attiwapiskat, a project worth $6.7 billion in potential revenues. In 2010, DeBeers told its shareholders that barely 1 per cent of its yearly profits went toward Impact Benefit Agreements negotiated with communities like Attiwapiskat. Thousands of kilometres west in booming Alberta, the Lubicon Cree's story is similar. Despite having never signed a treaty that relinquished their land, they have seen over $14 billion in resources taken away without any form of compensation. Dru Oja Jay describes the resulting conditions:

*The community has gone without running water, endured divisive attacks from the government, and suffered the environmental consequences of unchecked extraction. Sour gas flaring next to the community resulted in an epidemic of health problems, and stillborn babies.*

*Moose and other animals fled the area, rendering the community's previously self-sufficient lifestyle untenable overnight. In 2011, an oil pipeline burst, spilling 4.5 million litres of oil onto Lubicon territory. The Lubicon remain without a treaty, and the extraction continues.*[13]

Similar stories are evident across North America, sowing deep resentment and anger. On some occasions the anger has boiled over, leading to an upsurge of indigenous protest — that was the case by the end of the 1960s, and once more in the late 1980s and early 1990s. Each time, decision-makers have responded with a mix of coercion and limited dialogue, all of which has done little to change a colonial paradigm. In fact, an insatiable appetite for resource extraction has entrenched this power structure, creating instance after instance where governments help to circumvent indigenous rights.

In 2012, Canada's federal government expedited that process through proposed "omnibus" legislation (Bill C-45) affecting forty-four different aspects of federal law. Critics argued these changes were designed to facilitate extractive projects, whether through relaxed environmental laws or further intrusions into indigenous rights. In one notable instance, through changes to the *Navigable Waters Act*, 99 per cent of lakes and rivers were removed from the list of waterways under federal environmental regulations. Most of the newly deregulated waters ran through First Nations land; indigenous leaders believed that the state, through this measure, intended to silence their opposition to resource development, notably against pipelines linked to tar sands expansion. On December 4, 2012, when a delegation of chiefs travelled to Canada's federal Parliament to voice their concerns, they were refused entry. Video of that refusal went viral through the Internet, helping foster a new moment for indigenous protest. Activism soon coalesced around Idle No More, a grassroots movement representing a new generation's outrage and hope for a better tomorrow.

How this bold movement started said much about its most telling characteristics. It began as a teach-in organized in Saskatoon by Nina Wilson, Sheelah McLean, Sylvia McAdam, and Jessica Gordon, four indigenous women who were furious about the federal government's stepped-up intrusions. The event was framed under a banner that read "Idle No More," making clear its goal was to stimulate activism and reignite a wider sense of indigenous pride. That pride soon took concrete forms as First Nations marches, round dances, and drumming circles were soon widely seen in urban areas, interacting with holiday shoppers and raising awareness about the issues at stake. On December 10, co-ordinated events like these put Idle No More on the map; on this day as well, Attiwapiskat's Chief Theresa Spence and four other indigenous leaders began a hunger strike in Ottawa, a short walk from the Canadian Parliament. The strikers announced their full support for Idle No More and demanded an urgent meeting with Canada's prime minister and Governor General, representing the original treaty partners. On December 16, the Assembly of First Nations (AFN) — an indigenous federation funded in part by Indian and Northern Affairs Canada — announced its support for this objective. In very short order, an inspired grassroots movement was shifting larger forces.

The days that followed saw even more indigenous activism, often joined by others from non-Aboriginal backgrounds. Time and again, the movement's organizers were women, with a noticeable presence of indigenous youth in successive demonstrations. The prominent role of youth was not surprising, given demographic trends; today, 75 per cent of First Nations within Canadian borders are under age thirty, leading some to claim Canada's future is "young and aboriginal" in certain regions.[14] As these young faces emerged alongside others, many chiefs quickly supported Idle No More, taking pains to thank organizers for their leadership, pride, and enthusiasm. But from the onset, it was clear this movement would not wait for official support. It would champion grassroots activism and organize outside Canada's *Indian Act* rules. Pam Palmater — a university professor, member of the Mi'kmaq Nation, and frequent Idle No More spokesperson — made that point explicit:

> *The Idle No More movement, initially started by women, is a peoples' movement that empowers Indigenous peoples to stand up for their Nations, lands, treaties and sovereignty.*
>
> *This movement is unique because it is purposefully distanced from political and corporate influence. There is no elected leader, no paid Executive Director, and no bureaucracy or hierarchy which determines what any person or First Nation can and can't do.*
>
> *There are no colonial-based lines imposed on who joins the movement and thus issues around on & off-reserve, status and non-status, treaty and non-treaty, man or woman, elder or youth, chief or citizen does not come into play. This movement is inclusive of all our peoples.*[15]

Art Manuel, a celebrated indigenous leader, has offered a similar observation. What he saw was an entirely different approach to political activism, one not easily satisfied by common ploys:

> *Idle No More is a movement led by young people and women, and they have had it with discrimination and poverty — it's fine for the AFN to gain concessions for more talks at higher levels, but that won't satisfy this movement.*
>
> *Clean across the country, the kind of changes Idle No More wants aren't going to be negotiated through talk at a*

*table. Idle No More is finding its feet, it's learning and grow-
ing, it's broadly-based and it is learning how to put pressure
on the Canadian system to move.*[16]

This rebellious, inclusive approach would endear Idle No More to
many, even to local organizers initially doubtful of its potential. An
example was Kirsten Scansen, who wrote about her own experience:

*At first I was skeptical about the Idle No More movement. I
didn't want to lead my people to the government and beg for
rights and responsibilities that the Creator gave to us. But I
became involved with Idle No More because I could feel the
energy of the youth rising and I did not want this energy to
go to waste. I wanted to show them that the energy which we
as peoples often internalize in negative ways is better directed
to challenging the colonial framework that operates in all our
lives.*

*As the movement grows, the challenge of Idle No More
is to continue moving beyond rhetoric and towards a fundamental reconfiguration of the colonial structure of Canada.
Above and beyond, it must always be more than an emotion-
ally frothy appeal to the Canadian government for justice and
morality. We must be strategic, yet we must also act on the nation-to-nation spirit and intent of Treaty. The message of love,
peace, and non-violent protest is essential to the movement.*

*With this spirit at the forefront, we must seek to educate
Settler populations and heal our Indigenous nations from
the processes of genocide which we have experienced. Idle No
More means re-establishing ourselves as sovereign nations,
and empowering Settler people to fulfill their responsibilities
as partners in sacred relationships of Treaty.*[17]

In vivid prose, Scansen recounts the moment her Idle No More activism collided with the local power structure in Prince Albert, Saskatchewan. Her reflections are worth quoting at length:

> *In solidarity with the wider movement, myself and a small group of committed people organized a teach-in, march and round dance in Prince Albert's downtown core for December 21. I phoned city planners out of respect to advise them of our routes and to possibly have some cooperation with local police officials. I was told by a city employee that the route requested would probably be denied. I thought nothing of this possibility until the mayor phoned me on my cell phone and left me a message. He stated that he would "not allow" the route down busy streets, and that our rally could not be "permitted".*
>
> *To be sure, I did not call for their permission. Asserting Indigenous sovereignty does not require permission. Protecting treaty rights and fundamental human rights does not require permission. However, the reality of my communication with the mayor begged the question: was he implying that force would be used upon my people to prevent the protest? Since we were not breaking laws, what basis did he have to assert jurisdiction over our rights to freedom of assembly and free speech? Should Idle No More Prince Albert back down from asserting Indigenous sovereignty and use the dusty backroads suggested by the mayor? Upon consulting with Idle No More Prince Albert, the answer to this last question was an overwhelming "NO!"*
>
> *One cannot fully comprehend the true nature of the colonial relationship until being forced to ask yourself whether or not 500 people are being led into a potentially violent confrontation with the Royal Canadian Mounted Police. One cannot fully comprehend the true nature of colonialism until*

*the right to life, liberty, and security of 500 people, including children, youth, and Elders, is at risk.*

*Regardless of the unwelcoming political climate, the rally went ahead as planned. Idle No More Prince Albert was very much a success. Nobody was hurt and nobody was arrested, although there were a handful of irate drivers. In Prince Albert, we fought for our right to fight for our rights, and we won. The sound of drumming had not rang so freely in the city for hundreds of years. The spirit of Idle No More makes it possible to decolonize times and places, and to live out the freedom that guided the lives of our ancestors. For Prince Albert, the movement has meant a reconfiguration of Indigenous and Settler relationships; we asserted Indigenous sovereignty by re-establishing the justness of our presence in the city.*

*Idle No More presents a challenge to the old colonial order that forms the basis of Canadian society. This movement has been about challenging oppression in very real and very meaningful ways. It has meant questioning the legitimacy and authority of colonial laws by pushing the limits of these laws. Idle No More means not only speaking of Indigenous sovereignty, but living out our inherent sovereignty as nations.*

*This is especially important in the case of Omnibus Bill C-45, where our fundamental human rights to clean water, lands and foods are at risk. Essentially, Harper and the Conservative government of Canada are legislating the extinguishment of our Indigenous nationhood. Our response has been two-fold: to re-situate ourselves as nations, and to rejuvenate the commitment of our people and Settler society to the Treaty relationship.[18]*

In these words, we get a ground-level sense of the confidence that was building on Indian land and how it quickly led to widespread action. By the end of 2012, over a hundred Idle No More events had taken place, some of which were far from North American shores. By early 2013, the movement was dominating airwaves, earning the kind of media attention normally reserved for mainstream political actors. That attention drew outpourings of support from a wide range of sources — including former Canadian prime ministers and several established progressive groups. On the heels of this, the AFN and some chiefs released statements calling for action in Idle No More's name. Reminding everyone of Idle No More's purpose, however, its founders released a statement emphasizing the activist layer of the movement's base:

> *The Chiefs have called for action and anyone who chooses can join with them, however this is not part of the Idle No More movement as the vision of this grassroots movement does not coincide with the visions of the Leadership. While we appreciate the individual support we have received from Chiefs and councillors, we have been given a clear mandate by the grassroots to work outside of the systems of government and that is what we will continue to do.*[19]

The statement went on to insist Idle No More was not a repudiation of existing First Nations leadership, only a shift outside its traditional boundaries. The movement would make appeals on a grassroots basis, and mobilize its support toward shifting the fortunes of indigenous peoples everywhere. On January 4, 2013, Idle No More founders, following elaborate consultation and discussion with community groups, also clarified the movement's two main goals: "1) The establishment of a nation-to-nation relationship between First Nations and the Government of Canada, rather than a relationship as defined in the Indian Act; and 2) social and environmental sustainability."[20]

By this point, many activists I spoke to felt Idle No More had moved beyond the limitations of Occupy Wall Street, for the movement's goals also focused political demands on tangible reforms. Acknowledging indigenous sovereignty (and dispensing with Canada's *Indian Act*) was an obvious goal, and a learning opportunity for those unaware of our colonial past. Indigenous communities had long been leaders of progressive organizing on the fronts of social and environmental sustainability, too. Campaigns for affordable housing, enhanced health care, nutritious food, even progressive taxation — any number of other demands were ably included in Idle No More's unifying vision.

As indigenous organizers told white sympathizers, this unity often emerged from what Idle No More activists held in common. Unlike Occupy, they shared a long history, with roots reaching back through centuries of oppression. That meant access to common stories, powerful traditions, community organizers, leaders, and pre-existing sources of institutional support. That was certainly Bill McKibben's view after seeking out indigenous allies in climate justice organizing:

> *Eighteen months ago, when we at the climate campaign 350. org started organizing against the Keystone XL Pipeline, the very first allies we came across were from the Indigenous Environmental Network — people like Tom Goldtooth and Clayton Thomas-Muller. They'd been working for years to alert people to the scale of the devastation in Alberta's tar sands belt, where native lands had been wrecked and poisoned by the immense scale of the push to mine "the dirtiest energy on earth." And they quickly introduced me to many more — heroes like Melina Laboucan-Massimo, a member of the Cree Nation who was traveling the world explaining exactly what was going on.*
>
> *When, in late summer 2011, we held what turned into the biggest civil disobedience action in 30 years in this country, the most overrepresented group were indigenous North Americans — in percentage terms they outnumbered even the*

*hardy band of Guilty Liberals like me. And what organizers!*
*Heather Milton-Lightning, night after night training new*
*waves of arrestees; Gitz Crazyboy of Fort Chipewyan, Alberta*
*absolutely on fire as he described the land he could no longer*
*hunt and fish.*

*In the year since, the highlights of incessant cam-*
*paigning have been visits to Canada, always to see native*
*leaders in firm command of the fight — Dene National*
*Chief Bill Erasmus in Yellowknife, or Chief Reuben George*
*along the BC coast. Young and powerful voices like Caleb*
*Behn, from the province's interior; old and steady leaders*
*in one nation after another. I've never met Chief Theresa*
*Spence, the Attawapiskat leader whose hunger strike has*
*been the galvanizing center of #IdleNoMore but I have no*
*doubt she's cut of the same cloth.[21]*

By early January 2013, the organizing talents of Idle No More activists were obvious, but objections soon emerged from some indigenous
leaders. As the fourth week of Chief Spence's hunger strike approached,
some questioned her demand for a joint meeting with Canada's prime
minister and Governor General. Matthew Coon Come, Grand Chief
of the Grand Council of the Crees, was publicly urging for diminished
expectations. A high-level meeting with Canada's prime minister and
relevant cabinet ministers, he argued, was an "acceptable compromise"
to begin "a new process" in seeking redress for long-ignored promises.
The AFN's leadership agreed, and responded positively when the Prime
Minister's Office announced a meeting of this nature for January 11,
2013.

That development, however, evoked outrage from other indigenous
voices who supported Chief Spence's position. Given the original treaty
partners, it was crucial, they argued, to ensure Crown representatives
(like the Governor General) were involved in high-level discussions;

doing otherwise would undermine positive legal precedents and the goal of restoring nation-to-nation treaty obligations. Regardless, the January 11, 2013, meeting went ahead as planned, with the AFN delegates engaging Prime Minister Stephen Harper and various cabinet ministers in a day-long session. Grand Chief Coon Come emerged from the meeting to say the prime minister had "moved a couple of posts forward," sentiments echoed by Shawn Atleo, the AFN's Grand Chief.

But detailed notes taken by AFN staff and later released publicly suggested the opposite was true. The prime minister, with typical condescension, is recorded as stating that First Nations shouldn't be "looking for a cheque" in resource development on indigenous lands.[22] The broader goal, he claimed, is "participating in all aspects of development and spin-off benefits."[23] Indigenous leaders have heard this pitch before, only to be shunted aside later in settler documents fortified by legalese. More informative were comments Harper made that referenced tensions between Idle No More, existing indigenous leadership, and the shape of public opinion on aboriginal issues. Those contending forces, Harper claimed, present two realities: "The first is the pressure felt by First Nations leaders. The second is the negative public reaction that this invokes."[24] Evident here is Harper's cold political calculus: Idle no More, he believes, is no threat to him, but it is worrisome to indigenous leaders and to wider prejudices in settler society. Ironically enough, aspects of this position are likely true.

Clearly, controversy remains among indigenous leaders, all of whom are grappling with how to respond to Idle No More. Many, as already explained, welcome the movement, and are actively thinking about how this energy can break logjams that have flummoxed the wisest elders. Others likely perceive Idle No More as an unaccountable political actor, one that could potentially undermine projects requiring a longer perspective. But whatever the outcome of such debates, settler society should hardly be surprised this vigorous debate exists, for assuming a "common mind" among First Nations is yet another trope of colonial prejudice. Bill Namagoose, Executive Director of the Grand Council of the Crees, made this point after the January 11, 2013, meeting between the AFN and Canadian prime minister. "There's a double standard," he said, "if we expect Aboriginal people to be totally unanimous on everything, whereas Canadian society can be divided on all sorts of things. In the mainstream media, you can have a hundred native people in the room, 99 agree and one of them doesn't agree — the one that didn't agree will make the headlines."[25]

More importantly, ignorance is rife among non-Natives on indigenous concerns, and that is a crucial challenge progressives must address. Many have accepted the notion, constantly reinforced at a variety of levels, that government does "too much" for First Nations, and that "internal corruption" is the largest issue facing indigenous communities. This is why Chief Spence was widely attacked following accusations — later proven to be misleading — about financial mismanagement in Attiwapiskat. Within weeks of her hunger strike, these well-timed charges spurred a barrage of personal attacks, and not just from the usual suspects. Senior right-wing politicians also got in on the act. At a fundraiser in Orleans (an Ottawa suburb), Patrick Brazeau, a former Algonquin chief and outspoken Senator, led the audience in mocking Chief Spence's weight and appearance ("She's still fat," he claimed, despite the hunger strike).[26] Not to be outdone, Royal Galipeau, the riding's federal politician and former Speaker of Canada's federal Parliament, claimed he "noticed that manicure of hers. I tell you Anne [Galipeau's spouse] can't afford it."[27] Remarks like these were common online and through various talk radio programs, and would never be condoned if made against white leaders. The fact that no outcry happened from mainstream sources testifies to the racist and sexist assumptions deeply ingrained in settler society. Idle No More, to be sure, presents a "teachable moment" to question this status quo and shift public attitudes in a more progressive direction, but far more work remains to be done.

Nevertheless, Harper is wrong to underestimate the threat Idle No

More poses to neoliberal plans and the corporate giants poised to fulfill them. As Clayton Thomas-Muller told me, the embers of Aboriginal resistance were already burning before Idle No More; the movement simply carried them to a higher, more uproarious fire. That fire presents the best chance in generations to right past wrongs; its momentum touches the very lands corporate giants are seeking for development at the expense of us all. It is no exaggeration to claim, as Idle No More founder Sylvia McAdam does, that a sustainable future requires unity with indigenous peoples. Activism with this in mind must guide progressive strategy in the months, years, and decades ahead.

## SOLIDARITY WITH PALESTINE: OLIVE TREES, CATERPILLARS, AND FLOTILLAS

*Please tell people: what's happening in Palestine isn't a "conflict". It isn't a war between equals. It is an illegal occupation funded by Western dollars, and that funding must end. We need your help to make this happen.*

— *Emad Burnat*[28]

*The international media and our government are not going to tell us that we are effective, important, justified in our work, courageous, intelligent, valuable. We have to do that for each other, and one way we can do that is by continuing our work, visibly.*

— *Rachel Corrie*[29]

On a memorable day as I walked the corridors of Toronto's York University, a heated debate broke out before my very eyes. On one side were supporters of the Israeli government (largely Jewish students and campus conservatives) who handed out flyers that read "more hummus, less Hamas." They appealed to passers-by to partake in their food (which, ironically, was an Arab snack) and talk about threats to Israel, "the only democracy in the Middle East." On the other side were Arab students and progressive activists, who assailed the effort as yet another example of colonial prejudice, and held their ground amidst taunts and racist insults. As someone raised in white, rural, Anglo-Saxon Ontario, I found this spectacle astonishing; I knew of no other issue that invoked such heated debate, and this despite being familiar with the pro-choice movement that had faced violent attacks by anti-abortion extremists.

As I've learned since, considerable world attention has been focused on the Israeli occupation of Palestinian lands, and for good reason. Many activists I know regard Palestine as a defining subject in global politics, and the Israeli state's actions leaves little doubt as to why. As several compelling accounts make plain, Palestinians have undergone enormous suffering since the 1948 seizure of their land and subsequent military occupation of what remains in the West Bank and Gaza Strip. As over four hundred thousand settlers have established militarized outposts in the Occupied Territories over the ensuing decades, Israel's grip over Palestine has increased steadily, interrupted at times through human rights reports, peace negotiations, and two major Palestinian intifadas (uprisings).

From the start of the last intifada of 2000 until 2008, over five thousand Palestinians were killed and twenty-eight thousand injured by the Israeli Defence Forces (IDF). From 2008 to present, a period that includes Israel's "Operation Cast Lead" at the end of 2008 and early 2009, over seventeen hundred Palestinians were killed and five thousand injured. Israel today holds over ten thousand Palestinians in its prisons, including children and teenagers; many of them have undergone lengthy hunger strikes to challenge their jailers. Since 1948, over twenty-four thousand Palestinian homes have been destroyed by the IDF, leaving thousands homeless and confined to vast refugee camps that critics call the largest open-air prisons in the world.

The results of these efforts have been harrowing. Over a decade ago, the Palestinian Red Crescent Society observed that "in the West Bank, 57.8 per cent of households were below the poverty line, while in the Gaza Strip the figure reached 84.6 per cent. Translating these figures on an individual level, more than two-thirds of the Palestinian population is living on less that $1.90 a day."[30] The UN Office for the Coordination of Humanitarian Affairs and the World Bank have updated these figures, pointing out that unemployment since has ranged from 39 to 70 per cent.

In this context, freedom of movement for Palestinians today is practically non-existent. Stringent military checkpoints and curfews (often amounting to days of house-bound confinement) are commonplace in the West Bank and Gaza Strip. Since 2007, the entire Gaza Strip has faced an Israeli military blockade that prevents most imports and exports. In the West Bank, entire towns have been separated from each other, sliced through by "Jewish-only" highways for settlers, creating Bantustans on the model of South Africa's earlier apartheid regime. Indeed, Desmond Tutu, one of the most recognized spokespersons of the South African liberation movement, felt compelled to say as much after a visit to the Occupied Territories in 2002:

> I've been very deeply distressed in my visit to the Holy Land; it reminded me so much of what happened to us black people in South Africa. I have seen the humiliations of the Palestinians at checkpoints and roadblocks, suffering like us when young white police officers prevented us from moving about … I have experienced Palestinians pointing to what were their homes, now occupied by Jewish Israelis. I was walking with Canon Naim Ateek (the head of the Sabeel Ecumenical Centre) in Jerusalem. He pointed and said: "Our home was over there. We were driven out of our home; it is now occupied by Israeli Jews."[31]

The parallels here are hard to deny. Those who pass through military checkpoints today in the Gaza Strip or West Bank face hours of delay en route to work. Prominent Palestinian leaders are assassinated at will by Israeli snipers, while entire towns are terrorized through targeted killings at times involving innocent civilians, even children. Houses are routinely destroyed or raided by the IDF for suspected militants. Ambulances are regularly stopped at checkpoints, resulting in lack of access to medical care or, not infrequently, death before treatment. Israel has justified these measures as acts of self-defence against suicide bombers, but even mainstream Israeli politicians like Avraham Burg, Labour Party MP and Speaker of the Israeli Knesset from 1999 to 2003, are less convinced:

> *Israel, having ceased to care about the children of the Palestinians, should not be surprised when they come washed in hatred and blow themselves up in the centres of Israeli escapism. They consign themselves to Allah in our places of recreation, because their own lives are torture. They spill their own blood in our restaurants in order to ruin our appetites, because they have children and parents at home who are hungry and humiliated.*[32]

Under these conditions of abject suffering, the IDF has carried out — or overseen — a systematic assault on Palestinian infrastructure. Available resources have been rerouted to Israel or settlements, while Palestinian olive trees and water systems are frequently poisoned or destroyed. The latest effort of the Israeli government in this regard has involved the construction of a 670-kilometre wall, standing eight metres in height, meant to cordon off the West Bank from Israel to thwart potential suicide bombers. The wall has gone well beyond the "green line" separating Israel from the West Bank, annexing 975 square kilometres to Israel and displacing over a hundred and sixty thousand Palestinians. The wall has been condemned by human rights groups the world over, and was even deemed illegal by an International Court of Justice judgment rendered July 9, 2004. None of this, however, has dissuaded Israel from continuing the wall's construction, maintaining its blockade of Gaza, and building new settlements in the West Bank.

In this dispiriting context, the way grassroots activists have supported Palestinians has been nothing short of remarkable. José Bové, the militant French farmer renowned for "dismantling" a McDonald's in his native Millau, emerged in the Occupied Territories in March 2002 as IDF forces besieged the offices of the Palestinian Liberation Organization and carried out horrifying massacres in Jenin and Ramallah. Bové's justification for being there made plain that his was a gesture of solidarity, not sympathy: "I'm a farmer, and these people are farmers too. So I am fighting with them to help them protect their land."[33] Bové was expelled from the Occupied Territories, but not before shedding an international spotlight on the Palestinian cause.

Less widely known, however, was the group of activists Bové joined during his appearance in the Occupied Territories. While there, Bové participated in actions organized by the International Solidarity Movement (ISM), a Palestinian-led international organization founded in 2001 to "support and strengthen the Palestinian popular resistance by providing the Palestinian people with two resources, international protection and a voice with which to nonviolently resist an overwhelming military occupation force."[34] At considerable risk to themselves, several thousand ISM volunteers, most of whom are internationals outside of the immediate region, have delivered on these ambitious grounds. Through human rights observation and non-violent civil disobedience, they have (among other things) sat in Palestinian homes facing demolition, accompanied Palestinians in ambulances through IDF checkpoints, defended Palestinian olive trees and infrastructure, and helped organize protests against settlements and the "security wall" in the West Bank and Gaza Strip.

Since its inception, the ISM stressed to its international volunteers the importance of going to Palestine for the "right reasons." In this sense, "right" was explicitly defined as being advocates for action *chosen* by Palestinians, *planned* by Palestinians, and therefore *respectful* of the rights of Palestinians as equals. The Canadian branch of the ISM makes this point clear in its campaign leaflet to potential volunteers:

> *If you decide to go to Palestine, it is absolutely critical that you go for the right reasons ... you need to have a sense of proportion about your role, and your potential impact, as an outsider. And you need to understand that you are there to learn from Palestinians, and to help them resist the Occupation by carrying on with their daily activities and work on their own terms, not the other way around. Hopefully, you are there because you recognize that your own liberation is bound up with the liberation of all peoples, including Palestinians. This is not "charity" work that the ISM is engaged in.*[35]

By early 2003, the Israeli government was clearly perturbed by the ISM's presence, and a number of outright attacks on ISM activists took place. Three of these — against American students Rachel Corrie and Brian Avery, and British student Tom Hurndall — occurred over the course of one month, all of which resulted in death. The violence facing Palestinians for decades was perpetrated against internationals, and outrage teemed from Western activist movements in response. Dr. Samir Nasrallah, whose house Rachel Corrie sought to defend from an IDF bulldozer, offered poignant remarks about what ISM's work meant for Palestinians:

> *Now there are no internationals with us in Rafah, this isolated town on the Egyptian border. The last ones left to renew their visas, intending to return, but the Israeli army prevented their re-entry into Gaza. The hardships my family and I experience continue and have, in fact, worsened since the internationals left. We lost our house soon afterwards, as if the*

*Israeli army was just waiting for the ISM to leave.*

*As for Rachel and the message she delivered to us and to the world, she was in pursuit of the truth. She dedicated her life to that. She conveyed the truth as she saw it, reporting the crimes of the Israeli army against innocent Palestinian civilians. The hands of the occupation killed her in cold blood as if to say to us, "I will deny you your spoken voice."*

*I don't feel safe as long as our voice does not reach the outside world. I call on my ISM friends to return to us. I ask you to come back because Rafah needs you. Tanks roll in and out with total ease, killing and destroying at will. And, without you, no one sees and no one hears.*

*There is not a day when my family and I don't think of Rachel, I told her family when they came to visit us that Rachel was a loss to my family, a loss to the whole Palestinian people, just as she was to them. Everyone lost her.*[36]

Shortly after the killings of Corrie, Hurndall, and Avery, the Israeli government officially forbade the ISM from entering occupied Palestine, although a steady flow of internationals has continued despite these orders. While largely unreported in the mainstream press, these efforts have been publicized through the Internet, raising awareness about the Palestinian cause. These activists have also returned from their work abroad to give thoughtful seminars at home, frequently speaking to audiences in the hundreds.

An address on November 20, 2002, by Neta Golan and George Rishmawi at the University of Toronto was a fitting case in point. Golan (an Israeli organizer) and Rishmawi (a Palestinian organizer) both emphasized the role the ISM offers in providing hope in an otherwise hopeless situation. Internationals, Golan insisted, "bring the attention of the international community," and give voice to an otherwise ignored situation."[37] I spoke to Penny McCall-Howard, a Canadian volunteer with ISM, who insisted her presence in the Occupied Territories "made the difference between visibility and invisibility, and at least twenty Palestinian lives within two weeks."[38] Joshua Brown — a Johns Hopkins University student present for the forty-nine-day, twenty-four-hour IDF curfew in the Gaza Strip from August to September 2002 — told me: "The strength and spirit of the Palestinian people is beyond description and inspirational during this current incursion."[39]

Statements like these have caused a stir, particularly on campus, where some pro-Israel groups have challenged Palestinian solidarity work. The ISM has carried on undeterred, and framed its summer delegations of international activists as "Freedom Summers" on the model of the US civil rights movement. Shortly before his death in 2004, renowned Palestinian scholar Edward Said described the ISM's work as a genuine attempt to "recognize the Palestinian reality." Following a short meeting with Rachel Corrie's parents, he wrote the following words as a tribute to the ISM's approach and its resonance for activists worldwide:

> Rachel Corrie's work in Gaza recognized … the gravity and the density of the living history of the Palestinian people as a national community, and not merely as a collection of deprived refugees. That is what she was in solidarity with.
>
> And we need to remember that that kind of solidarity is no longer confined to a few intrepid souls here and there, but is recognized the world over. In the past six months I have lectured in four continents to many thousands of people.
>
> What brings them together is Palestine and the struggle of the Palestinian people which is now a byword for emancipation and enlightenment, regardless of all the vilification heaped on them by their enemies.[40]

Since 2003, a further development in Palestinian solidarity work has involved targeting Caterpillar Inc., the corporate supplier of the

IDF's gigantic bulldozers. The campaign was originally launched by the US-based Stop US Tax-Funded Aid to Israel Now (SUSTAIN), but has since been joined by a larger "Stop Caterpillar" initiative fusing many Palestinian solidarity groups. As is the case with ISM, these organizations were launched by activists based on campuses and in faith communities. One of the stated objectives of the "Stop Caterpillar" campaign, however, is to move beyond these audiences, most notably through appeals to unions. Given that Caterpillar has an established anti-union reputation, that objective is possible, but the campaign was not able to earn support from unions representing Caterpillar workers.

That did not deter activist interventions at Caterpillar's Annual General Meetings, which eventually moved from Chicago to Arkansas to avoid engagement with Palestinian supporters. When challenged, Caterpillar has said "it's impossible" to keep track of the millions of products they've sold around the world. On other occasions, it claimed sales to Israel are done with the backing of US government programs, so complaints should be registered at the White House. And yet, revelations have surfaced about Caterpillar appearing on a high-profile "US development aid" panel organized by the powerful American Israel Public Affairs Committee (AIPAC). Clearly, Caterpillar's relationship with Israeli decision-makers isn't as arms-length as the company suggests.

Not surprisingly, this double-speak has not deterred activists I've spoken to — if anything, it has encouraged them to be more ambitious. Indeed, from the early efforts to challenge Caterpillar, a wider movement has now emerged for boycotts, divestment, and sanctions (BDS) to challenge Israel's treatment of Palestinians. The campaign is modelled on the South African example of the 1980s and early 1990s, where Nelson Mandela and others urged BDS measures to challenge Afrikaner apartheid. In July 2005, 171 Palestinian groups issued a call for BDS, and the movement has steadily gained influence since.

In March 2006, an "Israeli Apartheid Week" was organized at the University of Toronto to host discussions, raise awareness, and build support for DIY activism and BDS measures. Today, Israeli Apartheid Week is a global phenomenon, with over a hundred cities hosting activities in 2013. As these events have taken place, the tactic of BDS, while controversial (even in progressive circles), has made an impact at the highest levels of Israeli politics. In May 2011, Ehud Barak, Israel's minister of defence and deputy prime minister, had these words for Israel's far-right voices, who have dismissed BDS campaigns as idle threats:

> There are elements in the world, quite powerful, in various countries, including friendly ones, in trade unions, [among] academics, consumers, green political parties . . . and this impetus has culminated in a broad movement called BDS which is what was done with South Africa.
>
> This will not happen overnight. It will start coming at us like a glacier, from all corners . . . to me, this uncontrollable process looks more dangerous than what the [Israeli] public perceives at the moment. We have been ruling over another nation for 43 years, this is unprecedented.
>
> Perhaps China can allow itself to control some small nations in various corners of its empire, and perhaps Russia can. We cannot, there is no chance that the world will accept this. The far right is exposing Israel to dangerous and unwarranted isolation.[41]

In addition to BDS appeals, other activists have expressed solidarity with Palestinians by challenging Israel's naval blockade of the Gaza Strip. Their movement was established under the original auspices of "Free Gaza Movement" flotillas, where activists set forth on boats to defy Israel's blockade and bring needed supplies. From 2008 to 2009, three successful flotillas took place that included high-profile politicians, journalists, and human rights advocates, some of whom were Israeli participants. Huwaida Arraf, a movement organizer, offered this reaction after a successful fifteen-hour flotilla in 2009: "We recognize that we're two humble boats, but what we've accomplished is to show that average people from around the world can mobilize to create change. We do not have to stay silent in the face of injustice. Reaching Gaza today, there is such a sense of hope, and hope is what mobilizes people everywhere."[42] With high-profile activists aboard, sentiments like these received wide coverage, even in the mainstream press. That exposure clearly infuriated the Israeli establishment, whose approach to the flotillas changed with each one that came.

In 2008–09, Israeli boats made contact with activist flotillas but did not prevent them from docking and delivering supplies. That changed during "Operation Cast Lead," as two flotillas were rammed, shot at, and forcibly taken to Ashdod, an Israeli port. That violent trend sadly escalated the following year with a tragic incident aboard one of six boats in a May 2010 flotilla. At 4:30 a.m., in international waters, an Israeli boat opened fire on the MV *Mavi Marmara*, the lead vessel in the flotilla that held mostly Turkish activists. After Israeli speedboats had attempted unsuccessfully to board the boat, fifteen commandos descended from a hovering Apache helicopter, opening fire almost immediately on activists below. Of the nine activists killed, five were shot in the back, execution-style, leaving little doubt about who the aggressor was. The rest of the boats were taken by force to Ashdod, and activists were asked to acknowledge their intent to defy Israel's naval blockade and waive their legal right to appeal in Israeli courts. A 2011 flotilla was boarded by commandos before it left Greece after Israel made appeals to Greece's erstwhile progressive government. Undeterred, flotilla activists used an array of clever tactics to briefly leave port and later challenge both Israel and Greece for their heavy-handed interventions.

David Heap, a movement organizer, told me about packed press conferences held afterwards featuring high-profile activists like author Alice Walker and First Nations elder Bob Lovelace. Walker likened the flotillas to modern "freedom rides," a reference to the bus campaigns that spurred the US civil rights movement of the 1950s and 1960s. Lovelace urged listeners to remember that "colonialism and democracy can't walk hand in hand," and that charges of flotillas being a "provocation" ignored something he learned long ago: "You *never* ask the oppressor for permission."[43] These statements earned global media coverage that emboldened activists and long-suffering Palestinians. Ironically enough, Heap says, Israel's obstructionism helped facilitate the movement's appeal. And that appeal has not ended, despite well-financed obstructions; flotilla activists formed an international coalition to finance *Gaza's Ark,* a vessel with the mission to bring Palestinian exports to global locations. At the same time, the project also called global attention to Israel's treatment of Gaza's fishers, whose livelihood faces constant threats by gunboats. This blending of local concerns with international support has earned broad resonance, and it is powerful enough to continue to do so in the months and years ahead. It is yet another example of grassroots activism and its ability to challenge the mightiest of adversaries.

## CONCLUSION: COGS AND WHEELS

Small forces can accomplish a great deal. At a time when so many are cynical about politics and the potential for making serious change in our lifetimes, the cases in this chapter show activists and movements breaking through mainstream barriers. This is true for campaigns blocking pipelines, challenging colonial mindsets, or assailing modern (but no less real) forms of apartheid. Each has challenged top-down politics with grassroots activism, and made elites squirm as a consequence. Each reveals how grassroots movements can act like mighty cogs turning larger wheels, which then create new experiments in progressive organizing.

Consider the nuanced sense of place documented in these cases, where local and global distinctions are blurred by activists to the point of distraction. Today's green activists, for example, often see their organizing terrain on a variety of levels, from local community struggles to international mobilizations against the fossil fuels industry. The organizers behind Idle No More fuse new relationships of indigenous solidarity to support in settler communities, both within and beyond the boundaries of North America. The place of solidarity activism with Palestine has also been cosmopolitan, and often in the face of severe repression; lessons learned abroad are communicated back home and often revitalize local campaigns.

A similar dynamism is also apparent in the ideas grassroots movements espouse, and how they soon have an impact on received wisdom elsewhere. Market-based green alternatives are unlikely to inspire today's climate justice campaigners who are driven by deep ethical commitments and ideas that see sustainability, simplicity, and direct democracy as a complete package. In very short order, Idle No More has challenged us to grapple with what "decolonization" means; in doing so, it has presented uncomfortable historical facts, revived ancient traditions, and linked these to modern efforts to uphold treaty commitments. Solidarity movements with Palestine have taken discussion of colonialism to the global level, compelling us to question the world's silence on Israeli crimes. These are the achievements of movements that think original thoughts and, in doing so, create the conditions for new breakthroughs. Without that, progress just doesn't happen.

Last, but not least, one is struck by the organization of grassroots movements, whose boldness and creativity demonstrate that the future is truly unwritten. On paper, networks of green organizers shouldn't be able to stall energy giants, but activist mobilizations have had that very result. Networked round dances, flash mobs, and blockades shouldn't shift the edifice of Canadian federal politics, but they have; before Idle No More, a neoliberal government, arguably the most aggressive in decades, was only too willing to force through its resource-hungry reforms. Now it faces stiff resistance that has given confidence to a new generation of warriors, including women and young people who feel more empowered than they have in decades. Who would have thought that flotillas, activist interventions at shareholder meetings, and week-long discussion forums would be assailed by Israel at the highest political levels? These are the achievements of a new generation of Palestine solidarity campaigners who have perfected what some call the "war of the flea": A weighty adversary grows irritated after numerous small bites and lashes out for relief. This is precisely what Israel has done when its siege on established opinion is challenged.

The brashness of these activists has made inroads with engaged volunteers. It offers tremendous hope. A grassroots approach to activism is what makes this possible. The next chapter turns to examples of this approach among trade unions.

*Police and demonstrators clash at the 1999 World Trade Organization meeting in Seattle.* Steve Kaiser

*Activists demonstrate outside the UN climate change conference in Copenhagen on December 12, 2009.* niOS

*Tunisian protestors carry a mural of street vendor Mohammed Bouazizi, whose death by self-immolation sparked the Arab Spring.* CJB22

*Arab Spring demonstrators in Cairo's Tahrir Square call for the ouster of Egyptian President Hosni Mubarak in early 2011.* Hossam el-Hamalawy

*Wisconsin demonstrators inside the State Capitol Rotunda during protests against proposed austerity measures in early 2011.* WI-AFL-CIO

*Former federal NDP leader Jack Layton and his wife, MP Olivia Chow, with environmental activists in Toronto on Earth Day in 2011.*
Sima Sahar Zerehi

*Toronto library workers meet in August 2011 with Toronto resident and distinguished author Margaret Atwood to finalize the details of the "My Library Matters to Me" writing contest as part of wide-spread opposition to proposed library cuts.* CUPE Local 4948

*Toronto's Nathan Phillips Square covered in tributes to Jack Layton one week after his funeral in August 2011.* Jackman Chiu

*Environmental protestors in front of Parliament Hill on September 26, 2011.*

Ben Powless

*Library workers in front of the Toronto Reference Library on March 23 participate in a read-in as part of their 2012 strike.* CUPE Local 4948

*A young Torontonian on Earth Day 2012 supports 350.org, a leading environmental organization that promotes activism in both developed and developing countries.*
Sima Sahar Zerehi

*A green activist in Toronto calls for an enhanced Kyoto Protocol on Earth Day in 2012. The Protocol was adopted by the United Nations Framework Convention on Climate Change in 1997 and came into force in 2005. The Conservative government renounced the agreement.* Sima Sahar Zerehi

*Students protest against increases in post-secondary tuition fees in Montreal as part of the Quebec Solidaire movement on August 22, 2012.*
Mathieu Breton

*Francoise David, Ahmir Khadir, and Quebec Solidaire activists await the outcome of the Quebec elections in Montreal on September 4, 2012.* Pierre Ouimet

*The Chicago Teachers Union protests against Bill SB-7 in a September 2012 mass march in downtown Chicago.* Lee Sustar

*Occupy Toronto participants vote on issues on October 27, 2012. This approach to decision-making was typical of Occupy encampments across North America.*
Sima Sahar Zerehi

*A cartoon published in December 2012 shows Canadian Prime Minister Stephen Harper on the run from Idle No More, an Aboriginal activist movement that brought public attention to the injustices experienced by Aboriginal people across Canada.* Marty Two Bulls

*Idle No More activists in Saanich, British Columbia demonstrate their support for Chief Theresa Spence during her hunger strike in 2013. Chief Spence waged a hunger strike to compel a meeting with both the Canadian government and Canada's governor general to discuss Aboriginal issues.* Caelle Frampton

*Idle No More demonstrators commemorate the International Day for the Elimination of Racial Discrimination in Ottawa on March 21, 2013.* Ben Powless

# 3

# BUCKING A LOSING TREND:
## GLIMPSES OF GRASSROOTS UNIONISM

*In our hands is placed a power greater than their hoarded gold,*
*Greater than the might of armies magnified a thousand-fold,*
*We can bring to birth a new world from the ashes of the old,*
*For the union makes us strong.*

*— Ralph Chaplin, "Solidarity Forever"*[1]

So ends the song that has since become a mainstay of the North American labour movement. Ralph Chaplin wrote "Solidarity Forever" as an organizer for the Industrial Workers of the World (IWW), a progressive union bent on uniting workers into a force capable of remaking society. At the time, the small ranks of organized labour were bastions of privilege for skilled craft workers, but the IWW (nicknamed the "Wobblies") aimed at changing this dismal reality. Chaplin's intent was to write a song "full of revolutionary fervour," complete with "a chorus that was singing and defiant."[2] It was a song intended to inspire workers and remind them of their power in collective action.

Soon after it was written, "Solidarity Forever" delivered on these grounds, and the proof lies in its continued use today. But the song, as further credit to Chaplin's efforts, is not only an example of union defiance, it is also a suggestive time capsule for union activism. "Solidarity Forever" was composed in 1912, during the pitched battles of West Virginian miners and mill workers in Massachusetts. In these and other places, IWW organizers appealed for unity among unskilled workers (few of whom, like craft workers, were Anglo-Saxon whites), in the face of huge obstacles.[3] The song offers a vision beyond that divisive, violent reality toward a more hopeful future, where workers themselves play a decisive role in campaigns for social justice. The notion of labour as the basis of all wealth is announced proudly, with unions heralded as the antidote to militarism and greed.

And yet, while Chaplin's song is still sung for labour events, one is struck by how odd its message appears now, even for those inclined to agree with it. Unions that once struck fear in the hearts of employers now face attacks on several fronts and often grope for an excuse to exist. In the private sector, a small minority of the workforce is represented by unions, and even the most powerful among them face strong pressure to give back historic gains. Public-sector unions, while far more numerous, are no less challenged; a weary public turns on them with the slightest prodding by right-wing pundits. Ken Georgetti, president of the Canadian Labour Congress (CLC), recently explained why this is so: "There's been a change in the paradigm . . . people used to aspire to belong to a union to get the benefits and be well off. Now the aspiration is, 'I'd be happy to take those benefits away from someone because I don't have them.'"[4]

How does one grasp this vexing position for organized labour, particularly given the progressive climate engendered by grassroots politics in recent years? If dissent is back in vogue, why haven't unions, as long-standing progressive organizations, grown in membership or influence? Why have the prime beneficiaries of the 2008 economic crisis been bottom-up movements (like Occupy and Idle No More), populist neoliberal voices (like the Tea Party), but not unions, whose historic role has been challenging ruling elites and defending our society's have-nots? Is this a result of poor strategy, flawed ideas, or bad habits? This chapter explores these questions, starting with a reflection on the crisis of working-class politics. I then survey recent glimpses of grassroots unionism in the CLC's recent pension campaign, with the Chicago Teachers Union, and with Toronto's library workers — all of which suggest lessons for organized labour for the battles that lie ahead.

## THE CRISIS OF WORKING-CLASS POLITICS AND PROMISE OF GRASSROOTS UNIONISM

*There's class warfare, all right, but it's my class, the rich class, that's making war, and we're winning.*

*— Warren Buffett[5]*

This section's title, for some, may seem parachuted from the past. These days, progressive readers are no longer used to discussions of labour conflict as struggles between a "working" and a "ruling" class. They are more accustomed to populist language that brackets out these distinctions: "we're in this together"; "fighting for fairness"; "we are all affected"; "defending the middle class." These are today's union slogans, each of which speaks largely to today's crisis of working-class politics. As Jim Stanford explains, in most advanced capitalist economies, 85 per cent of employed people (aged eighteen to sixty-four) must work for wages, while a smaller minority have other options. But despite those realities, polling research suggests people don't see workplace conflict in such polarized terms. Instead, most see themselves as "middle class," as heroic strivers above the drudgery of daily work, while their lives suggest another conclusion. Those "classless" instincts, as Warren Buffett explains succinctly, are not shared by employers who today are waging a largely one-sided class war.

So what explains the resilience of "middle-class" perceptions? In an insightful article, Arun Gupta links its emergence to the "Leave It to Beaver," postwar phase of consumer-driven capitalism:

> By the 1960s the promise of prosperity for all, which defenders of the middle class today harken back to, seemed within reach. Yet working-class consciousness was being sapped by consumption. No longer was the goal to transform social relations and bring forth the "New Man" (and Woman), it was to get a new Pontiac, an in-ground pool, a bigger house, the latest doodads. The middle-class lifestyle frayed the bonds of worker solidarity.
>
> Ultimately, the concept of the middle class is inherently anti-political. It is defined by consumption: a mortgage, multiple cars, stylish clothes, furniture and electronics, and affordable luxuries. We can't have a yacht, but we can go on an annual cruise. We can't buy a villa in Tuscany, but we can holiday in one. We can't afford a private chef, but we can visit Le Bernardin on a special occasion. Luxury goods makers from Prada and LVMH to Mercedes Benz and Tiffany have aggressively expanded their businesses by creating lines of downscale luxuries for the middle class.
>
> When we struggle for better wages and benefits and more social welfare, what is the goal? If it's for a growing middle class, we've been there, done that and failed miserably. What do we say to the more than 2 billion Chinese and Indians who want a middle-class lifestyle? In a time of runaway global warming, fighting for the middle class is like fighting for global ecocide.[6]

The "middle-class" narrative, as Gupta explains, is a compatible fit for our "classless," consumption-obsessed culture, but it hardly describes the world in which we live. Recent studies of global labour markets indicate that, with the unemployed counted, almost half of the earth's seven billion people can be described as working class, a number unprecedented in human history. The oft-cited trends of "deindustrialization" and "footloose capital" are trounced by the reality of numerous places where manufacturing remains crucial and work is geographically fixed.

Further still, as the Occupy movement explained well, the growth of a global working class has happened alongside galling increases in the gap between rich and poor. A study by the World Bank found the earth's richest fifty million people owned more assets than half of humanity, hardly suggesting the end of inequality and social class. Robin Blackburn's impressive study of pension markets confirms the difference between workers who hold stock and others who control it; while workers' pensions may indeed be a dynamic source of capital today, this hardly demonstrates worker *control* over these assets, a reality most seem reluctant to acknowledge. Control over capital remains within the grasp of a precious few the world over, and white collar "post-industrial" or "immaterial" labour has hardly shifted this balance in favour of workers. Overall, then, the realities of social class remain very much alive, and the precariousness facing the vast majority dependent on wages intensifies daily.

But arriving at this analysis is far from enough. Arguments around our "classless" society are easily challenged, but the uneven realm of working-class consciousness presents more troublesome questions. As Karl Marx, the first grand theorist of capitalism, once famously explained, there is a huge difference between a working class "in itself" hired to serve owners, and a working class "for itself" conscious of its subordinate position and willing to challenge the system. The best writing on unions asks how to foster the latter of these two conditions: How can union pride can be restored in a neoliberal era, when being a "worker" is somehow considered an admission of inferiority? This is a question the social philosopher André Gorz noted in his writing on the "lost magic of work":

*Even at its height, wage-based society was torn and "fractured" by class divisions and antagonisms. The workers were not integrated into society, but into their class, their trade union, their working community, and it was from their struggles to transform their work, lives and society that they derived their "identity", dignity, culture and cohesion.*

*And it was against their cohesion, "identity" and class organization that what is known as "business" found the absolute, unanswerable weapon; the evanescence [or fading away] of work; its conversion into an individualized, discontinuous activity; its abolition on a massive scale — insecurity of employment for all.*

*"Fear and tremble." The ideological message has changed. Where once it was, "never mind what you do, so long as you get paid at the end of the week," it is now, "never mind what you've been paid, so long as you have a job."[7]*

With these conditions in mind, intense debates have emerged about effective union organizing, democratic reform within unions, empowering equality-seeking workers, and wider questions about the political role of unions beyond servicing collective agreements. Many of the most extensive contributions have come from US writers, as that country's pitiful unionization rates have given rise to considerable reflection. A decade ago, Steven Lerner, the architect of the first "Justice for Janitors" campaigns in Denver and Los Angeles, suggested several proposals for "union renewal." Citing alarming trends in union density, he supported the further creation of "general unions" (which require mega-mergers), massive increases in organizing new members, and a willingness to target certain geographical areas with an array of campaign tactics up to and including civil disobedience.

Lerner's work drew a flurry of responses, most of which addressed the organizations proposed for his drastic reforms. Kate Bronfenbrenner offered the first critique, suggesting that Lerner's proposals to shore up union density, while important, did not address complexities involved in revitalizing unions. Gaining the trust and confidence of workers, she reasoned, was far more important than proposals to boost trade union membership numbers. The specific manner in which reforms are carried out, for Bronfenbrenner, is equally important to the goal of union renewal. Merging existing unions, she also explained, is more controversial for unions whose membership base lies in dwindling economic sectors.

There was substance to Bronfenbrenner's case. Lerner's proposals, while visionary, did not discuss the role of union members in transforming working-class politics. His call for mass action and militant tactics, given that the process of mobilization remained unexplained, runs the risk of supporting what some call "militancy without democracy," where union members are called out and dismissed like a stage army. Kim Moody warns of that very outcome, claiming that reducing union power to financial or physical resources misses the point. Contrary to accepted wisdom, Moody insists, "many factors determine success, [and] the quality of leadership is more important than its quantity; the degree of democracy and membership participation is more important than the union bank account."[8] At issue here is the role union leaders and staff play in the orchestration and execution of campaigns. On this matter, Dan Clawson has urged against "staffing up" as a solution:

> The most serious limitation of the "new" labour movement,
> a limitation closely related to the problems with debate and
> democracy, is the failure to empower or activate the rank and
> file. The model is still staff-driven. At the staff level, there
> has been a clear paradigm shift in terms of the kind of people
> hired and the language they speak. A substantial propor-
> tion of the new staff are past participants in, or at least are
> comfortable with the culture of, the new social movements …

> *[Many union leaders are] willing to be arrested at demonstra-*
> *tions, but they make little or no effort to empower rank and*
> *file movements.*[9]

In the years since Clawson wrote these words, there has been limited discussion in unions about the dominant role of staff. The same is true for related academic debates, which, as Stephanie Ross explains, typically endorse "social movement unionism" as the antidote to workplace-focused "business unionism." That explanation differentiates between unions wanting to change society and others seeking to protect their narrow piece of it; but absent from that narrative is the role of union members, whether at the workplace or in related issues that their union supports. Today, many union leaders support bottom-up movements, and support the idea of working in coalition with them. This is a positive development, but one that won't go far if union members are not invited to share in this work, participate in change-making processes, and develop their own capacities as activists and leaders. "Social movement unionism," in that important sense, ducks the central question of union democracy.

So, while there is great interest in thinking through new strategies for unions, those emboldened by these discussions can't avoid the challenges posed by grassroots politics. Some leaders and activists have made strides in important directions, but it is unclear how this has affected internal union practices and the views of members beyond the existing leadership. The example of the AFL-CIO co-ordinating a "freedom ride" for immigrant workers in 2003 would have shocked Wobbly organizers of old, as would claims from union leaders during Occupy events that "we are 99 per cent." Such statements, however, are frustrated by unwelcome trends. As recent internal union studies have shown, the wider malaise that workers feel with conventional politics *includes* existing frameworks of trade unionism. In this cynical context, workers often treat unions as insurance agencies rather than sites for collective action.

Meanwhile, as unions face these divisions, employers are seizing their opportunities. They have no qualms breaking the law while unions, for the most part, are reluctant to move beyond the limited framework of modern industrial relations. As firms hire union-busting consultants to flout labour law and drag out appeals, unions have responded, in large measure, with technocratic strategies and fiery rhetoric. A common trend in collective bargaining is to offer concessions to gain momentum in other areas. In this cynical situation, workers are being asked to forgo hard-fought gains with the promise of returns in the long run.

It should be hardly surprising that, in the midst of these circumstances, many workers (both union and non-union) have bunkered down to life under neoliberalism, yielding to the conditions of "evanescence" Gorz cites above. Tax cuts or overtime work are preferred over union militancy and other forms of collective action. Voting cynically for the "lesser evil" (in union or government elections) appears as the best option, if workers even vote at all. And yet, as Sam Gindin reminds us, to conclude that these trends imply working-class support for neoliberalism misses the point. To discover why most workers are dissuaded from other options, one must first ask whether any meaningful alternatives exist:

> *The barrier to popular resistance today is neither that people think the world is fine, nor that people are passive; rather it is that with no reason to believe that real change is on the agenda, people actively pursue other survival options ... The tragedy of this reaction extends beyond the obvious limits of its solutions.*
>
> *Worse still is the individualism and fragmentation such responses reinforce. If incomes are improved through longer hours, more debt, tax cuts, and moving away — then class consciousness and class formation develop radically differently than if wage increases and social programs are won on picket lines, in the street, and through mobilized communities. With class solidarity and ideological independence undermined by*

*the form personal coping takes, workers are condemned to
face the same constrained options in the future as they do in
the present.*

*The political dilemma is therefore not fatalism in the
sense that people are passively accepting their fate, but the
fatalism of acting within the given "structured options" —
rather than imagining, believing in, and organizing to expand
the possible options.*[10]

While Gindin and Gorz help clarify practical obstacles to union activism, it would be wrong to conclude that their provocative descriptions are applicable to all workers, or even unique to our neoliberal era. Indeed, Clawson makes a convincing case that spikes in labour organizing have arrived with profound shifts in orientation, often in moments seemingly inhospitable to unions. In the mid-nineteenth century, this involved British Chartism moving beyond government petitions to mass mobilizations against laws preventing unionization. In late nineteenth and early twentieth centuries, it meant challenging the exclusive model of craft unionism. In the postwar era, this meant determined efforts to organize public-sector workers and, in particular, the specific needs of women, who predominate in this sector.

In all of these cases and still others, what accompanied a spurt of union organizing was a wider politicization of society that gave a different emphasis to workplace activism. Anarchist and socialist movements were at the heart of union activism in the late nineteenth and early twentieth centuries, and feminist movements played a strong role in public-sector organizing in the latter half of the twentieth century. This is the inspiring history of grassroots unionism; there are also practical reasons to pursue member-led reform. As Jane McAlevy, a talented union organizer, notes in a recent book, member-driven "deep organizing" is crucial to lasting success. After observing McAlevy and others, Clawson noted the following:

*The moral argument for democratizing unions and involving the membership is compelling, but there is also a practical argument. Democratic and participatory unions, especially those open to progressive politics and connections, are more effective …*

*Employer arguments about the union as an "outside force" have some plausibility if existing unions are run by staff, not workers; if the staff differ significantly from the workers (in education, income, race, gender, neighbourhoods where they live, whether they drink coffee or latte); and if the union organizer is someone new to the town, who will depart as soon as the organizing drive is over.*

*If area unions are run by friends, neighbours, and fellow members of your congregation; if the organizing drive involves meetings with enthusiastic workers who are already members of the local undertaking the organizing drive; if the campaign started because non-union workers kept comparing their situation to the wages, benefits, security, and sense of power of their union neighbours; then employer anti-union campaigns face serious obstacles.[11]*

Simply put, direct democracy is the soul of grassroots unionism. It empowers union members to be leaders, and realizes this requires substantial change for unions themselves. It means bringing union activism down to earth, and grounding it in the lives of workers and the communities where they live. Above all, it reconnects unions with people, the source of their power. Today, there is much talk in organized labour about "branding themselves better" to withstand employer attacks — but the idea that a better pitch is needed misses the point. Effective union organizing will not be driven by brilliant ads, or by focus-group-tested messages that get released, like carrier pigeons of old, only to bring back good news later. Effective union organizing must begin by developing the political capacities of union members, the vast majority of whom are spectators in politics. But if members are politically conscious, sufficiently organized, and inspired by grassroots activism, unions can blunt the worst aspects of employer attacks and even win major victories. The rest of this chapter reviews glimpses of such promise.

## WHEN RESISTANCE ISN'T FUTILE: UNDERSTANDING THE CLC'S PENSION CAMPAIGN

*You may ask yourself, what is that beautiful house?*
*You may ask yourself, where does that highway lead to?*
*You may ask yourself, am I right, am I wrong?*
*You may say to yourself, my god, what have I done?*

— *Talking Heads, "Once in a Lifetime"*[12]

In April 2004, I left Toronto's activist scene for Wakefield — an artistic riverfront community 30 kilometres north of Ottawa. My partner and I bought a small, lovely house perched on a bluff overlooking the Gatineau Park (and, less interestingly, the local highway). The move was initiated by a job my partner took up at the local children's hospital; meanwhile, I spent the year commuting to North Bay to teach in Nipissing University's Social Welfare and Social Development Programme. After my contract position ended, I was hired to work in the Social and Economic Policy Department of the Canadian Labour Congress (the political voice for unions in English Canada), where I stayed for seven years.

More than once, I remember pulling away from our Wakefield driveway, asking myself if I had made the right decision. That was certainly the question asked by many activist friends, who worried my energy, skills, and time were wasted in the halls of union officialdom. The experience, they said, would either transform me into a cynic or deflect my attention from more important things. As I considered that view, the Talking Heads' "Once in a Lifetime" was a recurring anthem for me. I had turned down union staff jobs before: Why take this one, and where was it headed? Was I making a huge mistake?

Some reading this book are likely considering their own employment options, and wondering if grassroots activism is possible in union staff jobs. What follows, in many respects, is my response to that question. My time as a union researcher, educator, and organizer has taught me it is valuable to pursue union staff work, but only with eyes wide open. The union establishment is an important, progressive voice, but one with limited exposure to grassroots politics; it is unlikely to change quickly, and it is open to elite overtures that move it in unfortunate directions. That said, this structure will only change (and has only ever changed) when bottom-up activism asserts itself and finds support from union leaders willing to take political risks. That was the story of the CLC's pension campaign, whose story I recount here.

In my years as a CLC researcher (2005–08), the primary file I held was pensions, a complicated subject made more challenging given a lack of consensus among unions. For years I worked with others to devise a campaign that could unite public- and private-sector unions, both of which were mired in their own defensive struggles. In the aftermath of the 2008 financial crisis, however, the world was thrust into uncharted economic and political territory. Advocacy groups like the CLC were challenged to offer campaigns that addressed the calamities of market collapse, and pensions were a key subject in the mix.

The CLC's pension campaign had three core demands: to increase benefits for public pensions, to double future benefits for the Canada and Quebec Pension Plans (CPP/QPP), and to create an insurance system for workplace pensions. As the campaign's lead researcher, I had designed its appeal on a "pension story" basis, avoiding the common temptation to use elaborate graphs and pie charts. My aim, following the lead of Marshall Ganz and others, was to promote story-based organizing that could put a human face on our empirical research. Toward that end, we held activist training sessions to organize supporters, but to also create space for people to share their own pension stories. With their consent, we took their picture, recorded what was said, and created an organizing infrastructure where pension stories could be used to influence decision-makers. When those appeals went ignored, pension activists held rallies, marches, and even a few office sit-ins.

In October 2009, we organized a town hall meeting in Ottawa that was typical of the approach used in the CLC's pension campaign. It began, as usual, with a brief discussion panel at the front of the room. I had designed the presentation given by CLC Executive Vice-President Barb Byers, who spoke after John Gordon (then president of the Public Service Alliance of Canada) and Don Sproule, president of the Nortel Retirees. Both men were well received, with each pointing out the flaws in Canada's pension system. But when Byers spoke, the crowd noticed a change in strategy; she avoided a deluge of facts and figures. Instead, she justified the CLC's pension campaign by citing three stories we had heard in our training sessions (and did so while a a photo of the person being named was projected on a large screen):

> Meet Gail, she's 63. She used to work as a cook in a union-ized retirement home at $17 an hour. But when the home closed down four years ago, Gail couldn't find work. She sold her house, her assets, anything that wasn't tied down. She went from earning a decent wage to going on unemployment insurance, and later welfare. She now uses food banks, lives in a tiny apartment, and lives on an after-rent budget of less than $300 a month. Gail is living proof about why we must increase benefits for public pensions.
>
> Now meet Colin. His mom is one of 103 (largely women) workers at a unionized group home just West of Ottawa. These brave folks went on strike for 10 weeks to get a decent pension (which ultimately didn't happen). The employer even hired scabs to oppose this attempt at pension justice. Colin is

*holding a picket sign that reads: "I shouldn't be mom's Pen-sion Plan." Remember him the next time you hear someone criticizing "rich union pensions," and tell this story to anyone who opposes expanding the Canada and Quebec Pension Plan.*

*Lastly, meet Loretta. Loretta works at a Pulp and Paper company in Nakawic, New Bruswick. Her employer declared bankruptcy in 2004 after underfunding the pension plan over five years. As a result, Loretta's pension went from 92 percent funded to 48 percent funded. And when the employer emerged from bankruptcy protection, workers realized how much they lost in pension given our unfair bankruptcy rules. For Loretta, it meant $400 in pension after sixteen years of service. Not $400 a month, or $400 a year, but a one-time payout of $400. Those who say we can't insure workplace pensions should walk a mile in Loretta's shoes.[13]*

Powerful stories like these were ignored by elite pension discussions, but the CLC's pension campaign created a structure to flip that script. Our initial training sessions empowered a movement, which quickly made its presence felt in government pension consultations.

At a federal consultation in Ottawa on March 13, 2009, union activists accounted for most of the 150 people in attendance. This hardly surprised government officials who were aware of union passion on pension issues. What shocked them, however, were ideas that came from the front of the room. Bernard Dussault, the chief actuary of the Canada Pension Plan and Old Age Security from 1992 to 1998, had been invited as an expert to share his thoughts on specific reforms. But Dussault, a major player in the pension debates of the 1990s, did not restrict his comments to such narrow parameters. He instead proposed a dramatic expansion of CPP benefits that would eventually see all Canadians earn 70 per cent of their salary in retirement. He made a case for shifting the Canadian pension system to a European model and away from its largely neoliberal design. The direct losers would be banks and financial services companies that would almost certainly lose clients for Retired Registered Savings Plans (RRSPs) and other savings schemes. Dussault's vision shook the pension establishment, and unions now realized they had an powerful ally in the case for pension reform.

As the federal consultations moved to six other Canadian cities, halls filled with angry union members and retirees. Soon after Ottawa, a conference room in Halifax meant for 80 participants was swamped by 150 people. This was the moment when Loretta Kent told her story, which was followed by a standing ovation from the entire room (industry experts included). In Toronto, a room for 150 was packed by over three hundred participants, and autoworker retirees were prominent in the group. One after another, they berated the government for failing to adequately protect their pensions and provide decent options for the next generation. As Len Wallace, a retiree leader for Canadian Autoworkers Union (CAW) spoke, heads nodded around the room. "Why should politicians and CEOs," he fumed, "get amazing pension plans, but not fight to ensure everyone else gets the same? What's the message to young people there? Do our kids have to be politicians and CEOs to retire with dignity?"[14]

In Vancouver, a room meant for 225 was filled well beyond capacity, and once again retirees made their presence felt. Art Kube, past president of the Council of Senior Citizens Organizations of British Columbia, reminded government officials not to use consultations to delay reform. "Consultation is fine, and talking is fine," Kube said, "but we've had many years of that. We want action. And let me remind you of the obvious: seniors vote, and we vote for people who care about pensions. You get this issue wrong, and you could be out of a job."[15]

The 2009 federal pension consultations confirmed what we had said all along: Pension anxiety was wide and deep, and action was required to fix the system. The CLC had prepared briefings and materials for union participants in the consultations, and these proved useful for the predict-able deflections that came from the front of the room. This included fed-eral-sector employers, who sought concessions despite holding relatively well-funded pensions (83 per cent, on average) after the 2008 financial crisis. A joint submission by seven federal employers (employing over 50 per cent of all federal-sector workers) once again demanded greater access to pension surpluses and weaker pension funding rules. As they made these demands, our pension stories became a powerful source of resistance.

On April 23, 2009, another event added to our pension momentum. Following a call from the CAW, over fifteen thousand people demon-strated at the Ontario Legislature in Toronto to "protect our pensions." Rally participants included angry Nortel workers and pensioners facing significant concessions from a bankrupt employer, irate CAW members, and concerned citizens. A Toronto "Stewards Assembly" held two weeks later (called by the Toronto and York Region Labour Council) drew over 1,800 participants, from rank and file union stewards and elected union officials, and pensions were a hot topic. The *Globe and Mail* took notes at both events, capturing several compelling stories for an influential series than ran six months later, entitled "Retirement Lost." By this point, politicians could no longer, after bailouts for finance companies in 2008, ignore pleas to fix our pension system. Momentum for change was starting to build — pension anger and anxiety had traction in the mainstream press and the public mind.

On September 11, 2009, Saskatchewan, Alberta, and British Columbia threatened to go it alone on pension reform in the absence of co-ordin-ated action from Ottawa, and referenced CPP reform among other options. On September 15, the arch neoliberal *Financial Post* ran a lead story entitled "Pensions Loom as Election Issue" that featured angry Nortel retirees and quoted the CLC's plan to expand the CPP. The fol-lowing day, David Dennison, president and CEO of the CPP Investment Board (CPPIB), commented on the public debate over the fund's future.

The CPPIB had usually restricted its public relations to investment issues, but Dennison confirmed the depth of Canada's pension problems and acknowledged a range of potential CPP reforms including the CLC's proposal. On October 16, the *Globe and Mail*'s "Retirement Lost" series was released, beginning with these words:

> *Canadians can no longer assume they will retire with secur-*
> *ity. Many are seeking increasingly scarce work while others*
> *flail as their once-flush retirement accounts hemorrhage. A*
> Globe and Mail *series beginning today shows that the crisis*
> *in Canadian pensions is not looming; it is here, and has been*
> *for some time. A concerted national effort, involving changes*
> *in policy, behaviour and mindset from governments, busi-*
> *nesses, unions, pension overseers and individual Canadians,*
> *is needed to repel the crisis.*[16]

A week later, over three thousand Nortel workers and retirees joined union activists on Parliament Hill, demanding justice at a company once thought to be the jewel of Canada's "Silicon Valley North." Earlier that month, Nortel CEO Mike Zafirovski appeared before the House of Commons Finance Committee and was forced to account for demanding a 30 per cent reduction in pensioner cheques while authorizing a $45 million bonus scheme for top executives. This was a "hairshirt" moment for corporate Canada, and we did much to publicize the exuberant heights to which executive pay and pensions had soared. Politicians promised reforms due to an unrelenting wave of negative publicity, grassroots mobilizations, and appeals for change. After being ignored or dismissed by the pension establishment, the logjam that kept progressive options off the table had finally been broken.

Almost immediately, Canada's federal political parties began jostling for position on pension issues. The New Democratic Party and Bloc Québécois supported our demands, while the Liberal Party proposed an expansion of the CPP through a private-sector model. The ruling Conservatives, however, were cool to any ambitious plans. Reacting to the Liberal proposal, federal Finance Minister Jim Flaherty accused his opponents of a "knee-jerk reaction to a serious issue," while his staff warned against policy ideas that might "saddle taxpayers with big obligations."[17] This was the first sign of a counter-attack to the CLC's new momentum on pensions, with more to come soon.

As provincial, federal, and territorial finance ministers prepared to meet in December in Whitehorse, Yukon Territory, similar appeals continued from government reports and spokespersons. Jack Mintz, a University of Calgary professor, wrote a report for the Whitehorse meeting emphasizing the perceived merits of the status quo. Bob Baldwin, a former CLC researcher, produced a study for the Ontario government that downplayed ambitious reform, preferring instead to suggest "key subordinate questions," while "mixing and matching" various policy ideas.[18] Neoliberal voices seized on the ambiguity produced by these claims. The Canadian Bankers Association released a paper calling for raised RRSP limits (2009), while the C.D. Howe Institute published a study attacking federal public-service pensions (using, critics charged, questionable assumptions to balloon the perceived costs). David Dodge, former governor of the Bank of Canada, likened an expansion of the CPP/QPP to a "nanny state solution," and urged the finance ministers to embrace policy options that allow "choice" in retirement planning.[19]

These arguments gave politicians an excuse to deflect appeals for substantial reform, but they confirmed the CLC's pension campaign had traction. The province of British Columbia said as much through its own independent study. Nevertheless, the Whitehorse talks ended with no commitment to reform and gave most space to Mintz and other opponents. The positive outcome was a pledge to hold further public hearings, leave "no policy option off the table," and articulate a clear direction on pension reform at the next finance ministers' meeting in June 2010.

If Whitehorse was a tough moment for the CLC campaign, it was also clear that momentum for progressive options had not stalled. In fact, the CLC's lesson from Whitehorse was that more grassroots mobilization was needed to push politicians in the right direction. So, from January to April 2010, we worked with others to host large pension forums that invited attendees to share anxieties and concerns. The anger expressed at these forums generated more political action as labour activists pressed local politicians, held rallies, and occupied constituency offices of pension industry supporters. This second wave of activism morphed into a broad movement for pension justice.

The movement's climax was in March 2010, when unions hosted a "Pension Summit" in Toronto that offered space to divergent perspectives to debate the way forward. Almost six hundred delegates attended, including federal Finance Minister Jim Flaherty, Canadian Federation of Independent Business CEO Catherine Swift, pension consultant Keith Ambachtsheer, and influential employer-side actuary Malcolm Hamilton. But these voices did not dominate the proceedings. Union delegates posed tough questions and realized how brittle the neoliberal establishment was. It was a moment when organized labour discovered a sense of its power, and one could feel received wisdom starting to shift.

Incredibly, this shift was also on display a month later at an elite pension conference hosted by Jack Mintz at the University of Calgary. Ken Georgetti was invited to speak on a panel with industry heavyweights (who, we can presume, were expected to criticize the CLC pension campaign). But when Robert Brown, a former executive for PricewaterhouseCoopers, spoke after Georgetti, he said that expanding the CPP was likely the "best of all available options." Georgetti nearly tumbled from his chair, and that reaction was modest compared to Mintz's gaping jaw. Without question, the CLC notched a minor victory in the heart of Canada's neoliberal policy establishment. In June, this was followed by a resolution passed at the Federation of Canadian Municipalities convention, where delegates (including the mayors of Canada's large cities) backed the CLC's call to expand the CPP. Our movement was making an impact at the highest official levels of Canadian politics.

This was confirmed in June 2010 when Flaherty announced an new consensus among his colleagues on pension reform. The policy direction, he argued, would involve a "modest expansion of the Canada Pension Plan," while encouraging the financial sector to offer new retirement savings products.[20] Alberta stressed its objections to the reform, but it emerged as a lone voice (with, perhaps, quiet support from Quebec and Saskatchewan). Union activists celebrated the result and took pride in creating a historic moment in Canada's long-running pension debate.

The rest of the summer, however, was unkind to organized labour. By the time union activists returned for Labour Day weekend, momentum for CPP reform was sputtering. In November, the federal government unveiled legislation enabling Pooled Registered Pension Plans (PRPPs), the latest neoliberal policy option. PRPPs would be voluntary and did not even require employer contributions. Critics from across the political spectrum argued PRPPs would do little to expand the scope of workplace pension coverage.

The CLC fumed about PRPPs receiving higher priority than CPP reform, and this fact was confirmed a month later when Prime Minister Stephen Harper confirmed the latter was officially off the table. "Canadians," Harper insisted, "are looking for options . . . not a hike in their CPP premiums."[21] The union reaction was furious: Flaherty's constituency office was occupied by enraged protesters, and the CLC later filed two access-to-information requests aimed at exposing who had undermined CPP reform. In the lead-up to a meeting in late December, a joint letter from the governments of British Columbia, Ontario, Prince Edward Island, New Brunswick, Manitoba, and Nova Scotia urged Ottawa to recommit to CPP expansion, but Flaherty rebuffed this overture the following week. The window of opportunity was now abruptly closed.

Despite this unfortunate result, the CLC's pension campaign is a good news story in otherwise tough times for unions. As observers sift through the tea leaves of this experience, it will be important to understand where this movement came from and how it can be restored. At a time when many question the political capacity of unions, this was an example of collective action winning positive results. Not mentioned in the above narrative, for example, were legislative changes Canadian governments felt compelled to make in response to widespread pension activism. These included guaranteed wage payouts in the event of corporate bankruptcies, strengthened rights for pension plan members, and guidelines to prevent federal-sector employers walking away from unfunded liabilities in their pension plans. These were not the specific objectives the CLC sought, but they were significant in their own right and more than the unions could have won without their round of activism. The episode also offers important lessons about what kind of activism is effective in today's challenging times.

The first lesson is the necessity for unions, where possible, to pursue broad and inclusive campaigns. This time, the CLC departed from an expert-led focus on pensions and embraced demands that bridged the concerns of union and non-union workers. In this vein, the decision to champion CPP reform and public pensions was important; industry critics could not easily criticize unions for being "self-interested," and non-union workers could be credibly told that unions were fighting for everyone. The precise opposite would have happened had we focused on protecting the pensions of unionized workers. Such defensive campaigns do not appeal to a wider public grown weary from decades of neoliberalism. If organized labour is unable or unwilling to mount broad campaigns, employers will do so, and redirect public anger against "privileged unions." This is why the AFL-CIO's recent pursuit of the *Employee Free Choice Act* (for "card check" union certification) was doomed to fail; the CLC learned a similar lesson after fighting for "anti-scab" legislation in 2007.[22] These goals, while important, will not appeal to a broad enough base, and will cater to the perception that unions are driven by self-interest. To regain momentum, unions must demonstrate their capacity to win victories for all workers. This was the first strength of the CLC's pension campaign — it offered a compelling vision of "retirement security for everyone," and forced opponents to defend a flawed status quo.

The second lesson, and the second strength of the CLC pension campaign, was its effort to harness the fears, energies, and dreams of everyday union members. When it first realized its opportunity to mobilize on pension issues, the CLC could have simply presented its spokespersons to "multi-stakeholder" meetings and the media. Instead, we recognized the power of workers' stories, and invited the workers into a focused campaign. For that to happen, we financed an extensive, two-year process of pension education to ensure local stories were crucial in our appeal for pension reform. We empowered union members to argue the merits of richer public pensions through the meagre realities of a retiree on their street. The argument for pension insurance, likewise, was articulated locally as a backstop to prevent more Nortels, Abitibi-Bowaters, or AV Pulp and Papers from tearing communities apart. The costs of CPP expansion were explained as a sacrifice of a few take-out coffees or magazine subscriptions per month. From these local, accessible perspectives, union activists could speak from a position of strength, recruit supporters, and apply significant pressure to intransigent decision-makers. This was a welcome departure from the CLC's earlier pension education efforts: intermittent regional courses, and research papers published for specialist audiences. Solid research would remain a key element of the campaign, but a newly mobilized layer of activists gave the CLC new momentum on pension issues. This vindicated those who insist that "staffing up" or "hyper-professionalizing" takes unions away from union members, their primary source of strength. If the grassroots of organized labour take ownership of campaigns, mass participation can happen, and much is possible. If union activists are asked to act as a stage army, far less enthusiasm can be expected. For genuine success, labour's rank and file must be the driver of change.

The closely related need to sustain local activism is the third and final lesson from the CLC's campaign, and it is likely the most difficult to understand. As our movement grew, it wasn't clear how mobilization would continue beyond various government events. And yet, many of the campaign's most impressive moments came because activists themselves scored blows against the forces of pension austerity. Our movement's meetings, rallies, and sit-ins happened because union members gained a sense of their power and focused it against a common adversary.

By June 2010, an apparent victory (through CPP reform) caused many to think change was coming from above. The truth, of course, was otherwise. It is unclear who bears the blame for this widespread misperception. CLC leadership urged vigilance following Flaherty's June 2010 announcement, and called on local pressure to "get the job done." Pension activists sent in numerous requests for campaign materials and further training. However one interprets the federal government's final decision, it clearly believed that betraying an earlier pledge would not entail significant political consequences.

As it happened, this turned out to be true — in Canada's May 2011 federal election, the ruling Conservatives won their first majority government. CLC supporters (particularly the NDP) also did well, but not well enough to ensure greater adequacy, fairness, and security for Canada's pension system. That weighty task remained to be accomplished. It is one organized labour is well advised to take seriously.

## CHICAGO TEACHERS, DIRECT DEMOCRACY, AND GRASSROOTS UNIONISM

*Some people think you elect a president and the president makes*
*all the decisions for the union. No, that's not it, that's not how it*
*works. In the past, what we saw in Chicago was leadership that*

*tried to stifle opposition. I think that opposition deserves to be
heard and deserves to be part of the process.*

— *Karen Lewis, President, Chicago Teachers Union*[23]

By any measure, Karen Lewis is not your typical union leader. She
didn't spend years revolving through low- and middle-ranking union
positions, only to emerge on top later with the backing of union power
brokers. Instead, she was a chemistry teacher serving a low-income area
in Chicago. Disgruntled with the state of the Chicago Teachers Union
(CTU), she and seven others established a rank and file caucus that
swept the union's internal elections in 2010. Under Lewis, the CTU
became a tenacious force prepared to face a formidable adversary. That
adversary was none other than Rahm Emmanuel, former White House
chief of staff to President Obama from 2008 to 2010, who many claim
left Washington, DC, to bring Chicago's teachers to heel. Thankfully,
events turned out rather differently and confirmed the value of grassroots unionism. As I was writing these words, the CTU's experience was
being widely debated by union activists — a hopeful development for
those who want new relevance and energy for organized labour. We turn
to the CTU's story now.

In 2005, Arne Duncan, then chief operating officer of Chicago Public
Schools (and later the US secretary of education), gave a lengthy list of
public schools he believed encouraged a "culture of failure." Low student
test scores and high drop-out rates, Duncan claimed, required an ambitious
approach to education reform, one where enhanced teacher-testing provided incentives for improvement. Duncan's "culture of failure" list included
a preponderance of schools in poor neighbourhoods serving black and
Latino families. Many of these schools operated without adequate heating,
sound infrastructure, arts or music programs, or access to crucial "wrap-
around" services like counsellors, social workers, and nurses. Many of them
were surviving in areas with high unemployment and gang-related violence.

These conditions, of course, were hardly the fault of Chicago's students, parents, and teachers. They were the consequence of neoliberal reforms at the municipal, state, and federal level, all of which preached the merits of low taxes, private-sector-led job creation, and the privatization schemes of large corporations. The University of Chicago, which housed the public policy laboratory for neoliberal thinkers like Milton Friedman, was the birthplace of this strategy, and its application to public education was an early test case. Friedman and his disciples preached the merits of allowing public schools to fail, so private charter schools could be established in their midst, often using the same infrastructure. Several major US cities like Philadelphia, Cleveland, and Detroit have seen widespread charter school takeovers; the most galling case was New Orleans in the aftermath of Hurricane Katrina, where officials glowed about a once in a lifetime chance to create the education system people deserve. In short order, public facilities built up over 150 years became commodities run by a well-connected elite.

By the time Duncan gave his 2005 speech, the case for charter schools was well established; if public schools were "failing," then it made sense to offer parents "more choice," and private charter schools would motivate the public system to improve. In practice, as the CTU explained later, this was a "real estate plan" first, with education reform given as a secondary excuse. Charter schools wanted the "markets" served by public schools, and they had friends in high places to facilitate that objective. Teachers' unions, however, remained a formidable obstacle — despite the overall decline of unions, this sector remained well organized. Almost one in three union cards issued in the United States belonged to workers in the public school system.

In 2005, Jackson Potter was teaching at Chicago's Englewood High School, where he was also the union's local delegate. The day after Duncan's "culture of failure" speech, Potter was summoned to a meeting with Ted Dallas, then vice-president of the CTU. In vivid terms, Potter recalls what happened next:

*I walk through the door and he says: "Jackson, come here. I
gotta tell you something. Today, the board is going to come
and tell you guys your school is closing." I'm like, "holy shit,
what is going on?"*

*And he says, "there's really not much you can do. You
should get your resumes ready, start sprucing up everything in
them, and get the applications out, because this doesn't look
too good."*[24]

This was the moment Potter realized the stakes at hand. He was, as
he recalled later, "confronted with the realization that this union is not a
fighting union. There is not a bone in its body where it's willing to really
put itself out there on behalf of its membership or on big public policy
issues that affects large swaths of public schools across the city. They are
much more comfortable in back-room deals."[25] After that realization,
Potter could have shrugged his shoulders, conveyed the sad news, and
set to work on his resumé. Instead, he found others who opposed the
leadership's defeatist posture and started fomenting dissent in the union.

From those initial conversations, Potter met Al Ramirez, Karen Lewis,
Jen Johnson, Jesse Sharkey, and others who went on to found the Caucus
of Rank and File Educators (CORE). The dissident caucus initially
started as a reading group aimed at helping CTU members establish
the larger agenda behind their employer's plans, and the best prospects
for union resistance. (The first book they studied, fittingly enough, was
Naomi Klein's *The Shock Doctrine*.) Given the CTU's uninspired leadership, however, CORE quickly morphed into a more ambitious force. Jen
Johnson offers these reflections on CORE's early months:

*Our goal was to push the leadership in the right direction. It
was not our expressed intent to take over the leadership of the
CTU when we founded CORE. We held community forums and
reached out to community organizations. We really just tried to*

*build a framework of increasing rank and file participation and community participation in important fights for education.*

*We had events like the CORE forum at Malcolm X College in 2009, where, in the middle of a blizzard, 500 people showed up to talk about charter school proliferation, school closings, and the devastation in communities of color. We said: "Oh my gosh! If 500 people will show up in the middle of a blizzard, then I think we are tapping into something real."*

*Over the next year we continued to build internally, school by school, literally going to schools before our day of work and after our day of work, dropping off fliers and having one on one conversations, sponsoring regional meetings, inviting everyone we knew to get involved in some way to build an organization that would see itself as leading the fight back against school closings and charter proliferation.*[26]

By the spring of 2009, CORE was a known entity in Chicago's black and brown neighhourhoods. It forced city officials to hold public meetings about school closure announcements, and then used the meetings to mobilize further community-union support. It leafleted schools, as Johnson says, and recruited workplace leaders who could join in CORE's work. At times, CORE even compelled city officials to delay or rescind school closures, and this with only a grassroots network of volunteer organizers. That soon earned CORE a solid reputation in Chicago's black and brown communities, who knew all too well what school closures meant for them. It meant fewer resources, fewer black or brown teachers, and more chaos in long-suffering neighbourhoods.

By this point, the CTU's leadership saw CORE as a political threat. By early 2010, CORE organizers had decided to field a slate of candidates for the union elections in a four-way race, most of whom were activists steeped in community organizing. They faced repeated accusations of being "socialists, communists, and troublemakers" from incumbents who, according to one account, spent at least $250,000 to cling to power. On June 13, 2010, CORE prevailed nonetheless with almost 59 per cent of the vote. Karen Lewis's first public address as CTU president made clear a new era had begun:

> *Today marks the beginning of a fight for true transparency in our education policy — how to accurately measure teaching and learning, and how to truly improve our schools and how to evaluate the wisdom behind our spending priorities. This election shows the unity of 30,000 educators standing strong to put business in its place — out of our schools.*
>
> *Corporate America sees K-12 public education as a $380 billion trust that — up until the last 15 years — they haven't had a sizeable piece of. So this so-called school reform is not an education plan. It's a business plan, and mayoral control of our schools and our Board Of Education is the linchpin of their operation.*
>
> *Fifteen years ago, this city purposely began starving our lowest-income neighborhood schools of greatly needed resources and personnel. Class sizes rose, schools were closed. Then standardized tests, which in this town alone is a $60 million business, measured that slow death by starvation. These tests labeled our students, families and educators failures, because standardized tests reveal more about a student's zip code than it does about academic growth.*
>
> *And that, in turn — that perceived school failure — fed parent demand for charters, turnarounds and contract schools. People thought, "it must be true, I read it in the papers. It must be the teachers' fault." Because they read about it, every single week. And our union, which has been controlled by the same faction for the last 40 years — 37 out of 40 — didn't point out this simple reality.*

> *What drives school reform is a single focus on profit. Profit.*
> *Not teaching, not learning, profit.*[27]

Lee Sustar has documented CORE's emergence (and the CTU's transformation), and describes Chicago's press corps as "speechless" after hearing these words. "The local media," he claimed, "isn't used to an assertive teachers' union leader — certainly not one who declares that she's standing up to the politicians and business interests that have made Chicago a laboratory for "school reform" for the last 15 years."[28]

In short order, the CORE leadership delivered on these words, but first by changing the CTU's internal structure. Exorbitant salaries and perks enjoyed by previous officers were eliminated. The new CTU leadership would earn the average teacher's salary, and the savings created were used to establish an organizing department of seven staff. The members of this intrepid crew, who include some of Chicago's best movement organizers, were responsible for membership mobilization and building solidarity with community allies. They oversaw "listening teams" of staff and volunteer organizers who were dispatched to canvass every school and engage union members in conversations about the next round of bargaining. The CTU's executive and bargaining team were expanded to include rank and file members, and a new "community advisory board" with twenty-eight members created a direct link between the CTU, local activists, and representatives from other unions. In a matter of months, a top-down, executive-driven union was transformed through bottom-up reforms, and not a moment too soon.

Rahm Emmanuel took office as Chicago's mayor in February 2011, and his early decisions sent a clear message to the CTU. He first appointed Juan Rangel, the head of a charter school network, as his education adviser. He then went directly to school principals and asked them to sign waivers allowing for a longer school day with no additional staff compensation; the offer was incentivized with grants of $150,000 for every school that signed, and free iPads for teachers. Thirteen of these waivers were signed before the CTU had the initiative stopped at Chicago's Education Labor Relations Board, but the union's takeaway message was clear: Emmanuel was determined, brash, and willing to go over their heads at a moment's notice.

That fact was confirmed three months later, when Emmanuel worked with state legislators to pass Bill SB-7, which required (among other things) that the CTU get 75 per cent of its entire membership to authorize strike action. This was an exceptionally high standard bemoaned by teachers and cheered by anti-union boosters. But Lewis, to everyone's surprise, offered the CTU's endorsement of SB-7, and did so without informing the wider membership immediately. She insisted, in her defence, that the union needed at least 75 per cent of members to vote for a strike for any strike to be effective. That did not prevent anger from erupting in the CTU's ranks, particularly because its new leaders had pledged to embrace grassroots democracy.

The CTU weathered the SB-7 controversy, which was quickly followed by more attacks from the mayor's office. In June 2011, Emmanuel announced he was rescinding the 4 per cent wage increase specified in the CTU's collective agreement, while he also increased salaries for public school executives. These moves roiled teachers who were already seething. Undeterred, Emmanuel declared his objective to seek a district-wide school day extension (without additional compensation for teachers). The CTU knew the idea was popular with parents, and didn't succumb to mudslinging in the press. Instead, it dispatched more listening teams to parent groups, most of whom realized what Emmanuel was doing. A longer day was fine, the CTU heard, but teachers should not work for free. That sentiment was mobilized, directed at the mayor's office, and resulted in the hiring of five hundred additional CTU positions by July 2011.

These early skirmishes convinced the CTU's activist base that a showdown with Emmanuel was inevitable. As bargaining approached in

2012, the union repeated this message wherever possible, and that led to strike readiness work long before the mass rallies. By February 2012, in a discussion paper called *The Schools Chicago's Children Deserve*, the CTU articulated its vision for the future of Chicago's public education system. It was a defiant call against cutbacks, racist discrimination in school funding, and quick charter school "turnarounds" of public schools. It gave voice to those who had suffered enough, and wanted to fight for a better future.

On May 23, 2012, a mass rally of four thousand CTU members filled a downtown auditorium to capacity, while two thousand more filled an adjacent park. Eight days later, a staggering 90 per cent of CTU members participated in the union's strike vote, with 98 per cent of voters authorizing strike action. Teachers would not stomach a 20 per cent work day increase, a meagre 2 per cent pay raise, the constant threat of school closures, and the continued encroachment of charter schools. They also rejected employer calls for narrow "teacher testing," and "merit pay" that flouted hard-won seniority rules. The message to Emmanuel was clear: CTU members were fed up; if the mayor wanted a fight, their union was ready.

By late August, the CTU had filed its ten-day strike notice. It quickly held "practice strikes" (information pickets) at several locations, and established a strike deadline for September 10. Many readers will be familiar with what happened next: Emmanuel, expecting to call the union's bluff, refused to budge in negotiations, which launched the first CTU strike in over twenty-five years. He then spent eight days on television taking gulps from his water bottle, exasperated at the rising fortunes of the CTU. Polls confirmed the public had swung behind the union, and that sentiment was clearly linked to its reputation for fighting school closures and criticizing the differential treatment of black and brown students. For days, mass rallies of CTU members adorned with red T-shirts filled Chicago's downtown core, channelling outrage in a way few had expected. As this happened, unbeknownst to CTU leaders, the offices of sixteen city aldermen (deemed "aldersheep" by union activists) were occupied by over two hundred CTU members. A silent march of thousands snaked through Chicago's wealthier neighbourhoods, even passing by Emmanuel's house, to question who the city served. International attention was drawn to the city that featured an anti-union mayor who had served an allegedly pro-union White House.

Toward the end, when CTU negotiators felt they had a tentative agreement worth showing the membership, Emmanuel was infuriated to learn that didn't mean an immediate return to work. Instead, the union stayed out until its rank and file members had sufficient time to understand and approve the tentative agreement. This did not stop the city from seeking a court injunction, but the presiding judge could sense the prevailing winds. The injunction was denied, and CTU members returned to work with their heads held high. They had fought off most major concessions, including merit pay and mandatory teacher testing. They had secured modest wage increases and a commitment from city officials to find jobs for CTU members displaced by school closures. More positions were created for social workers, counsellors, and nurses in under-serviced schools. But above all, CTU members learned that fighting back makes a difference, particularly if activists believe in a culture of grassroots unionism. Three months before the CTU's strike, Toronto's public library workers drew a similar conclusion. We turn to their story now.

## THE EMPLOYER AS ORGANIZER: THE RISE OF TORONTO'S LIBRARY WORKERS

*I wish I knew her name.*

*She is at the Lillian Smith library and I was looking for some books to help the four and five year olds I work with in day care, to understand more about the Underground Railroad and other events to celebrate Black History Month.*

*She went out of her way to find me appropriate books and*

*turned me on to authors and stories I did not know. The kids have loved the books and talk about what they've learned all the time. Even their parents have noticed their interest.*

*Thank you. If we didn't have librarians like this wonderful woman, what would we do?*

— *Estelle Amaron*[29]

Like Chicago's teachers, Toronto's library workers have staffed a cash-strapped system for decades, and have done so despite their library system's widespread popularity. In 2012, the operating budget of the Toronto Public Library (TPL) was $20 million shy (in 2002 dollars) of its amount in 1992, while its use had increased by 17 per cent over the same period. Although some of this trend could be explained by automation, this austerity has been largely borne by library workers, who suffered job reductions and precarious work arrangements. Despite staffing the most widely used library system in the world — with over nineteen million visits, and thirty-three million items circulated in 2012 — 523 of TPL's unionized positions have been cut since 1992, a reduction in service of almost 25 per cent. By 2013, over half of the TPL's unionized staff (almost twenty-four hundred people) were part-time, many of them "pages," a position historically reserved for student interns. Wage rates varied widely between about 440 librarians, 699 pages, and hundreds of public service assistants who provide the TPL's innumerable programs.

This is the cynical context TPL workers and their union (Local 4948 of the Canadian Union of Public Employees) have faced for decades. By 2011, that trend took a dramatic turn for the worse. In October 2010, Rob Ford — a conservative populist on the Tea Party model — was elected as Toronto's mayor on a wave of support from suburban boroughs. Ford came in after David Miller's two terms, totalling seven years. When elected, Miller was widely seen as a progressive, and he did oversee some progressive reforms, notably on green retrofits and urban revitalization. Once in office, however, Miller implemented many of the neoliberal reforms he earlier opposed; he also, most notably, precipitated a bitter thirty-nine-day strike with city workers, and engaged in divisive rhetoric in doing so.

As several Toronto activists have told me, Ford's victory was helped by the frustration progressives felt toward Miller. Nevertheless, the result stunned Toronto's downtown core, home to many talented organizers and grassroots movements. Ford's election also showcased the disconnect between these neighbourhoods and Toronto's suburbs; downtown activists (supposedly) sipping fair trade lattes were often far removed from the (claimed) strip mall culture of outlying areas. This distance bred jealousies, misperceptions, and vast audiences for neoliberal populists like Ford who insisted on ending the "gravy train at City Hall." By December 2010, with the Ford administration installed, the tenor of Toronto's civic politics had changed. Doug Ford, the mayor's brother (and a city councillor from suburban Etobicoke), announced, "We're going to be outsourcing everything that is not nailed down."[30] As their first act in office, the Fords made good on that pledge by forcing the closure of Toronto's Urban Affairs Library, which had long served a bustling clientele of municipal researchers, civic administrators, and downtown library users. They claimed the move would save the city $100 million in 2011 and $629,000 in 2012.

Opponents argued these numbers were exaggerated and the act betrayed the mayor's campaign promise not to cut key services. For a time, the TPL board defied the move, but after extensive debate a majority opted otherwise. The rationale for giving in was articulated by Kathy Gallagher Ross, a citizen board member who worried about provoking the Fords: "I just think we must think about the library. We must think about what's going to happen next year, and think about what we have already done by putting ourselves in conflict with the mayor, and the mayor's office and the mayor's policies . . . I think we are sabotaging what we love in the library by not being more careful."[31]

As Maureen O'Reilly, President of CUPE 4948, told me, the union fought the Urban Affairs Library closure despite the timidity of the TPL board.[32] Members held rallies, leafleted passers-by, lobbied city officials, and raised awareness, where possible, through media interventions.[33] These efforts proved unsuccessful, although they provided an important training ground for later battles, notably the union's mobilization against the mayor's 2011–12 budget proposals. In crafting those proposals, elite consultants from KPMG were hired to find the "gravy" in Toronto's public services, and library services were soon in their crosshairs. Among other things, KPMG's June 2011 report recommended closing library branches, reducing library hours, and implementing a 10 per cent cut to all TPL programs (a reduction sought for most other city services as well).

O'Reilly recalls this moment as a "gift," for it infuriated an already bitter union membership. As a life-long librarian with twenty-seven years experience, O'Reilly understood what decades of austerity meant for TPL workers. In 2011 the city had cut 107 TPL jobs, reducing an array of popular services. The 2012 budget proposals would only compound this problem, and the CUPE 4948 leadership knew library advocates had reached a breaking point. Months before, they had laid the foundations for a new campaign, dubbed Project Rescue, to raise the union's civic profile and reinforce its image as a defender of TPL's mandate. This involved setting up a sophisticated website (capable of several campaign functions), polling TPL user attitudes, and forging new relationships with city authors and library users. That work revealed what the union already knew: The public supported the TPL and opposed any further cuts to the system. And yet, when the union launched Project Rescue on July 14, 2011, it did so to limited fanfare; union members, despite appeals from union leaders, were not drawn to the campaign. A select few in the local media covered the launch, which made many question the union's ability to fight the mayor's austerity plans.

Nevertheless, Project Rescue caught the attention of Doug Ford, who took issue with its appeal during a talk radio appearance a week later. In classic demagogic style, he pronounced that Toronto had "more libraries per person than any other city in the world. I've got more libraries in my area than I have Tim Hortons."[34] Those claims, both of which were false, elicited a firestorm of anger, ably tapped by CUPE 4948 through its revamped website and social media presence. There and elsewhere, O'Reilly noted that Ford's Etobicoke constituency had thirteen TPL branches and thirty-nine Tim Hortons franchises. The *Toronto Star*, after interviews with TPL officials, raised other pertinent comparisons: "Toronto has one library for every 28,120 citizens, fewer than Hamilton (one branch per 21,629); Ottawa (27,527); and Vancouver (27,976)."[35] Despite repeated media requests, Doug Ford declined any further comment. His remarks were ridiculed online, with thousands of missives launched under the Twitter hashtag #booksnotdonutsforford (a memorable entry was entitled "Love in a time of gravy"). Barely a week after the union faced the brunt of Ford's attack, Project Rescue had notched a propaganda victory.

Two days later, that victory was boosted by another unexpected event. Margaret Atwood, arguably Toronto's most famous author, also took issue with Doug Ford's library claims. On July 22, 2011, through her Twitter account, Atwood released this statement to her 225,200 followers: "Toronto's libraries are under threat of privatization. Tell city council to keep them public now."[36] The statement included a link to a Project Rescue petition launched by CUPE 4948 on its campaign website, which soon crashed after thousands signed almost instantaneously. In the thirty minutes it took to fix the problem, the petition amassed over 17,300 signatures. The union sought a private meeting with Atwood, whom it had already approached to help resist library cuts. This time, CUPE 4948 asked for help in making appeals to prominent authors; within hours, Atwood had enlisted ten authors to help facilitate a writing contest — "My Library Matters to Me" — that highlighted the value of libraries from a community perspective. The contest would be judged by CUPE

4948 members, and winners would enjoy lunch and literary tours with participating authors.

The Fords had kickstarted an anti-library-cuts movement that was now gaining steam. At a marathon twenty-two-hour meeting beginning at 10 a.m. on July 30, 2011, a city committee including the mayor listened to deputations from residents who opposed the city's austerity measures. By all accounts, the two highlights of this meeting involved libraries. At 3 a.m., O'Reilly presented the committee with thirty-nine thousand names on CUPE 4948's Project Rescue petition; as she explained to me, this drew thunderous applause and chants of "save our libraries" lasting several minutes.[37] Shortly before, Anika Tabovaradan, a fourteen-year-old student, wept openly as she lamented the potential loss of her local library branch. "I'm no taxpayer," she said, "but when I get to use the computers in the library and do my homework, I'll be able to get a good job someday . . . and when the day comes to pay taxes, I'll be glad you supported young people paying the extra taxes to keep the system going."[38]

As O'Reilly told me, heartfelt statements like this flooded the e-mail accounts of city councillors, whose staff counted 61,246 messages on library cuts alone (more than triple what any issue had galvanized before).[39] Much of this traffic was facilitated by CUPE 4948's website, but a larger bottom-up movement was in motion, and it made library workers believe that a fightback was possible. The movement had even had an impact on Mayor Ford, who, by August 2011, pledged that no library branch would be closed in the hunt for cost savings.

Two months later, however, the public learned that library cuts would be demanded in other areas. On October 13, 2011, Toronto's city librarian released a report that recommended $9.7 million in cuts, a figure that represented 5.9 per cent of the TPL's operating budget.[40] This was below the 10 per cent target the mayor had sought from all city programs, and the report listed additional austerity measures required to meet that higher threshold (including elimination of Sunday service at eight branches, and summer closings at nineteen others). News of these proposals evoked public fury, which soon found its voice at the next TPL board meeting. Thirty people signed up to offer oral remarks about library cuts, while over a hundred crammed an overflow room to watch the proceedings.[41]

What happened next testified what library workers had accomplished. This time, a majority of board members shifted from deference to determination. They defied the mayor's 10 per cent target and endorsed the city librarian's lower goal of 5.9 per cent in TPL cuts. This was, as the union acknowledged, a pyrrhic victory — a further 109 TPL jobs would still be lost with the lower figure, in addition to some services. Even so, the mayor's allies considered the decision as a betrayal. Paul Ainslie, board chair and close Ford ally, reacted with these words: "A majority of the Board just abrogated their duties, shirked their responsibilities ... I'm fully expecting the City Manager to be furious. I think the Mayor's going to be furious. I think the Budget Committee will be furious. I'm furious."[42]

The Fords fought back and issued ultimatums through allies on the city's Budget Committee demanding the full 10 per cent cut. That belligerence, as it happened, drove fence-sitters to the library workers' side. Critics noted the mayor's office, the office of the city manager, and several other municipal services were spared the 10 per cent target. Many of Ford's allies complained they couldn't support reduced library hours or summer library closures, and CUPE 4948's polling research ascertained why: When asked, a majority of Toronto's voters had said reduced library services would factor into their decision at the ballot box.[43] By January 2012, however, Ford pushed on undeterred, forcing decisive votes on various austerity measures. He lost a majority of these votes, including a 22–21 decision that confirmed the more modest 5.9 per cent cut to libraries. Conservative luminaries soon expressed their unease and worried the Fords were "tarnishing their brand." A *Toronto Life* feature article cited a top Ford adviser: "There are only so many votes you can lose," the anonymous source said, "and then you end up becoming sort of neutered."[44]

At this point, CUPE 4948 was ensconced in collective bargaining with TPL board negotiators. There too, the union faced a similar intransigence. In February, the union filed for a "no board report" with the province of Ontario; the measure was granted, putting the union in a strike position as of March 12. Union members, riding a wave of public support, had given a 91 per cent mandate for strike action. The union ensured that members realized the stakes at hand. Activist flying squads created two years earlier had already begun organizing in November 2011, as dozens of library workers booked off for full-time union work.[45] This meant visiting all ninety-eight TPL branches, updating bulletin boards, and engaging members in a conversation about strike readiness. Of all the issues raised in these conversations, the abysmal conditions of part-time workers emerged as a unifying concern. In March 2012, for the first time in its history, a majority of TPL staff were part-time, a trend management wanted to expand dramatically.

In March, a union rally put a human face on this problem. A featured speaker was Mary Bissell, a librarian with twenty-five years experience who had been stuck in part-time work for six years. Speaking to a large crowd, Bissell described what her employer's austerity plans meant to her: "The reality is the more full-time jobs they cut, the fewer full-time opportunities there are . . . there's a disturbing trend towards a retail model of staffing at TPL, and part-timers being used to fill holes in the schedule means we feel interchangeable."[46] Bissell said it was common for part-timers to work three-and-a–half-hour shifts for twelve consecutive days, and lamented the consequences of that staffing model for workers' lives. O'Reilly then spoke passionately about recent library worker activism and the current stakes of collective bargaining: "We fought back on library closures, cuts to service hours, cuts to collections, and cuts to programs," she said. "But we were not able to prevent staff cuts, and now they want even more from us at the bargaining table."[47]

In the end, like Chicago's teachers, it took a strike for TPL management to understand why the cuts were unaffordable. In a last-ditch effort before the strike deadline, the union appealed to Jane Pyper, Toronto's city librarian, to speak to the negotiators so management could grasp why job insecurity was not in anyone's interest. When that failed, the union knew it had to strike. Organizers had given considered thought to the tactics that could inspire union members, mobilize public support, and back management off its most aggressive demands. When the picket lines went up city-wide on March 19, the public saw CUPE 4948's experiments in grassroots unionism. Supporters were invited to join "read-ins" and "knit-ins" on the largest picket lines, most notably the throngs circling the entrances of City Hall, who at times amounted to over a thousand people. The union produced seven strike bulletins in nine days to keep members abreast of developments, and 60 to 70 per cent of the members actively participated in strike activities.[48] The strike's appeal was sufficient to motivate low-level TPL managers, most of whom were former CUPE 4948 members, to visit strike events, offering food and water to those they met.

On March 30, when CUPE 4948 members returned to work, they did so after fighting off most of management's austerity proposals. Several aspects of the collective agreement were preserved or improved, but one concession stuck in everyone's craw. The city won its bid to change job security rules for TPL staff. Previously, the rules had required management to find jobs for workers whose services were cut. The language of that provision was now changed; that right would be extended only to workers with eleven years of tenure or more. That meant at least 50 per cent of CUPE 4948's membership was vulnerable to job loss, a threat that the union forestall given more public funding for TPL services. As I was writing these words, that was the latest goal for the union's Project Rescue — a political force library opponents ignore at their own peril.

# CONCLUSION

*Now the labor leaders are screamin' when they close the missile plants,*
*United Fruit screams at the Cuban shore,*
*Call it "peace" or call it "treason"*
*Call it "love" or call it "reason"*
*But I ain't marching any more.*

*— Phil Ochs, "I Ain't Marching Anymore," 1965*

At a time when the AFL-CIO was ensconced in its support for American militarism, folksinger Phil Ochs, in his redoubtable style, offered these lyrics to describe a process he felt was well underway. Long before many US soldiers — most of whom, as is still the case, were poor and working class — refused to serve in Vietnam, Ochs could envision an uprising that today's power-brokers still remember. That uprising would not come, as Ochs tells us, from union leaders stumping for war-mongering industries, or "responsible" corporate citizens like United Fruit. In Vietnam's unfolding saga of violence, what truly mattered were grassroots anti-war movements in working-class communities, and the wider refusal among soldiers to fight in a conflict both immoral and wrong.

To capture this mood, Ochs once introduced "I Ain't Marching Anymore" as a "turning away" song, in language that reflected the fear and optimism of his times: "So what can you do? I mean, here you are, a helpless soul, a helpless piece of flesh amidst all this cruel, cruel machinery, and terrible, heartless men. So all you can do is turn away from the filth, and hope. Hope to build something new someday. So here's a turning away song."

Grassroots unionism begins from a similar premise. Those interested in fighting effectively have needed to "turn away," for the most part, from the dominant strategies of organized labour. That was certainly my goal in the early stages of the CLC's pension work, which had historically been mired in expert-driven discussions. I remember the first CLC pension meeting I facilitated in Ottawa in late 2005, and the opaque jargon participants used during the course of our discussions. As we debated what the CLC should do, it was clear we were trapped in a parallel world only intelligible to pension specialists. Meanwhile, millions of union members faced vexing questions about their pension security, not to mention the fortunes of their family and friends less fortunate. In 2005, we lacked a compelling, intelligible vision to inspire workers to fight for pension justice. By 2010, we were staring down pension experts and running a campaign that changed Canada's pension debate.

We did that by building the capacities of union members, often to remarkable ends. And, as debates unfold about how to change the world, that kind of grassroots unionism, as we've seen in this chapter, offers glimpses of hope. The rise of Toronto's library workers, as we saw, was also facilitated by the union's embrace of grassroots campaigning, a strategy bearing great likeness to smaller, effective bottom-up movements. The energy of the Chicago Teachers Union, in like terms, started with CORE's dogged community organizing against school closures and racist bias in the delivery of public education services. With that reputation established, CORE's leaders went on to transform their own union, driven largely through bottom-up reforms. An emphasis was placed on grassroots organizing, listening to members, widening the scope of decision-making, and, in real terms, building a new generation of activists to resist proponents of austerity. That work, of course, continues — as these words were written, the Chicago Public School Board announced its intention to shut an additional fifty-four schools, affecting over thirty thousand students, largely in poor black and brown communities. On March 28, 2013, that led to a downtown march of over five thousand CTU members, all of whom pledged to put their "bodies on the line" to resist the mayor's attacks. There is no reason why unions elsewhere cannot aspire to the same proud, defiant spirit.

Of course, some will read that last sentence with a hefty dose of cynicism — the larger picture for unions today hardly portends that outcome. But even if most are skeptical about the likelihood of union renewal, recent glimpses of grassroots militant unionism suggest other possibilities. If rank and file workers were so inclined (and prepared), far more than motions at union meetings could be mustered to challenge proponents of neoliberal austerity. The efforts of the CLC, Chicago teachers and Toronto library workers could be communicated beyond the usual activist websites and progressive magazines. These transformative struggles could be trumpeted as models for the big battalions of organized labour to understand, emulate, and champion.

This is also true when unions engage in grassroots politics outside the workplace. As I explained in chapter one, the relationships established between unions and other movements were decisive in Seattle in 1999. In that case, small groups of activists (in and outside organized labour) worked together to challenge the AFL-CIO, but only after trust was won beforehand through joint campaigns. A lesser-known fact about Western labour history is the comparable role of activists who led campaigns for industrial trade unionism. The Knights of Labor, the IWW, the Scottish Clydeside Workers movement, the One Big Union movement, and the Trade Union Education League (those unfamiliar with these names should stop reading and start googling) were built by grassroots activists seeking a better future for the average person. Each was often divided on questions of tactics and strategy, but organizers were committed to building independent thought and action in unions. The top-down, bureaucratic approach to unionism was repellent then, as it should be now.

Altogether, nothing short of a revolution is needed in unions to change their otherwise dismal fortunes. For that to happen, organized labour will need political momentum driven by their rank and file. That is what the CLC's pension campaign, Chicago's teachers, and Toronto's library workers suggest to the rest of us. They may be glimpses of grassroots unionism, but they are also pioneers; their energy and defiance embody the spirit of our activist times. Teeming networks of rank and file activists were once the anchor of unions, and will remain crucial to their uncertain future.

# 4

# MIRRORS OR MIRAGE?

## POLITICAL PARTIES AND GRASSROOTS MOVEMENTS

*If voting ever changed anything, they'd make it illegal.*

*— Emma Goldman*[1]

So declares a familiar slogan, one that resonates loudly the world over. When governments of numerous stripes implement the same unpopular neoliberal policies, when deep-pocketed interests hold sway in well-crafted election campaigns, and when the mainstream media offer a predictably stale, personality-based focus for political debate, many have opted to either vote cynically or not at all. A widespread frustration exists with political parties everywhere, and a persuasive logic fuels it. What is the point of voting if, regardless of the political party, politicians simply break promises in office? Scandals involving collusion between government and business draw outcry in extreme circumstances, but even these seem fleeting. Most people regard such practices as an ugly feature of modern politics; politicians are widely regarded as corrupt, in the process of being corrupted, or eminently corruptible. Ursula

Franklin, a renowned physicist and peace activist, captured broad opinion with these words: "I once thought politicians were well-intentioned but ill-informed; now I think they are not only ill-informed, but equally ill-intentioned."[2]

Today, mainstream politicians hold power through divisive agendas: "cracking down" on "deviants" or "violence" in racialized communities, rooting out social assistance "fraud," opposing same-sex marriage, attacking unions, increasing the state surveillance of alleged "terrorists," slashing or privatizing utilities and social programs, or siphoning public funds into grossly unequal personal tax cuts. As depicted in *Wag the Dog,* Barry Levinson's memorable film, divide and conquer remains the tactic of choice for those who form governments.

And yet, there has also been cause for hope in recent elections, something I have seen first-hand (and heard from others close to the action). In recent years, as thousands have been drawn into grassroots activism, political parties have emerged, at times, to champion this upturn. When this has happened, activists have seen an image of themselves in certain Left parties or political leaders who typically appeal to those sceptical of "politics as usual." These moments have often produced remarkable outcomes, leading some activists to argue that elections are not a foregone conclusion. They compel us to reconsider the relationship between Left parties and movements engaged in grassroots activism.

That, of course, hardly settles a long-standing question: Can political parties be a genuine, supportive reflection of social movements, or are they always — as Emma Goldman implies — a mirage that appropriates activist energies? To explore that narrative, I review the work of three Left parties and the intersection of each with movements engaged in grassroots activism: the federal New Democratic Party under Jack Layton's leadership; the rise of Québec Solidaire; and the lessons learned before, during, and after Barack Obama's historic 2008 campaign for the US presidency.

## MAN, OR MOVEMENTS? UNDERSTANDING THE RISE OF JACK LAYTON'S NDP

*Jack was the guy you could call and say, "What the fuck is going on?" — and instead of getting defensive, he would come to the meeting. I always saw him as an intermediary between government and the people who like many of us located in community, worked as change agents.*

*But he did it from government. Jack made the personal political, made us forget our fears and reminded us of our goodness. In his life and in his death he raised us with hope.*

*. . . I know, St. Jack of Layton, right? But he was not that; he was just a man doing what he could do, should do, not accidentally but strategically in response to community initiatives and with organizers and activists. He worked with us in order to work for us. He acknowledged the work of people on the front lines of communities, didn't throw away the t-shirt after the parade, inhaled, and understood the power of civic engagement to effect change.*

*And he did it from the municipal level all the way to the top. He brought our community experts with him, knew where to find us, and in his success, we saw our own.*

*— Jane Doe, feminist organizer and activist*[3]

In the Canadian electoral context, May 2, 2011, was a key historical moment, rather like November 4, 2008, for Obama supporters. After spending decades in the political wilderness, the federal New Democratic Party (NDP) emerged as Canada's official opposition — winning an unprecedented 103 seats (of 309) in the House of Commons. Previously, leadership of the opposition had been held by Liberal and Conservative parties, whose roots date back to Canada's founding in 1867. The roots of the federal NDP, in contrast, are more recent; the party emerged in 1961 when the social democratic Co-operative Commonwealth Federation (CCF) merged with the Canadian Labour Congress (the political arm of unions in English Canada). The federal NDP continued its commitment to the CCF's core principles, with great emphasis on the party's role in fighting for public health care and other social justice concerns.

By 2011 the NDP had regularly formed governments at the provincial level, often to the consternation of many supporters. Commitments to enact major policy reforms were frequently ignored, relations with social movements were often tense, while tepid campaign platforms were routinely proposed to silence establishment critics. This has led many to echo Louis St. Laurent, a former Liberal prime minister who once claimed NDPers were merely "Liberals in a hurry." But the federal NDP's May 2011 breakthrough, for many, heralded something different. It certainly wasn't due to the party's program which, as before, was crafted to fit mainstream, neoliberal assumptions; among other things, the NDP pledged to support cap-and-trade emissions schemes, reward "small business job creators" (through tax cuts), and maintain lower corporate tax rates relative to US standards. The difference in 2011 was the overwhelming public response to Jack Layton, the federal NDP leader, who was widely perceived as an honest, empathic, and idealistic exception to an otherwise cynical rule.

Many knew Layton had fought a recent battle with cancer but still insisted on campaigning vigorously; in doing so, he emerged as a symbol of defiance in tumultuous times. In place after place, Layton pumped the air with his cane, appealing to the same feistiness that created Occupy Wall Street. In the press, he was cast as an inspiring everyman, or "*un bon Jack*" for French-speaking discussion. With Layton's untimely death in August 2011, that sentiment reached a fever pitch. Millions were drawn into a process of collective mourning as televised images of Layton's state funeral dominated the airwaves. Urban landscapes were filled with chalked testimonials to his work, many of which referenced the closing words of his last public statement: "Love is better than anger, hope is better than fear, optimism is better than despair. So, my friends, let us be loving, hopeful, and optimistic, and we'll change the world."[4]

And yet, since those handwritten tributes have washed away, we are left with a tough question: How did Layton earn wide support despite the NDP's modest vision, when most politicians are scorned for similar caution? A common answer, one heard in many NDP circles, credits the "great persona" of Layton himself, who had a unique ability to communicate progressive ideas to mass audiences. That was certainly the narrative behind *Jack*, a recent biopic by the Canadian Broadcasting Corporation focused on the NDP's 2011 breakthrough and the drama of Layton's cane-waving appeals. The film's early moments, however, touched on Layton's initial years in Toronto politics, and it was here one detects the cause for the NDP's future electoral gains. Layton's success came from his affinity with activist movements and his ability to listen to, learn from, and broadcast their stories using the platform of electoral politics. Jane Doe's words (cited at the top of this section) make this very point, and it is one shared by countless other movement organizers (including myself). The balance of this section is therefore quite personal, for Layton is someone I saw up close for several years, but rarely as an NDP member.

As a graduate student in Toronto, I had run across Layton several times — both in his days as a city councillor and during his later role as a federal politician. My first conversation with him, in 1999, was about a book — Susan Faludi's *Stiffed: The Betrayal of the American Man*. I was selling books for a socialist group, and Layton was curious about the political drift of Faludi's contribution to masculinity studies. "So much of that literature," he lamented, "is thinly-veiled bitterness about feminism. But if someone like Faludi takes this seriously I want to know her perspective." We debated the impact of various feminisms on progressive movements, with both of us, as feminist allies, lamenting there was much left to be done. It was a thought-provoking conversation, largely because I knew Layton had co-founded the white ribbon campaign to challenge violence against women eight years earlier.

The next time I talked to Layton was January 25, 2003. He was presenting his candidacy for federal NDP leader during a convention held at Toronto's Exhibition Place. Layton, to a great extent, had inherited many supporters of the New Politics Initiative, an ambitious, movement-inspired reform movement inside the NDP that had won 40 per cent of the vote at the party's federal convention in 2001. In 2003, however, I met Layton as a supporter of Joe Comartin, a leadership candidate who enjoyed close ties to peace activists and Muslim communities. As the leadership convention approached, some worried the NDP would support Canadian participation in an Iraq war if it was sanctioned by the United Nations. That was the view of the ruling federal Liberal Party, and I was part of a broad effort to urge against this outcome. After winning the leadership handily on the first ballot, Layton announced, to a densely packed convention hall, that the NDP would never endorse Canadian participation in the Iraq War — with or without a UN mandate. He used the media attention on that day (and several days after) to promote peace marches on February 15, 2003. And on that date, as I discussed earlier in chapter one, the world was rocked by unprecedented anti-war mobilizations. Canada saw its largest peace marches since the anti-conscription fights of the First World War, and a political context that convinced then Prime Minister Chrétien to stand behind his earlier commitment. On March 18, 2003, after Colin Powell's infamous appeal was rejected by the UN Security Council, Chrétien confirmed Canada would not participate in the Iraq War. It was a decision that enraged hawks and emboldened peace activists. It did not prevent the Iraq War and subsequent occupation from happening, but it isolated the pro-war apologists and reminded progressives of Layton's own commitment to peace and global justice.

Those commitments were on display again three years later, when Layton supported an appeal to withdraw Canadian troops from

Afghanistan. At the time, some prominent NDP leaders urged a more nuanced position supporting a role for Canadian "peacemakers," to ensure efforts to promote women's rights continued. In the lead-up to the NDP's 2006 convention in Quebec City, peace activists worked tirelessly to urge Layton and others to reject that view. They did so in alliance with Malalai Joya, an outspoken politician from Afghanistan's Farah province, whom the British Broadcasting Foreign Service called "the bravest woman in Afghanistan." On December 17, 2003, Joya, to the astonishment of the Afghan Loya Jirga (national parliament), decried the process by which former war criminals had political titles and operated with impunity. The warlords lived in mansions, she said, while ordinary Afghans were mired in brutal poverty; they facilitated a booming heroin trade, and pilfered development funds meant for the Afghan people. For these statements, Joya was labelled an "infidel" and "communist," with a one warlord screaming "Rape her!" as she spoke. Undeterred, she continued despite several assassination attempts, speaking out publicly around the world. On September 6, 2006, at Layton's invitation, she addressed the federal NDP convention. Her words resonated loudly:

> No nation can donate liberation to another nation. Liberation should be achieved in a country by the people themselves. The ongoing developments in Afghanistan and Iraq prove this claim.
>
> I think if Canada and other governments really want to help Afghan people and bring positive changes, they must act independently, rather than becoming a tool to implement the wrong policies of the U.S. government.
>
> They must align themselves to the wishes and needs of Afghan people and stop any kind of support to the warlords and reactionary and ignorant element within the system. Only by such policy, they can gain people's trust and will prove themselves as real friends of Afghan people.[5]

Convention delegates gave Joya a standing ovation, and soon after passed a resolution calling for the withdrawal of Canadian troops. Layton, anticipating this result, authorized the production of "bring them home" buttons for wide distribution on the convention floor. When the media pushed him about alternatives to war, he argued for negotiations with Taliban leaders. That statement angered many in the NDP and drew ridicule from both Liberals and Conservatives — many of whom branded Layton as "Taliban Jack." But before six years had passed, direct and indirect talks with the Taliban had become the actual (if not official) approach being used by governments seeking withdrawal of most combat troops.

At the time, I was proud to have helped Layton's "bring the troops home" appeal as a non-NDPer. Still, right after the 2006 motion was passed, he called my cellphone to relay the news, welcoming any help I could offer in refining NDP policy further. I listened to Layton's message in stunned amazement. What kind of politician, I thought, makes himself that available to outside pressure, and cares this much about what non-NDP activists think? Senior NDP staff often groaned when Layton offered his cellphone number to people like me, for it meant disgruntled calls later that cut into the leader's precious time. But that was Layton's calling card; he worked tirelessly to develop relationships with movement organizers who appreciated having that access. Those relationships facilitated the party's inroads into Quebec, in particular, where the federal NDP would later strike a loud chord.

Of course, Layton's focus on building movement ties didn't prevent accusations that he was abandoning core NDP principles. A notable case happened during Canada's parliamentary uproar during the 2008 global financial crisis. The minority Conservative government (elected only months before) had vastly underestimated its budget shortfall, and opposition parties were threatening to vote against the budget on that basis. Beyond that, however, were budget measures Conservatives used to antagonize opponents; a key target was withdrawing public-funding-per-vote legislation introduced in 2003, which by 2008 was a major source of revenue for opposition parties. The Conservatives, however, had pursued independent fundraising for years, enjoying a generous surplus for doing so. They calculated, likely correctly, that cancelling the public funding would cripple most opposition parties. And, they thought, the public would not support another trip to the voting booth so soon after the last election, a result opposition parties would likely not consider. For Conservative strategists, these factors meant a unique chance to quash their opponents, a ploy that could facilitate more dramatic moves later.

Of course, as Canadian readers know all too well, events took a much different course. What transpired instead was the most significant parliamentary crisis in recent memory, as opposition parties seized on the perception that the government had gone too far. Layton set in motion, his advisers now admit, well-laid plans to form a coalition government of opposition parties that could initiate reforms to meet the challenges of the global financial crisis. In 2004, the Conservatives had participated in such planning during an earlier Liberal minority government, but the NDP had opted against pursuing it then. In 2008, however, NDP strategists saw a moment that could not be missed. They quickly contacted Stéphane Dion, then Liberal leader, and Gilles Duceppe who led the Bloc Québécois. Opposition MPs were hastily canvassed, and that led to a collective letter to Canada's Governor General appealing for the dissolution of Parliament and formation of an NDP-Liberal coalition government supported by the Bloc. Brian Topp, the NDP's chief of staff at the time and a key coalition negotiator, recalls this moment as one where progressives "almost gave the Tories the boot." Topp, who had served an NDP provincial government in Saskatchewan, also hoped the experience of governing would moderate the federal party. As he has written since, "I liked the idea that the federal NDP would have a direct role in the government for many reasons, a key one being it would change the federal NDP, by giving it direct exposure to the realities of government."[6]

In coalition negotiations, Layton got agreement on reforms intended to mitigate the 2008 economic crisis. These included boosting unemployment benefits, child care benefits, financial stimulus and infrastructure spending, and job loss programs, and a commitment to discuss a North American cap-and-trade emissions scheme. These proposals, however, came at a serious cost. The NDP agreed to downplay its "bring the troops home" position on Afghanistan, and to withdraw its objection to corporate tax cuts. These moves, demanded by the Liberals, roiled the NDP's activist base and progressives outside the party — many of whom decried the move as a dangerous case of unprincipled pragmatism. What good was a coalition government, they asked, if it functioned inside a neoliberal, war-mongering framework? How could the NDP exchange core principles for seats in government? Layton's cellphone, no doubt, was deluged with calls from coast to coast.

The coalition government, of course, never came to pass. Dion's eleventh-hour coalition appeal (recorded, it seemed, from a cellphone camera) didn't help. But more significant was the Conservative branding of the proposed coalition as an undemocratic scheme of "separatists and socialists." That message was repeated to great effect, and it proved resilient in the closing days of the parliamentary crisis. After governing for a mere thirteen days, the Conservatives won the consent of Canada's Governor General to prorogue Parliament — effectively pausing the coalition effort until early in the new year. By that time, the Liberals were coalescing around a different leader, Michael Ignatieff, who quickly abandoned coalition efforts, and later supported the Conservative budget in late January 2009. Layton was left to wonder what might have been, while also dealing with movements that questioned his lurch to the right.

The last time I saw Layton in person was the fall of 2009, when the CLC was building the pension campaign discussed in the last chapter. At one memorable event, Layton walked over to congratulate me about the success of our work. I thanked him, but insisted credit was due to union activists at the community level, who were spearheading an effort that was making governments nervous. He laughed, shook my hand, and headed back to his seat where he was quickly surrounded by well-wishers. After the event was over, and many others had shared powerful pension stories, Layton sent me a memorable one-liner by e-mail: "Well done, brother — that's the kind of campaign we need!" Despite his six years in establishment politics, Layton could spot innovation from a community organizer's perspective. It was an affirming and humbling experience.

The last exchange I had with Layton was also by e-mail. The date was January 1, 2011, and he had sent an ambitious fund-raising pitch through his personal e-mail so the NDP could, as he put it, "show Harper the door" in 2011. My initial reaction was annoyance. I was frustrated at how Layton had handled a public feud the previous summer between the federal NDP's deputy leaders Libby Davies and Tom Mulcair.

The squabble emerged in June 2010 after Davies had been ambushed by pro-Israel videographers. Almost immediately, Davies was asked, "When do you think the [Israeli] occupation began, 1948 or 1967?" The initial response Davies gave was, "I don't know, it's the longest occupation in the world though, and it's got to stop."[7] After more pestering, however, she said "1948," the date of Israel's founding (and the expulsion of eight hundred and forty thousand Palestinians).

With the aid of the pro-Israel lobby, the video went viral. The usual pundits snarled, accusing Davies of questioning Israel's "right to exist." To make matters worse, Mulcair demanded that Davies retract her reference to 1948 and her support for the boycott, divestment, and sanctions campaigns against Israel.[8] Layton was quick to offer this statement: "I have spoken to the [Israeli] ambassador [to Canada], to indicate very clearly that those comments were not the position of our party and Ms. Davies has sent a letter indicating that she made a very serious mistake . . . I told her it was a serious mistake."[9] Davies had been an almost lone voice in Parliament to speak against Canada's uncritical support for Israel and the long suffering of the Palestinians. Layton's haste to reassure Israel felt like a betrayal for those committed to Palestinian human rights. I told him as much in the e-mail I sent back on January 1, 2011, and went on to say the federal party wasn't getting a dime from me.

And then, to my amazement, my phone buzzed with an e-mail message about ninety minutes later. It was Layton himself, responding to my concerns:

> *Hi Joel, thanks for your quick and thoughtful message. I want you to know that since those tough days, Libby and Tom are actually working together quite well, and the party has developed its policy in this area. I am impressed with your deep concern for human rights in Palestine and Israel, and that is a sentiment widely-shared in the party.*
>
> *It's too bad this issue is keeping you at distance from supporting our work. Are you aware of our actual policy in this area? You should talk to your friends on staff to have a look. It may not be exactly what you want, but it's won very broad support among NDP members. Let's keep in touch, ok? 2011 is going to be a very big year for us. In solidarity, Jack.*[10]

I trundled upstairs to show this message to my partner, who smiled widely after reading it. "That's what I call a bridge builder," she said, "no wonder people have such respect for him." I reflected on the testimonials from others who said similar things. Some of those were people from Quebec whom I had interviewed for research on Québec Solidaire detailed in the next section. They spoke about how Layton and others were working to build new relationships among activists, largely by facilitating discussion between progressives across federalist-sovereignist lines. That is the approach that gave the NDP its historic breakthrough in 2011.

More recently, though, some have accused the NDP of "sleepwalking to the centre" to resemble a "government in waiting."[11] As I wrote these words, Tom Mulcair, Layton's successor, was offering Margaret Thatcher's family condolences after her recent death. Two months before, Mulcair spoke to the Calgary Chamber of Commerce about developing "a partnership" with firms in the tar sands. A month before that, as Theresa Spence and other Idle No More activists fasted a short walk away from Mulcair's office on Parliament Hill, he was nowhere to be seen. The previous summer, as the streets of Quebec exploded in student protest, Mulcair insisted NDP politicians not vocally support the upstart movement. These moves demonstrate at best a distance, and at worst hostility, to values and movements Layton held in high regard. Are the federal NDP's movement-friendly days over? Only time will tell, but of this we can be certain: The movements that supported Layton and others like him gave the party the strength it needed. That strength will be tested once more for the battles that lie ahead.

## QUÉBEC SOLIDAIRE: A PARTY OF THE BALLOT BOX *AND* THE STREET

*Progressives in Québec need the support of progressives in the rest of Canada. That's why whenever asked about this question, this delicate question of the sovereignty of Québec, I insisted on saying to the late Jack Layton that we are surely to celebrate the first day of independence if it happens, but the next day at 8 o'clock in the morning, I will be in Ottawa, knocking on the door if I have to, to make a new proposal to the Canadian people for the foundation of a new alliance, of a new basis of community between the people of Québec, the people of Canada, and the First Nations (which were, of course, forgotten in 1867, and are still forgotten in 2013).*

— *Ahmir Khadir*[12]

For decades, Quebec progressives have faced a perplexing challenge. While Quebec has been a site of considerable militancy, with a political culture sympathetic to progressive causes, activists have experienced great difficulty capturing this mood in the electoral realm. Political upturns in Quebec have not seen the Left, but the provincial Liberal Party (PLQ) — and other parties that have split from it — capture the stage with ambiguous agendas. Larger forces have had their impact on Quebec politics; an oil crisis and the overheated US economy by the late 1960s and early 1970s dragged down corporate profits and forced the timid PLQ to set a course of austerity and anti-union reforms. When veterans of Quebec's "Quiet Revolution" — which, as Benoît Renaud (a widely-respected activist) insists, was neither "quiet" nor a "revolution" — split from the Liberals to form the Parti Québécois (PQ) in 1968, most progressives hailed the event as the best hope in generations. The PQ became a focal point in this period for anti-war protest and union activism.

When the PQ was first elected to government in 1976, it announced its intention to hold a "favourable prejudice toward workers." As time wore on, however, its practice became remarkably different. With government programs slashed, anti-union laws implemented, and a sovereignty referendum lost, widespread disillusionment put the PQ in crisis, allowing other progressives to put forward alternatives by the mid-1980s to late 1990s. Numerous efforts within and outside the PQ emerged, but none won widespread support in social justice groups. A neoliberal drift in politics hampered these attempts, but some modest gains were important. In 1998, Michel Chartrand, a renowned union activist, earned 15 per cent of the vote against Lucien Bouchard (then PQ leader and premier of Quebec) as a representative for the Rassemblement pour une Alternative Politique. In 2001, union organizer Paul Cliche won 24 per cent support during a by-election in Montreal's progressive Mercier riding, this time representing a party named Union des Forces Progressistes (UFP). Ahmir Khadir, a microbiologist and outspoken left sovereignist, followed Cliche as the UFP's candidate for Mercier; in 2003,

Khadir captured 18 per cent of the vote despite vitriolic attacks from the PQ establishment. I was in Montreal for the entire campaign as a volunteer for the UFP. My conversations with activists confirmed this was a new movement for the Quebecois left, one that could destabilize the long-standing bulwarks of elite politics.

Two years later, the Quebecois right — both federalist and separatist — issued its own challenge to the status quo. On October 27, 2005, twelve high-profile individuals published a manifesto calling for urgent austerity reforms, with the clear aim of influencing the PQ leadership race scheduled for November 17, 2005. The manifesto — entitled "A Manifesto for a Clear-Eyed Quebec" ("Manifeste Lucide") — cited Quebec's aging society and an increasingly competitive world economy, with particular reference to China and India, as reasons to embrace a neoliberal model of development. Its endorsers included former PQ leader (and federal Progressive Conservative Party cabinet minister) Lucien Bouchard, centrist economist Pierre Fortin, and media luminary Sylvie Lalonde. Unfortunately for them, the "Manifeste Lucide" drew tepid support from most PQ leadership candidates, but where it did resonate proved important. André Boisclair, the only candidate who endorsed the manifesto, went on to win the PQ leadership with the backing of the party establishment.

A quite different reply to the "Manifeste Lucide" had arrived two weeks before the PQ leadership race. On November 1, 2005, an alliance of progressive individuals (some of whom were leaders in large movements) issued a manifesto entitled "For a Quebec Based on Solidarity" ("Manifeste Solidaire"). For these authors, the issues at hand were not Quebec's demographic trends, unmanageable government debt, and challenges from emerging world powers like China and India. Exacerbating the impact of these challenges, they insisted, were policy choices that prioritized limitless growth, blind competition, and capitulation to transnational firms and "global markets." The "Manifeste Solidaire" prefaced its specific suggestions for reform with these remarks:

*We, too, think we are clear-eyed. An attentive, critical look at the fate of the world and Quebec's future shows us the disastrous results everywhere of decades of neo-capitalist economic policies. Social inequalities, poverty, financial crises and scandals, environmental degradation and climate change—all against a backdrop of bloody conflicts—are the visible consequences of laissez-faire policies that have relegated the responsibility for daily life and the future of the Earth and humankind to the illusion of a self-regulated market.*[13]

The impact of the "Manifeste Solidaire" was felt almost immediately, as sympathetic media coverage widely transmitted its claims. Ahmir Khadir and Québec Solidaire figured prominently in this coverage, but Françoise David (a celebrated Quebec feminist) did also; David, by this point, had worked with allies to create a citizen's group (Option Citoyenne, or "Citizen's Option") that initially aimed to move all parties leftwards, but also (like the UFP) establish a broad party of the Left. Like the UFP, Option Citoyenne shared a vision inspired by the collectivist tradition of Quebec's social programs and "creative" responses to neoliberalism in Latin America and Northern Europe. Pushing aside dramatic claims about a future "demographic crunch" and stifling government debt, David pointed out that Quebec was creating record levels of wealth with fewer workers. At issue, she claimed, was the poor distribution of this wealth, and the sustainable development practices necessary to ensure a viable Quebec for future generations.

The "Manifeste Solidaire" was a fitting segue for merger talks between Option Citoyenne and the UFP which, by the end of 2005, had been approved after thirteen meetings. Controversy remained about the merger, most notably around the attention given to Quebec sovereignty as an aim, the role of democracy within the new organization, and how it intended to balance an electoral and movement approach. Moreover, a joint report issued to the memberships of Option Citoyenne and

the UFP also indicated a willingness to channel the goals of both parties into "plain language" demands that were "responsible, achievable,
and absolved of unrealistic promises."[14] Some openly worried about
the intent of these statements. Was the call for "responsible demands"
a thinly veiled argument for diluting activist goals? Did the insistence
on "achievable demands" mean accepting a policy framework shaped
by neoliberal ideas? Would abandoning "unrealistic promises" mean
a rejection of the idealism many had embraced in emerging forms of
activism? Tensions and concerns around these and other questions were
present in the minds of activists as the merger went forward.

Still, an abundant sense of goodwill was palpable at the Option
Citoyenne–UFP merger conference from February 3 to 5, 2006, which
I attended as a UFP member. The proceedings took place in a large university auditorium in Montreal that was filled to near capacity with 980
delegates and almost a hundred observers. Delegates to the conference
included several key activists who had built many of Quebec's most successful movements. Accompanying David, for example, were delegates
from Quebec's feminist movement, but also present were the ranks of
young anti-neoliberal and anti-war activists. A banner that hung over
the large hall captured the spirit of the weekend; letters forming the
word "*ensemble*" (together) reminded everyone of the co-operative spirit
that had make the conference a reality. In the common areas outside the
assembly hall, delegates scrawled inspiring messages explaining why they
had come, and what they wanted from a unified party of the Québec Left.
The statement released by the founding conference made this plain:

> *A new party has arrived on Quebec's political scene offering*
> *a progressive alternative to other existing political parties. A*
> *large and united alternative which is rooted in all regions of*
> *Québec. An alternative capable of carrying and realizing the*
> *hopes for change of so many women and men in Quebec! An*
> *alternative enabling us to build a world which fits our dreams.*

> *Our party completely devotes itself to defending and pro-*
> *moting the public interest (le bien commun). In other words,*
> *it puts the interests of the whole population before those of a*
> *greedy minority. It focuses its energy in searching for equal-*
> *ity and social justice, in respecting individual and collective*
> *rights. It recognizes the interdependence of human beings and*
> *of nature.*
>
> *This demands a profound transformation of Quebec. For*
> *our party, this means opposing neoliberalism, a modern ver-*
> *sion of capitalism, which dominates our societies and bank-*
> *rupts our future as well as the future of our planet.[15]*

In the end, the most memorable moment of the merger conference was before debate on the proposed statement of principles and party statutes. It occurred when delegates were asked to choose a name for the new party between four different options: Québec Solidaire, Union Citoyenne, Union Citoyenne du Québec, and Union des Forces Citoyennes. These four options came forward after a process begun four months beforehand; in a jointly written letter to Option Citoyenne and UFP members, the negotiating committee had asked for members to submit simple, straightforward names that reflected the new party's aims and ambitions. Over 150 names were brought forward, and the negotiating committee had pared these down to the four options presented at the conference.

There had been considerable debate prior to the conference about the best name for the new party. On the plenary floor, delegates continued the debate. Some worried about the potential association with the ultra-conservative Union Nationale regime of Maurice Duplessis from 1936 to 1959, should the party opt for a name that included "Union." Others worried about an obvious melding of the former Option Citoyenne and UFP in the name, and the potential conclusion that the party was simply a rehash of previous ideas rather than a push in a new direction. Still others suggested Québec Solidaire's "QS" acronym could be too closely associated with the PQ's and called for a more distinctive name. Ultimately, a sea of red voting cards welcomed the name "Québec Solidaire." Ecstatic clapping, hooting, but also "twinkling"[16] evidenced the different activist cultures in the hall that greeted the new party's collectively founded identity.

Following the conference, Khadir said that it had exceeded his expectations despite the "inevitable controversies that arise when activists of different persuasions unite in common cause."[17] What mattered, Khadir insisted, was that Québec Solidaire had captured the "collective imagination of all Quebecois," unlike the "quasi-coronation of André Boisclair" as PQ leader. David credited the diversity of Québec Solidaire's membership for providing its new purpose, and claimed the party represented the best hope for progressives in decades. Such optimism appeared warranted; a foray had been made in an exciting direction. After three decades of experience, a significant Left alliance declared its independence from the PQ, and had done so as proud defenders of movement work. "We have left the margins," announced David, "we are now a legitimate player with Quebec's other major parties."[18]

PQ leaders reacted with a mix of interest, indifference, and scorn, but few contested the importance of this political moment. In a frank discussion with the English-Canadian mainstream media, Khadir pitched Québec Solidaire's vision of independence as distinct and necessary: "We're here to reposition the debate around social issues, economical issues, environmental issues, instead of always talking about the flag."[19] A poll taken soon after the merger conference found 20 per cent of voters supported this message. Quebec's first-past-the-post electoral system remained a formidable obstacle for translating support into seats in the National Assembly, however. Although Québec Solidaire enjoyed a solid reputation, debates around "strategic voting" hamstrung the party's reach beyond its activist base.

As Khadir (and others) had noted before, sovereignist voters feared strengthening the federalist Liberals more than they feared the neo-liberal drift of the PQ. Many voters agreed that both parties espoused similar ideas, but were concerned that a vote for Québec Solidaire (and not the PQ) would empower the Liberals. That message was repeated constantly from PQ-allied pundits, but Québec Solidaire steadily gained strength with its patient appeal for independent thinking. In December 2008, that hard work paid off — Khadir was elected in Mercier, beating the PQ's Daniel Turp by 810 votes, a margin of 3 per cent.

It didn't take long for Khadir and QS to make an impression. Days after the election, Khadir participated in a protest to support an Iraqi journalist, Muntadhar al-Zaidi, who had thrown his shoes at George W. Bush during a press conference in Baghdad. Khadir and others lined the streets, throwing shoes at a large photo of Bush in front of the US consulate in downtown Montreal. Gilbert Gagnon, a college teacher, was so incensed that he wrote a letter of protest to the Speaker of Quebec's National Assembly. Khadir's response was to shrug his shoulders and insist voters wanted a politician who was willing to be outspoken.

QS continued that approach through 2009, when the Taylor-Bouchard Commission was convened to consider rules around the "reasonable accommodation" of religious minorities. Khadir, who had lived in Iran until age ten, had suffered religious intolerance; he and QS nevertheless opposed attempts to prohibit the wearing of religious symbols in work-places. He challenged these as thinly veiled Islamophobia, which had escalated since the recent "War on Terror" and its offshoots. Françoise David, acting as QS president, made similar assertions, often to howls of protest from some feminists. In December 2009, QS members once again chose principle over political expediency by voting for a resolution to support boycott, divestment, and sanctions (BDS) against Israel for its human rights violations against Palestinians. The motion was met with loud protest by pro-Israel voices that made predictable accusations of anti-Semitism. Undeterred, Khadir took part in BDS demonstrations, and did so months after he tabled emergency resolutions at the

National Assembly opposing Israel's Operation Cast Lead. In these and other instances, QS demonstrated a willingness to challenge dominant political thinking, while Khadir took that defiant spirit to the corridors of established politics. Despite the vitriol he often evoked, voters were appreciative; in December 2010, polls indicated Khadir was the most popular politician in Quebec, with an approval rating of 45 per cent.

The years 2011 and 2012 saw QS emerge once again as a champion of social movements. The catalyst this time was student activism, which had steadily grown in influence since the ruling Liberals had announced a tuition hike of 75 per cent over five years, in March 2011. By November 2011, as twenty thousand students marched to Premier Jean Charest's office, orange QS signs dotted the crowds. There was good reason for this: Many QS activists and organizers were veterans of the last Quebec student strike in 2005, while older members had links to student uprisings in previous decades. Indeed, student mobilization is a core theme in Quebec's progressive history, even for those not directly involved in campus life.

In the early weeks of 2012, it became clear the government was dug in for a long struggle. It accused students of being unreasonable in challenging financial times, and opposing what amounted to a "50 cent per day increase." Student organizers, however, were in no mood to capitulate, even in the face of public pressure. In the past, their movement had been divided by government negotiators who pitted "radicals" against "well-meaning lobbyists." This time, Quebec's three student organizations refused to meet with government negotiators alone, despite their differences. Two of the groups, Fédération Étudiante Universitaire du Québec (FEUQ) and Fédération Étudiante Collégiale du Québec (FECQ), were long-standing institutions representing students in colleges and universities. The third, Association pour une Solidarité Syndicale Étudiante (ASSÉ), had formed in 2001 to project a new vision of student activism. Unlike the FEUQ or FECQ, ASSÉ organized itself on a departmental basis (representing, for example, political science or sociology students at a given campus instead of the entire student body). It also championed a more progressive vision of post-secondary education (advocating, among other things, free education from kindergarten to university), and a direct democracy model for its decision-making that was rooted in local campus assemblies. As it organized against the government's tuition hike, ASSÉ formed CLASSE — a larger coalition that aimed to unite the broadest possible number of progressive students.

In the face of government intransigence, CLASSE declared its intent to mobilize a student strike through appeals to local student assemblies. That same month, assemblies representing thirty-six thousand students voted for strike action, while thousands temporarily occupied schools, bridges, and even metro stations. Police action was fierce, often devolving into pitched street battles. By early March, CLASSE announced an unlimited student strike, an appeal joined by FECQ and FEUQ in subsequent weeks. By mid-March, over three hundred thousand students had voted to strike, amounting to 75 per cent of all post-secondary students in Quebec. On March 22, over two hundred thousand students and supporters from across Quebec marched in downtown Montreal, hearing joint calls to action by FEUQ, FECQ, and CLASSE. A month later, over three hundred thousand marched to commemorate Earth Day, many of whom wore as their symbol a red square, which quickly became synonymous with the strike movement. For a time, government negotiators delayed the onset of the strike through a "tentative settlement" with student leaders that still maintained the tuition increase; this brief reprieve unravelled later when local student assemblies voted unanimously to reject it.

As this protest wave built, PQ and QS spokespeople wore the red square in the National Assembly and on protest marches. They assailed the Charest Liberals, accusing them of fomenting an unnecessary conflict. But in early May, the government raised the stakes by enacting "national security" legislation, Bill 78, which allowed police to prohibit demonstrations and local campus assemblies. Once the legislation was introduced, the PQ's timidity was more apparent; it asked students to obey the law and seek retribution later at the ballot box. Khadir and QS, however, took a far different position and earned wide praise with student activists. In a press conference held after Bill 78 passed, Khadir declared it was crucial for students and their supporters to "consider defying this unjust law."[20] The following day, as he left the National Assembly, Khadir encountered an "illegal" student protest and joined the crowd. For this act he was arrested and levied a $500 fine, joining 106 others who met the same fate.

Bill 78, as it turned out, was a decisive moment in Quebec's student uprising, a period many describe as the printemps érable (or "Maple Spring," in reference to Egypt's ongoing revolution). Many who previously opposed the student strike were appalled by the government's authoritarian measures. As student organizers appealed for civil disobedience, Bill 78 drew outrage from the Quebec Bar Association and most unions, including the Canadian Union of University Teachers. On May 6, 2012, the night after Bill 78 passed, police clashed with demonstrators, but that didn't contain the fray; in the months to come, streets were filled with pot-banging protests ("casseroles") that snaked through neighbourhoods. And when organizers appealed for a mass protest to mark the strike's hundredth day on May 22, the call was answered by over four hundred thousand people. The previous week, Line Beauchamp (Quebec's education minister) resigned her post and political seat, lamenting the state of talks with student leaders. The government cancelled classes at some schools while requiring them elsewhere, hoping to divide the movement. It then pushed for a September election, aiming to capitalize on public frustration with the student strike.

That choice, like many the Charest Liberals made, was a major mistake. The Liberals lost power along with fourteen seats in the National Assembly, including Charest's own seat in Sherbrooke. The PQ won seven new ridings, enough to form a minority government, while the right-wing Coalition Avenir Québec added ten more seats.

For progressives, however, the real story of the election was QS, who captured Gouin, a downtown Montreal riding held by the PQ since 1970. Its new spokesperson was Françoise David, who had inspired Quebecois with her August 2012 performance in the televised leaders' debate. David was alone in wearing the red square, and articulate in calling out the neoliberal uniformity of her opponents. She insisted that independence, in QS terms, "must be in favour of the 99 percent."[21] Unlike the PQ, which had historically said "independence first, politics later," David presented a vision of Quebec that was more democratic, inclusive, and intent on social justice.

The 2012 QS platform — entitled "Debout!" ("Stand Up!") — listed clear, costed reforms for a more environmental, feminist, and egalitarian future. QS did not win, as some had hoped, six to eight additional seats in the National Assembly, but its real victory was evident in its swelling membership ranks. Through its initial years, the party had attracted roughly three thousand members, an amount that plateaued at seven thousand with Khadir's breakthrough in Mercier. But in 2012 alone, after QS's outspoken support for the student strike, its membership doubled, and many strike veterans remained ensconced in the party's work. Many believed this boded well for QS's future, given a transfusion of youthful energy could elevate the party to new heights. Khadir later resigned as QS leader, a role that David took on; this move and David's new electoral platform were expected to create further inroads into the PQ's support. The collapse of the federal Bloc Québécois and rise of Jack Layton's NDP also suggest Quebec voters are looking for fresh alternatives to established options.

Some worry QS will succumb to pressures other left parties have faced when climbing the ladder of electoral politics. Many, for example, question the party's recent consideration of oil drilling in the St. Lawrence River and offshore regions in Gaspésie, a position that contrasts with QS's green leanings. Others think the party uses too much caution in refusing to offer advice to social movements, while QS members, as movement organizers, are frequently questioned for inspiration. This reluctance to lead is understandable given the dogmatic practices of some far Left groups, but it is also creating problems for QS activists.

The role of QS in the Quebec student movement is a case in point. In ASSÉ circles, the most activist wing of the movement, participation in elections is generally frowned upon. Leaders are expected to remain non-partisan, while influential voices in ASSÉ insist, like Emma Goldman, that elections don't matter. In this political environment, student supporters of QS find themselves holding back their party work, and that is making some frustrated.

These and other unresolved contradictions marked the party's first years. What was immediately clear, however, is that QS raised the expectations of Quebecois and emerged as a trusted voice for activist movements. That on its own is worth celebrating.

## YES, *HE* CAN: THE PROMISE AND PITFALLS OF PRO-OBAMA ACTIVISM

*What began twenty-one months ago in the depths of winter must not end on this autumn night.*

*This victory alone is not the change we seek — it is only the chance for us to make that change.*

*And that cannot happen if we go back to the way things were. It cannot happen without you.*

*— US president-elect Barack Hussein Obama*[22]

Like many, I recall where I was when these words were spoken. I was at home, gaping at the televised spectacle that met my eyes — a vast horde of well-wishers, numbering in the hundreds of thousands, greeted the first words of Barack Obama who would be sworn in later as the forty-fourth US president. The crowd gathered in the very place where, four decades earlier, thousands of riot police had brutally attacked anti-Vietnam War activists protesting the Democratic Party convention. But on November

4, 2008, that bloody scene was exchanged for a remarkable moment of mass euphoria. Young people screamed, older folks swayed, and television cameras captured a weeping Oprah Winfrey. Loudspeakers blared "The Rising," Bruce Springsteen's post-9/11, anti-war reveille.

For those long-abandoned by established US politics — notably youth, and poor black and Latino voters — Obama's win was a warm, historic embrace. When Obama said "this is your victory," it didn't sound like the saccharine platitudes all too common in elections. It was a message directed at Obama's network of thirteen million core supporters, and the thousands of full-time organizers who facilitated his improbable campaign. At first, the campaign had interrupted a planned coronation for Hilary Rodham Clinton as the Democratic Party's presidential candidate. It went on to mobilize millions of cynical or uninterested voters, even making inroads into Republican supporters. As many have explained, it was an election campaign and a powerful social movement, whose organizing strategies drew on powerful activist traditions. Before long, however, these were exchanged for top-down practices, leaving supporters to grapple with diminishing returns. In this section I explore that narrative, much of which yields insights about the relationship between political parties and grassroots movements.

As several accounts explain, Obama's rise to political fame didn't fit the traditional script. He was, like many skilled politicians, a gifted speaker and natural leader, capable of making strong connections with even skeptical audiences. But more than this, Obama was also drawn to community activism in his early years, and often at times when its fortunes seemed bleak. In 1981, Obama's first political speech was against South African apartheid, and it urged Occidental College to divest any financial holdings or academic ties with the Afrikaner regime. The next year, Obama transferred to Columbia University where, as a political science student, he sought an outlet for his interest in community activism. After several false starts, he found his opportunity in Chicago's poor neighbourhoods; in 1985, he became a community organizer for the Developing

Communities Project (DCP), a church-based initiative to revitalize areas hammered by the shuttering of US Steel and other major employers.

Obama has described his three years of DCP organizing as a formative experience: "the best education I ever had," he has said, "better than all my years at Harvard Law School."[23] Much of his first book, *Dreams from My Father*, details his efforts working with community activists to, among other things, ban asbestos from public housing complexes, or open job centres in places left abandoned by city planners. To facilitate such efforts, Obama was trained by disciples of Saul Alinksy — an unorthodox criminologist, union organizer, and political activist — whose methods emerged in Chicago's poor neighbourhoods.

Alinksy's method was driven, first and foremost, by skilled organizers who sought to agitate oppressed people and train them to fight back. His approach began with a detailed analysis of power relationships in a given community; with that in hand, organizers then asked how "have-nots" could be mobilized to shift that context. To inspire that outcome, Alinksy asked organizers to identify the "self-interest" of those oppressed, and focus on concrete reforms. Campaigns to win city services for black communities, for example, were preferred over "big-picture" discussions of racism. On this basis, campaigns were built that allowed the oppressed to take collective action against adversaries, and become leaders themselves. As this process developed, organizers were urged to lead from within the group; Alinksy's method was deeply suspicious of charismatic leaders and politicians in general. He had harsh words, for instance, for Martin Luther King Jr., who he believed rode the coat-tails of more talented organizers in the civil rights movement. In *Dreams from My Father*, Obama describes how he explained this strategy to fellow students:

> *When classmates in college asked me just what it was that a community organizer did, I couldn't answer them directly . . . Instead, I'd pronounce on the need for change.*
> *Change in the White House, where Reagan and his*

*minions were carrying on their dirty deeds. Change in the Congress, compliant and corrupt. Change in the mood of the country, manic and self-absorbed.*

    *Change won't come from the top, I would say. Change will come from a mobilized grass roots.*[24]

Obama's years as a community organizer, however, made him reconsider the limits of this strategy. He wasn't convinced that big-picture appeals were useless, particularly on the pervasive subject of racism. He didn't think charismatic leadership was misplaced, a view reinforced when local egos limited the potential of community activism. These disagreements festered in Obama's mind, and made him reconsider electoral politics as a place for activist work. In *Dreams from My Father*, he asks, "What if a politician were to see his job as that of an organizer — as part teacher and part advocate, one who does not sell voters short but who educates them about the real choices before them?"[25] At this moment in Obama's development, he parted ways with the Alinsky approach; while retaining its hard-headedness, he developed a vision to inspire voter participation through different means. To get there, Obama pursued a long march through establishment institutions — as editor of the *Harvard Law Review,* as a Chicago-based politician and, soon enough, as a rising star in the Democratic Party. In each instance, he used a close analysis of power relations, placating influential egos while mobilizing a core of supporters. He built extensive ties with establishment figures, while also using rhetoric that challenged politics as usual. It was a curious mix of top-down and bottom-up politics at the same time.

As an Illinois politician, Obama didn't gain wider notoriety in the state senate, but rather in an October 2002 speech to an anti-war rally in downtown Chicago. At the time, few US politicians opposed the Iraq War, and fewer still knew about Obama. His pointed remarks — aimed squarely at the liberal centre of anti-war opinion — would change that soon enough:

*I don't oppose all wars. After September 11, after witnessing the carnage and destruction, the dust and the tears, I supported this administration's pledge to hunt down and root out those who would slaughter innocents in the name of intolerance, and I would willingly take up arms myself to prevent such tragedy from happening again.*

*I don't oppose all wars. What I am opposed to is a dumb war. What I am opposed to is a rash war. What I am opposed to is the cynical attempt by Richard Perle and Paul Wolfowitz and other armchair, weekend warriors in this administration to shove their own ideological agendas down our throats, irrespective of the costs in lives lost and in hardships borne.*

*What I am opposed to is the attempt by political hacks like Karl Rove to distract us from a rise in the uninsured, a rise in the poverty rate, a drop in the median income, to distract us from corporate scandals and a stock market that has just gone through the worst month since the Great Depression . . .*

*You want a fight, President Bush? Let's fight to make sure our so-called allies in the Middle East, the Saudis and the Egyptians, stop oppressing their own people, and suppressing dissent, and tolerating corruption and inequality, and mismanaging their economies so that their youth grow up without education, without prospects, without hope, the ready recruits of terrorist cells.*

*You want a fight, President Bush? Let's fight to wean ourselves off Middle East oil through an energy policy that doesn't simply serve the interests of Exxon and Mobil.*

*Those are the battles that we need to fight. Those are the battles that we willingly join. The battles against ignorance and intolerance. Corruption and greed. Poverty and despair.*[26]

In these words, we get a sense of the Obama to come — the speech appealed to broad cynicism about the case for invading Iraq. It did not question why the US is loathed worldwide for its imperial ambitions, or why it has historically sought relationships with despotic regimes in the Middle East and elsewhere. The cozy ties between corporate giants and the Democratic Party aren't mentioned, even as Obama rails against energy policy designed for Exxon and Mobil. Instead, his patriotic case against "dumb wars" brackets out such questions; a Democrat version of "us-and-them" rhetoric replaces the bombast of Republican Party hardliners. It was a skillful pairing of mainstream politics with anti-war opinion, one widely noticed in activist circles. Two years later, Obama repeated that performance on a larger scale, in his keynote speech to the Democratic Party's National Convention:

> Tonight is a particular honor for me because, let's face it, my presence on this stage is pretty unlikely.
>
> My father was a foreign student, born and raised in a small village in Kenya. He grew up herding goats, went to school in a tin-roof shack. His father, my grandfather, was a cook, a domestic servant to the British.
>
> But my grandfather had larger dreams for his son. Through hard work and perseverance my father got a scholarship to study in a magical place, America, that's shown as a beacon of freedom and opportunity to so many who had come before him . . . While studying here my father met my mother. She was born in a town on the other side of the world, in Kansas.
>
> My parents shared not only an improbable love; they shared an abiding faith in the possibilities of this nation. They would give me an African name, Barack, or "blessed," believing that in a tolerant America, your name is no barrier to success.
>
> They imagined me going to the best schools in the land, even though they weren't rich, because in a generous America

*you don't have to be rich to achieve your potential.*

*They're both passed away now. And yet I know that,*
*on this night, they look down on me with great pride. And*
*I stand here today grateful for the diversity of my heritage,*
*aware that my parents' dreams live on in my two precious*
*daughters.*

*I stand here knowing that my story is part of the larger*
*American story, that I owe a debt to all of those who came*
*before me, and that in no other country on earth is my story*
*even possible.*[27]

If Obama's 2002 anti-war speech introduced him to peace activists, his 2004 keynote showcased him as unique leadership candidate for the Democratic Party. His remarks were noticed by Marshall Ganz, a Harvard University professor whose experience in progressive organizing stretched back for decades. Ganz was struck by Obama's "story of self" as a mixed-race child with an immigrant father and white mother, and how Obama linked that to a collective "story of us" about liberal principles and traditions. He quickly contacted a Harvard-based Obama adviser and asked for an audience with the Illinois senator. Three years later, that led to an activist strategy that propelled Obama's run for the US presidency.

That strategy began with "Camp Obama," small-scale training efforts co-ordinated by Ganz in 2007–08, which spread quickly to city after city. Participants typically had a few things in common: They were inspired by Obama's call for grassroots involvement in politics, his commitment to end the Iraq war, and his broader message for "hope", "change", and "tolerance." Beyond that, however, attendees were quite diverse: black and white, gay and straight, young and old filled rooms with nervous energy. Those who had marched with Rosa Parks sat with students engaged in campaigns for immigrant rights, or young mothers who wanted improvements to the health care system. All of them engaged in intensive, three-day training sessions that began with an overview of Obama's campaign, its general vision, and its plan to win the Democratic Party's presidential nomination and the White House. After an evening of introductory speeches, the next two days challenged participants to share their own "story of self," and see how it connected to Obama's campaign.

The idealism and passion on display at Camp Obama illustrated the promise of the movement that emerged. The process trained over three thousand full-time organizers who felt they were making a historic contribution to US politics. These remarks from Susan, a white working mother from Burbank, California, were typical:

*When I showed up yesterday I came with a lot of hesitation . . . it was because I was afraid to believe in a candidate again, and be disillusioned, again. And I was afraid to pick a losing cause, again.*

*And I'm a busy person — I'm a mom, I've got a job, we're leaving on family vacation and I thought, you know, I'll just show up, I'll see if it's worth my time, and then, I can leave. If it's not going anywhere, I can just leave. It's ok. This campaign isn't it for me.*

*And then I sat down, and Marshall started talking, and he started talking about working with Cesar Chavez, and marching in Mississippi, and I could feel my heart beating a little bit faster.*

*And then I sat down in my group, and men wept who saw Bobby Kennedy shot, and felt that loss of hope, and a loss of everything he embodied in that generation. And to have people like Marshall and those men sit there and say that, for them, Barack Obama was the return of that hope, I just began to have that hesitation melt away.*

*I felt my heart softening again, I felt myself able to give a little bit more of me to this process. I could feel that this campaign was about something really big, and really important, that it's the beginning if a healing of our nation, and a healing of our generations, and the generations that came before that.*

*The folks that marched with Dr. King, and people who are just graduating from high school were all working together, we're mentoring each other and we're moving forward.*

*And I realized it doesn't matter if Barack actually fails me, and it doesn't matter if we win. It does, of course, I'm in it to win it. But this campaign has made us win already.[28]*

Virginia, a Puerto Rican–American Camp Obama participant, arrived at a similar conclusion through a much different story of self:

*I loved this country when I was little, I cried singing "The Star Spangled Banner" . . . then I found out about genocide against Native Americans, and I found out about the Atlantic crossing, and I found out about sexism, and homophobia, I found out about classism . . .*

*And I became so bitter, I was the most bitter woman, I went from believing that this was the most wonderful country in the whole world . . . to watching my neighbourhood turn into a heroin-dealing death trap.*

*By the time I got out, I started going to college when I was a single mom, almost thirty years old. And I started getting the words, and the theories around all this stuff, it was the era of the PC [political correctness] police.*

*And I was the captain, I terrified them all. I told the white people that they just needed to go back to Europe . . . I told straight people I hoped their children were bisexual and transgendered.*

*I was so angry, so mean. I went from having a bunch of communities — single mothers, black folk, Latin folk, queer folk — to nobody needed to talk to me, 'cause I didn't have nothing good to say . . . then Obama comes along, and I didn't believe a word he said . . .*

*So I go digging, and I go reading, and this man rocked my world . . . and I realized that all of my bitterness was really grief . . . but I've learned from Obama that the moment you ditch that bitterness, the moment you change your focus, and the moment you start to be thankful for every connection, and every bit of kindness, everything starts changing.[29]*

Virginia's words testify to the spirit that would drive Obama's leadership campaigns — first for the Democratic nomination, and later for the presidency itself. In the fall of 2007, Camp Obama graduates spread out from coast to coast, devoting weeks of poorly paid work to evangelize about Obama's campaign. That laid the foundation for ObamaforAmerica.org, MyBarackObama.com, and the numerous other social media strategies to which most attribute Obama's success. But without Camp Obama, and activists inspired by story-based organizing, there was nothing of substance to tweet about. This was a movement initially built on face-to-face conversations and heartfelt appeals coming out of lived experience. Using the platform of social media, three thousand organizers built a massive community of 1.5 million volunteers, and those volunteers created an e-mail network of 13 million people, the largest activist campaign in US history.

There were several formative moments for this activism once its influence grew in earnest. The most significant, by far, was the public reaction to a speech Obama gave after losing the New Hampshire primary to Clinton. It was billed as the "Yes, we can" speech, and its appeal connected with the spirit of modern activism:

*There is something happening. There's something happening when Americans who are young in age and in spirit, who've never participated in politics before, turn out in numbers we have never seen because they know in their hearts that this time must be different.*

*There's something happening when people vote not just for party that they belong to, but the hopes that they hold in common.*

*And whether we are rich or poor, black or white, Latino or Asian, whether we hail from Iowa or New Hampshire, Nevada or South Carolina, we are ready to take this country in a fundamentally new direction. That's what's happening in America right now; change is what's happening in America . . .*

*We have been told we cannot do this by a chorus of cynics. And they will only grow louder and more dissonant in the weeks and months to come. We've been asked to pause for a reality check. We've been warned against offering the people of this nation false hope. But in the unlikely story that is America, there has never been anything false about hope.*

*For when we have faced down impossible odds, when we've been told we're not ready or that we shouldn't try or that we can't, generations of Americans have responded with a simple creed that sums up the spirit of a people: Yes, we can. Yes, we can. Yes, we can . . .*

*It was whispered by slaves and abolitionists as they blazed a trail towards freedom through the darkest of nights: Yes, we can.*

*It was the call of workers who organized, women who reached for the ballot, a president who chose the moon as our new frontier, and a king who took us to the mountaintop and pointed the way to the promised land: Yes, we can, to justice and equality.*

*Yes, we can, to opportunity and prosperity. Yes, we can*
*heal this nation. Yes, we can repair this world. Yes, we can.*[30]

This appeal inspired activists who were campaigning for Obama through the heady year of 2008. It inoculated them against Hilary Clinton's campaign and even against controversy generated by Reverend Jeremiah Wright, Obama's former spiritual adviser. It was adapted to a short music video featuring an array of celebrities, all of whom reinforced the liberal idealism of its message.

Soon enough, "Yes, we can" was everywhere — I heard it countless times in union meetings and in conversations with activist friends. Sales of Obama's books skyrocketed, and his campaign materials became widely visible in the United States and around the world. In January 2009, 1.8 million witnessed Obama's presidential inauguration first-hand, while 37.8 million US viewers watched on television. A new mood had arrived, filled with great hope and promise; Obama was hailed as the "organizer in chief,"[31] someone who would bring an activist approach to the seat of US power. As George W. Bush and Dick Cheney skulked back to Texas, an upstart movement cracked a wide grin.

And yet, this "organizer in chief" narrative was flawed from the start. Without question, Obama had an atypical path to the presidency — his early years in Chicago set him apart in mainstream circles. But as Ganz and others have said, Obama's training in Alinsky-style organizing was quite different from the grassroots, story-telling approach that would energize his 2008 campaign. In fact, Alinksy's method has been criticized for its reliance on skilled organizers, which some call a top-down approach with grassroots rhetoric.[32] Obama may have parted ways with Alinsky, but not, it seems, with the notion that skilled tacticians should guide political campaigns. In *The Audacity of Hope* (Obama's 2006 sequel to *Dreams from My Father*), he argued effective campaigns were "turned over to professionals"[33]; so it was hardly surprising that, by 2008, Obama's inner circle featured no one with experience in activist politics. Meanwhile, a mass movement had been built, creating a once-in-a-generation chance for major policy changes. But, when adversity presented itself, the Obama administration relied on the tactics of elite politics, not change-making from below.

Its approach to the 2008 financial crisis was a telling case in point. The crisis emerged in the final weeks of the George W. Bush administration, exposing a vast array of fraud in Wall Street's corridors of power. But in 2009, as progressives hoped Obama would seize the reins, they found him instead handing them over; the president surrounded himself with neoliberal thinkers such as Timothy Geithner and Larry Summers, whose ideas had facilitated the crisis. Obama's government didn't question Wall Street bailouts, it allowed them; adding insult to injury, when millions were losing their homes, Wall Street bonus schemes were left intact. People were furious, but no form of progressive activism had emerged that spoke for them.

Into this vacuum stormed the Tea Party movement, which quickly became a political force thanks to regular media coverage, generous corporate donations, and shrill sloganeering. Government town halls convened to discuss "Obamacare" were invaded by people questioning Obama's citizenship, warning of "socialism," and lambasting handouts to Wall Street tycoons and Detroit carmakers. The Obama regime, they claimed, undermined the "American way of life"; it tolerated loose immigration policy, gay rights, executive perks, and "intrusive" government. Home-made signs screamed epithets: Obama was an "undocumented worker", a "godless communist", or a trickster intent on forms of "white slavery". Tea Party rallies featured armed protesters proudly displaying their use of the US Constitution's Second Amendment. A "Restoring Honor" rally on September 28, 2010, offered these people a collective voice in Washington, DC, as eighty-seven thousand gathered to insist they too, like Martin Luther King Jr., "had a dream."

As the Tea Party's fear machine gained momentum, activism on behalf of Obama largely stood still. Obama For America (OFA), the umbrella group that housed the thirteen-million volunteer list from the presidential campaign, was placed under the oversight of the Democratic National Committee. In January 2009, Organizing for America, a separate group, was created with the intent of utilizing OFA capacities and creating an activist infrastructure to support Obama's policy initiatives. But in Obama's first term, such work was rarely done, and activists soon realized "Yes, we can" didn't include them. The president was more interested in accommodating conservative hardliners and offering only modest reforms. The 2009 *Lilly Ledbetter Fair Pay Act*, for example, allowed women to contest employment discrimination, but only through protracted legal means that only a few could likely afford. The 2010 *Patient Protection and Affordable Care Act* set limits and new rules for health insurance providers, but compelled people to seek private coverage (without any "public option"), leaving corporate control of US health care untouched. The anti-gay "Don't ask, don't tell" policy in the US military was repealed, but no new oversight measures were designed to challenge rampant sexist and homophobic behaviour. An executive order in 2012 stalled the deportation of over eight hundred thousand children of "undocumented" workers, but failed to provide any meaningful path to citizenship. (In fact, the rate of deportations increased under Obama from the years of George W. Bush.) The Guantanamo Bay prison remained open, while missile attacks (facilitated by remote-controlled drones) strafed the countryside of Pakistan and Afghanistan, killing innocent civilians.

This, needless to say, was not the "change" for which millions had mobilized. Progressives expected the audacity of hope, and a movement that would shake the foundations of establishment politics. Instead, they found themselves on the sidelines, watching Obama's elite team seek compromises in Washington, DC. Obama became, as Ganz explains, a transactional leader, and not the transformational President many wanted.[34] As the Tea Party rose, Obama refused to unleash the people power that drove his movement through to storied heights. The consequence was disastrous mid-term election results in 2010, when

Republicans gained 68 seats and control of the House of Representatives. Obama's supporters insisted the setback was due to a crushing recession and the upstart Tea Party. But Van Jones, a former top adviser to Obama on green jobs, saw it differently: "Our movement did not crash because the losers of 2008 created a fear machine. It crashed because the winners of 2008 mishandled, and inadvertently dismantled, the hope machine."[35]

In progressive circles, two general interpretations explain the pitfalls of pro-Obama activism. Some defend Obama's shortcomings, and insist it isn't his role to lead a grassroots process for change. "It's not Obama's job," says veteran activist Al Sharpton, "to lead his own civil rights movement."[36] The issue instead, Sharpton claims, is the pervasive fear among Democrat politicians to buck the Washington establishment, which leaves Obama little room to manoeuvre. Others, like academic Cornel West, insist Obama-backers like Sharpton are too focused on top-down political models. For West, Obama has become "a black mascot for Wall Street" because activists have forgotten the lessons of history. "We would have no Lincoln," West claims, "without organizers like Frederick Douglass" who dedicated their lives to building mass abolitionist movements.[37] It is up to activists, West claims, to pressure Obama to pursue a progressive agenda. The relationship between movements and elite power is important, but it takes the former to create transformational change.

As I was writing these words, Organizing for America emerged as its own tax-exempt group, no longer controlled by the Democratic National Committee. Its new mandate was to mobilize public support for reforms, as the Tea Party has done for Republican hardliners. Many of Organizing for America's senior staff were veterans from the 2008 campaign and trainers in the storytelling approach that drove Camp Obama. For some, this suggested a shift to the grassroots energy that can drive gains on gun control, immigration, green jobs, gay marriage, and other key files. And yet, the criticism that Obama's left-wing critics raise is that these moves were taking place while the president, in his "fiscal cliff" negotiations with Republicans, was contemplating massive cuts to long-standing programs like Social Security and Medicaid. That can only lead to more public outrage and tarnished hopes for those who once saw promise in the activism surrounding Obama's campaigns.

As progressives plot their next moves, the pitfalls of elite-led change must be understood; "Yes, *he* can" was never Obama's slogan, but it became the reality in practice. More authentic expressions of grassroots activism are required, of which there are many in US history. The words of Eugene Debs, an outspoken socialist who ran for president three times and earned 913,613 votes in 1920, should inform a new approach:

> *I do not want you to follow me or anyone else; if you are look-ing for a Moses to lead you out of this capitalist wilderness, you will stay right where you are.*
>
> *I would not lead you into the promised land if I could, because if I led you in, someone else would lead you out.*
>
> *You must use your heads as well as your hands, and get yourself out of your present condition.*[38]

## CONCLUSION

> *Spare a thought for the stay-at-home voter*
> *His empty eyes gaze at strange beauty shows*
> *And a parade of the gray suited grafters*
> *A choice of cancer or polio*
> *. . . They don't look real to me*
> *In fact, they look so strange*
>
> — *Rolling Stones, "Salt of the Earth"*[39]

On November 11, 2011, Joan Baez, a legendary folk singer from the 1960s, sang "Salt of the Earth" to Occupy Wall Street's Veteran's Day Rally in downtown New York City. Her version said much about the mood of our times — she adapted the lyrics to lament the imposing presence of Wall

Street itself, whose grey buildings, at close range, "looked so strange." Unfortunately, she didn't sing the song's lament about the "stay-at-home voter," a caustic reflection that captures the cynicism many feel about electoral politics. But Baez did attempt — and, judging from the sing-along that arose, she did succeed — in bridging one generation's anger with the next, offering a potential soundtrack for today's pioneers in grassroots activism.

Whether that energy finds resonance in political parties, however, remains an open question. And so, after all that this chapter has explored, I return to the question that I posed early on: Can political parties be mirrors for movements, or are they mirages that appropriate activist energies? Even a partial response must admit that the evidence to date yields different answers. The political parties I reviewed have appealed to emerging forms of activism and, at times, transformed the cynicism that normally confronts politicians. At the same time, some progressive electoral efforts, like the activism that surrounded Obama's campaigns, invoke the language of grassroots organizing while doing otherwise in practice. How does one make sense of such uneven returns? An honest answer, in my view, must reconsider the place, ideas, and organization of political parties, and what their interaction with social movements suggests. This can help activists understand how to participate in elections without casting their principles aside.

The political parties reviewed here (in their rhetoric, at least) see their place as being outside the neoliberal mainstream, and in tune with movements engaged in grassroots activism. They have championed "fresh ideas" to break through frustration with established politics, and forms of political organization aiming to convince voters that they can help transform society. For pro-Obama activism, that meant appealing to liberal values, the "American dream," the anti-war movement, civil rights history, and the push for universal health care. It meant using the tactics of community organizing, and training warriors for "hope" and "change"; to those who tempered such enthusiasm, Obama's campaigners responded with "Yes, we can." For Jack Layton's NDP, it also meant, at times, embracing the anti-war movement, feminism, and a "fighter" image to unite the Left across federalist/sovereignist lines. When some lampooned such alliances, Layton's reply, echoed by many NDP activists, was: "Don't let them tell you it can't be done." For Québec Solidaire, it meant projecting its work as a party of the ballot box and the street, and as an advocate for movement-inspired change; when the sincerity of that was questioned, the presence of QS in progressive movements has backed up its rhetoric and swelled its membership base.

Genuinely progressive parties, then, see their place as inseparable from movements for social justice, and succeed or fall short on that basis. They offer ideas that challenge neoliberal assumptions and break the corporate stranglehold on modern democracies. They propose forms of activist organization that build local leadership, and empower activists to be change-agents themselves. But when political parties fall short, or become unaccountable to the movements they champion, they cease to be progressive at all. With that in mind, it is sad to witness the present state of the activism surrounding Obama, which, despite its early promise, has shifted well inside the neoliberal mainstream. For similar reasons, progressives should also question the federal NDP's current direction and many decisions taken under Layton's tenure as leader. In doing so, they can hold up the example of Québec Solidaire, which, in spite of shortcomings, has remained a crucial ally of Quebec's progressive movements. Indeed, the constant scorn heaped on QS by establishment voices reveals the threat this party has become.

Another way to assess political parties involves challenging the notion of a narrow calculus of "electoral success" as measured by the number of politicians in a given parliament, and not by the influence of the party's message. The wish to elect members has often inspired political parties to abandon progressive ideas and give in to the pressures of established political discourse. And yet, as we see in this chapter, an activist approach to elections is possible, and it carries great potential. The most successful political parties in recent years have acted as mirrors of social movements and reflected the images of social movements. In the legislatures, neoliberals should see progressive political parties as the street-based dissent they loathe. In progressive parties, activists should see in the legislatures, at long last, an image of themselves. When this balance is achieved, elections can help activists organize and consolidate strength; the interplay can also create opportunities for progressive ideas to be liberated from their traditional obscurity.

The activism that accompanied Obama's early campaigns, the successes of Layton's NDP, and the rise of QS have all shown that this is possible. We must, without question, be attentive to their mistakes; but their successes remind us that progressives, where possible, must take elections seriously. For the vast majority of people, elections represent the height of politics. Activists can either ignore that reality or seek to work within it. If they opt for the latter, progressive ideas can reach a broader audience, make tangible gains, and advance existing campaigns for social justice. Activists are wise to maintain a critical approach: The relationship between political parties and grassroots movements is often tenuous. But this relationship, and its significance for progressive activism, must be understood.

# 5
# UNDERSTANDING ACTIVISM

*If there is no struggle there is no progress. Those who profess to favor freedom and yet depreciate agitation, are [those] who want crops without plowing up the ground, they want rain without thunder and lightning. They want the ocean without the awful roar of its many waters.*

*Power concedes nothing without a demand. It never did and it never will. Find out just what any people will quietly submit to and you have found out the exact measure of injustice and wrong which will be imposed upon them, and these will continue till they are resisted with either words or blows, or with both.*

*The limits of tyrants are prescribed by the endurance of those whom they repress.*

— *Frederick Douglass*[1]

Why protest? That is a fair question to begin any reflection on activism and on how one attempts to understand it. A common answer mirrors the reasoning used by Frederick Douglass, among the greatest (and least known) US revolutionaries. For him, the strength of a democracy is tested by the degree to which people will fight for it; those bemoaning protest, therefore, are either naive or intellectually lazy. They "profess to favor freedom," Douglass says, without supporting the agitation required to maintain its vibrancy. They accept received wisdom, without questioning its assumptions that facilitate injustice. They scorn unsanctioned expression and, in doing so, hollow out the content of democracy itself.

These are powerful ideas. I recall them often in my own activist work. Many, even those with high posts in our current social structure, will agree with them. But although many accept the constructive role of protest, fewer understand what draws people to it, and its impact in shaping established thought and institutions. This chapter is my effort to explore those questions at a theoretical level and engage with others who have done so already. My review includes contributions by progressive academics and movement thinkers, as well as theory on offer from activists themselves. Following that, I offer my own approach to understanding activism that appreciates its *place* (where it happens), its *ideas* (why it happens), and its *organization* (how it happens).

## THE TROUBLE WITH SOCIAL MOVEMENT THEORY

*It's hard to think of another time when there has been such a gulf between intellectuals and activists; between theorists of revolutions and its practitioners.*

*Writers who for years have been publishing essays that sound like position papers for vast social movements that do not in fact exist seem seized with confusion or worse, dismissive contempt, now that real ones are everywhere emerging . . .*

*This may be the result of sheer ignorance, or relying on what might be gleaned from overly hostile sources like the* New York Times; *then again, most of what's written even in progressive outlets seems to miss the point — or at least, rarely focusses on what participants in the movement think is most important about it.*

— *David Graeber*[2]

David Graeber — an anthropologist and activist in his own right — moves between the two worlds of academia and on-the-ground activist work. He played an important role in the early days of Occupy Wall Street's encampment in Manhattan's "Freedom Plaza." But long before that, Graeber lamented that most scholars and intellectuals did not understand modern forms of activism; they could not grasp its emphasis on direct democracy in action, grassroots forms of political expression, and the significance of protest without detailed demands. They could not appreciate the new culture of resistance that would not wait for peer review by specialists. Graeber saw that a re-imagining of activist efforts to think big, to challenge assumptions and authority structures, and demonstrate alternative ways of living was underway. Rather than demand (or announce) the manifesto, Graeber suggested, we must appreciate the innovative practices of today's activists, and their intent to advance progressive causes in new and exciting ways.

That advice was largely ignored by Social Movement Theory (SMT), the most popular academic approach to studying forms of activism. Soon I will speculate about why this is so, but first, it's worth understanding where Social Movement Theory comes from. The literature emerged during the late 1960s and early 1970s (a time of mass protest), but its rapid expansion took place during the 1980s and 1990s (when conservative, neoliberal movements were powerful, and progressive movements were relatively weak). It began at the margins of social science, though it stands as a major paradigm today. Its authors have included academics committed to proving that protest movements are a legitimate object of study. In the early years, they did so despite heated objections from conservative, "behaviouralist" scholars who likened protest to "mass deviance" or "imitated" forms of expression.

For the most part, two approaches defined scholarly inquiry into various forms of activism. The first of these, Resource Mobilization Theory (RMT), aimed to refute the notion that protesters were mindless deviants by charting the precise way activists mobilize and make decisions. Political Process Theory (PPT) emerged later in the 1970s and 1980s as a successor to RMT, and emphasized the nuanced "processes" and "repertoires" of action undertaken by protesters given various "political opportunities." At issue were the tactics (or "constituent mechanisms") that reappear in successive examples of dissent; a closer appreciation of these patterns, they argued, can suggest clues about why some protesters succeed while others fail. When critics from within PPT urged more "actor-oriented" studies exploring emotional reasons for protest, new conceptual tools were developed. More recent contributions have involved social-psychological discussions of "frame analysis," and studies concerned with the emotional capacities of those who engage in dissent.

From the late 1990s to the present, PPT scholars have also offered studies to understand the emergence of protest on a global scale. The first major work came from two international relations theorists, Margaret Keck and Kathryn Sikkink, who examined the US civil rights movement, movements for women's liberation, and environmental campaigns, to grasp how transnational activism develops, and what processes or criteria often contribute to successful campaigns. Overall, their major point was to suggest that transnational activism develops through repression or containment of dissent at the domestic level of politics. If dialogue between protest actors and governments is obstructed, hindered, or deflected, "political entrepreneurs" seek alternatives outside their own state, whether through shared information, conferences, or foreign travel.

With transnational resources, Keck and Sikkink explain, activists can enlist support from outside their own borders, and gain from a "boomerang effect" that emboldens local campaigns. Those engaged in such work, they argue, are bolstered by "shared principled ideas and values" transmitted through "voluntary, reciprocal, and horizontal exchanges of information and services."[3] Generally, they claim, the most successful activist networks bring the energy of globally shared concerns to bear on national or local politics. Key factors that contribute to success or failure are the strength and density of protest networks, the relative weakness of adversaries, and the resonance of the issue at hand for wider public opinion. From their case study research, Keck and Sikkink concluded that campaigns around bodily harm to at-risk populations or appeals for legally sanctioned equality of opportunity were most likely to win broad support.

Despite Keck and Sikkink's theorizing on the potential of transnational activism, for them — and for most academics who study dissent — nation-states are the crucial actors that shape the limits of progressive activism. Global support for activist campaigns can make a potential difference in changing activist fortunes, but not to the extent that the state is pushed aside as the agent responsible for shaping political outcomes. At the same time, these researchers also insist that global and national politics is "made up not only of states engaged in self-help or even rule-governed behavior, but of dense webs of interactions and interrelations among citizens of different states which both reflect and help sustain shared values, beliefs and projects."[4] To this extent, Keck and Sikkink endeavoured to trace the relationship between local activists and the energy of global campaigns, while retaining a sense of what transnational activism can accomplish given the reach of state power.

Keck and Sikkink's work won broad acclaim, most notably for its insistence on treating transnational dissent as a force in its own right. Their creative notion of a "boomerang effect" stimulated further academic work, most of which has continued the focus on the organizational choices of activists in given countries. Still, as this literature has grown, many have expressed concern about the preoccupation with certain case studies, while few have tackled broader issues or concerns linked to activism. Some scholars have attempted to move beyond this impasse, and offer contributions that identify "activist processes" that bridge the local trends to larger theoretical questions.

Sidney Tarrow, a widely recognized scholar for English-speaking readers, is among this group. He published his own assessment of transnational activism in 2005, and followed with a newer volume in 2012. Tarrow established his reputation through his earlier *Power in Movement* (1998), a book that set a new standard in Social Movement Theory by providing an array of concepts to understand processes and behaviours in contemporary protest. Throughout, he has sought out "robust" patterns of dissent, and surveyed various "mechanisms of protest contention" he believes arrive with activist movements. In elaborating on this approach, Tarrow explains "the logic . . . is that when mechanisms concatenate repeatedly in the same processes, we can say that those processes are robust; when such processes link domestic activists to international venues and to transnational networks and coalitions, they help to break down the walls between domestic and international activism."[5]

In 2005, Tarrow used the term "rooted cosmopolitans" to describe much of modern activism, for protest, he claimed, is often "an opportunity space into which domestic actors can move, encounter others like themselves, and form coalitions that transcend their borders."[6] In his latest work, he has also described protest movements as "strangers at the gates" who organize "on the boundaries of constituted politics, culture, and institutions."[7] This situation does not imply a lack of power, but it does mean activists exist "in an uneasy position which explains much of the ambiguities and contradictions in their strategies, composition, and dynamics."[8] Nonetheless, Tarrow believes, like Keck and Sikkink, that substantial change is possible given the interaction between activist movements, established political groups, and everyday citizens whose support determines the balance of power.

In many respects, Tarrow's work demonstrates the strengths and weaknesses of Social Movement Theory. In the best circumstances, such work brings a focused, cautionary approach to assessments of dissent, and tempers claims by others out of touch with activist potentials. But given the lack of dialogue between academics and activists, the literature can often seem lifeless and far removed from the daily setbacks, breakthroughs, and insights of protest movements. As a consequence, Tarrow's jargon is also unlikely to attract (unless it offers an academic career path) or, worse still, provide much engagement with activists on the ground. For that to happen, one must appreciate protest movements on their own terms. For me, this involves surveying the places, ideas, and organizations that facilitate activism, and pursuing conversations with those who create them. Doing so can help us understand *why* grassroots activism, after decades of existing on the margins, is back in vogue. It can also help us grasp *how* activists have broadened the appeal of progressive ideas, often in the face of considerable pressure.

To clarify the "trouble" with Social Movement Theory, it's worth returning to Graeber's earlier lament about the gulf between "theorists of revolution and its practitioners." Social Movement Theory has become, without question, a well-spring of scholarship, but it is not a home for activists seeking to engage with theory. That is because few scholars truly listen to (or support) emerging forms of progressive activism. Such an approach would likely be dismissed by academics as "anecdotal," "unscientific," or too close to advocacy; preferable instead is scholarly distance and the "objective" standpoint of "rigorous research."

In fact, scholarly distance contributes to the "gulf" Graeber notes between academics and activists, an unfortunate outcome for both parties. Social Movement Theory can yield interesting concepts (e.g., "boomerang effect", "rooted cosmopolitans", or "strangers at the gates"), and offer intellectual frameworks to understand forms of protest. But that approach, as Chris Dixon and Dennis Bevington argue, misses a crucial point: Appreciating the power of progressive activism involves political commitment and identifying where the author stands in relation to protest movements.[9] Politically engaged scholarship must evaluate activism on its own terms and ask why it is worth studying in the first place. Is it only for the benefit of social science, so academics can appreciate "robust processes"? Or is it to learn history's lessons, contribute to thoughtful dialogue, and facilitate, through whatever indirect means, that project of transforming society? To paraphrase a well-worn slogan: Are scholars content with interpreting progressive activism, or will they help it change the world?

Faced with these questions, Social Movement Theory seems consumed by internal debates and unwilling to move beyond specialist language. While scholars and activists can benefit from this literature, they must go elsewhere to grasp the larger context created by grassroots movements in recent years. Having reached similar conclusions, some academics offer theory that seeks a dialogue with protest movements, while others (like me) attempt theory-making based on experience in progressive activism and conversations with activists themselves. My shorthand for these people is "movement thinkers," for they represent a break from scholarly distance and an intention to grasp what movements say, do, and represent in practice. I turn now to a survey of their contributions.

## THE CONTRIBUTIONS OF MOVEMENT THINKERS

As we saw with Social Movement Theory, the activist uprisings of the late 1960s and early 1970s had a profound impact on progressive academics. This was also true for movement thinkers, however, who began challenging the Left ideologies prevalent during the 1960s, ranging from social democracy through Maoism. In the academic world, these writers coalesced around the "New Social Movements" approach. In other arenas, we saw new voices from emerging political actors, most notably representing feminist, Aboriginal, anti-racist, and gay/lesbian/transgendered movements. A recurring theme was the idea that protest results from the failed recognition of certain identities or moral claims, and that the "existing Left" had little interest in grasping these questions. As Janet Conway explains, the

> *last eruption of "new" social movements, in the 1960s and*
> *'70s, posed serious challenges both to the hegemonic discourses*
> *of science, progress and development and to the emancipatory*
> *narratives of modernity, most notably Marxisms.*
>
> *Subsequently, the proliferation of progressive movements*
> *around multiple and intersecting identities has unsettled*
> *practices and theories of oppositional politics constructed on*
> *unitary and unproblematic subjects (e.g., "the working class"*
> *or "women").*
>
> *New social movements — their transformative power*
> *and potential, their limits and defeats, their transmutations*
> *and their enduring presences — provoked revolutions in so-*
> *cial theory and theories of power and change as well as new*
> *approaches in studying the movements themselves as social*
> *phenomena.*[10]

More recently, authors inspired by similar ideas have analyzed today's protest movements, often with the aim of reorienting how activism itself is theorized and understood. In their books *Empire, Multitude,* and *Commonwealth,* Michael Hardt and Antonio Negri have offered the most debated contributions. Much of what they write takes issue with conventional ideas about global capitalism and progressive dissent. In contrast to earlier analyses of "imperialism," "anti-imperialism," and revolutionary movements, Hardt and Negri invoke the concepts of "Empire" and "multitude" to describe today's world economy and transnational resistance against it.

"Empire," they maintain, describes global capitalism as a "smooth space," a seamless entity where power relations are far-reaching but (unlike what imperialist analyses might attest) difficult to identify. In

Empire, any notion of national sovereignty or competition between imperial powers is dissolved; all that exists are global elites and an increasingly complex world system of ideological controls. For Hardt and Negri, Empire first emerged through US dominance after the Second World War, and grew in earnest during the late 1960s to early 1970s. Following this period, they argue, the rapid expansion of "immaterial labour" (a term they use to describe the rise of "service-sector," "knowledge-based" work, and decline of traditional manufacturing jobs) has compromised the power of nation-states, giving rise to the global dominance theorized in *Empire*.

As some critics have argued, this vision resembles a neoliberal vision of a world driven by unrelenting and invincible free markets. Hardt and Negri have responded by acknowledging progressive features in Empire, but claim the prevalence of "immaterial labour" has also created significant potentials for resistance. They theorize their conception of global resistance to Empire as "multitude," which they consciously juxtapose to earlier conceptions of "the people", "the masses", or the "revolutionary working class". Hardt and Negri think these notions of activism are outdated, limited, and incapable of grasping contemporary trends in global dissent. Their vision of an activist "multitude," instead, is theorized as being

> *composed of radical differences, singularities, that can never be synthesized in an identity … [yet featuring] the creation of new circuits of cooperation and collaborations that stretch across nations and continents and allow an unlimited number of encounters.*
>
> *This second face of globalization is not a matter of everyone in the world becoming the same; rather it provides the possibility that, while remaining different, we discover the commonality that enables us to communicate and act together.*
>
> *The multitude too might thus be conceived as a network:*

*an open and expansive network in which all differences can
be expressed freely and equally, a network that provides the
means of encounter so that we can work and live in common.[11]*

As is clear from this quotation, Hardt and Negri envision the multitude as not an entity in itself, but a meeting point between different perspectives: a network in sharing ideas and practices capable of changing
the world. In this network, those with radical perspectives encounter
others with less strident views, and develop "trust relationships" that can
lead to new experiments in progressive activism.

For Hardt and Negri, two features of the multitude offer great promise over earlier efforts in progressive activism. The first is its power in
"biopolitical production," a term they borrow from French philosopher Michel Foucault to explain mechanisms of social control and the
options created for activist resistance. With the dominance of "immaterial labour," Hardt and Negri claim, activists are furnished with new
abilities to think, debate, and campaign for support. The Internet, they
insist, demonstrates how the communicative basis of much production
in global capitalism also creates new opportunities for dissent.

At the height of their argument, Hardt and Negri claim the multitude's own capacities include the basis for a "post-socialist" and "post-
liberal" global democracy, one beyond the inadequate representative
democracy realized in some parts of the world. In the final words of
*Multitude*, they situate the capacity of progressive activism in realizing
this end as being somewhere "between a present that is already dead
and a future that is already living — and the yawning abyss between
them is becoming enormous."[12] In their more recent *Commonwealth*,
they discuss the way activist resistance creates new conceptions of "the
common," and redefines notions of shared concerns against the hyper-
individualism espoused by neoliberal thinkers. The multitude does this,
Hardt and Negri insist, when it seeks "exodus" from the sovereignty

of nation-states, and activists make good on the "threat to refuse their position of servitude and subtract themselves from the relationship."[13] In seeking "exodus" from state politics, they claim, the multitude's best option involves seeking genuine democracy at the global level, a project necessarily defined through networks of activists.

The second strength Hardt and Negri attribute to the multitude is the inclination among activists for participatory, grassroots organization, away from the centralized approaches used in earlier activist eras. On this note they write of an activist tendency

> *from centralized forms of revolutionary dictatorship and command to network organizations that displace authority in collaborative relationships … a tendency for resistance and revolutionary organizations not only to be a means to achieve a democratic society but to create internally, within the organizational structure, democratic relationships.*[14]

Further on this subject, they contend that

> *democracy on a global scale is becoming an increasingly widespread demand, sometimes explicit but often implicit in the innumerable grievances and resistances expressed against the current global order. The common currency that runs throughout so many struggles and movements for liberation across the world today — at local, regional, and global levels — is the desire for democracy. Needless to say, desiring and demanding global democracy do not guarantee its realization, but we should not underestimate the power such demands can have.*[15]

Richard Day has drawn similar conclusions in his assessment of the potential of progressive activism. For him, the most remarkable achievement of dissent in recent years is the shift toward "affinity-based organizing," a model he deems quite different from earlier activist projects that sought broad-based "hegemonic support." By "affinity-based organizing," Day refers to the activism first widely visible during the 1999 protests in Seattle against the World Trade Organization, where activists planned their dissent through networked groups that "self-organized" according to shared interests. For these activists, Day claims, the "logic of affinity" is situated outside the traditional realm of "revolutionary" or "reformist" politics.[16] Instead of seeking broad-based support to overthrow or reform the state, "affinity-based organizing" involves activists refusing to accept state-defined options, and instead carving out new niches of resistance with like-minded allies. Examples Day cites includes the work of web-based independent media, food collectives fostering locally grown products, and indigenous movements asserting traditional means of subsistence against rules imposed by labour markets or property relations.

In juxtaposing these examples to strategies for "hegemony," Day refers to ideas expressed by Antonio Gramsci, an early-twentieth-century Italian socialist who felt dissent must involve tactics aimed at undermining the legitimacy (or hegemony) of capitalism. As a sympathetic observer of the Russian Revolution in 1917, Gramsci believed Western capitalism posed a different set of challenges. In Western liberal democracies, he insisted, an important task involves contesting capitalism's appeal through overtures to the "hearts and minds" of its subjects. For this, an elaborate "counter-hegemonic strategy" was necessary, one equipped with an anti-capitalist critique, but also a set of compelling proposals for transforming state power and capitalism itself.

In extolling examples of affinity-based organizing, Day insists the search for counter-hegemony in activist projects was flawed from the start. He identifies a common tendency of liberal, Marxist, and even some anarchist thinkers, whose struggles for state power, he suggests, compromised the integrity of activist projects.[17] For Day, a more compelling approach emerges from the "post-anarchist" insights of Peter Kropotkin and Gustav Landauer. These thinkers, he believes, stressed the crucial goal of respecting the autonomy of all human beings, and engaging in small-scale radical projects with those of like mind (or "common affinities"). Such affinity-based activists, Day insists, can then align with others of like mind, and in the process create networks of "groundless solidarity."[18] Ultimately, Day insists, when a critical mass is drawn into alternative ways of living, its activities sap capitalism's legitimacy from the outside, "interrupt its flows," and allow for "conscious attempts to alter, impede, destroy or construct alternatives to dominant structures, processes, practices and identities."[19] Affinity-based organizing is therefore a better strategy for arriving at this goal, given its basis in "shared ethico-political commitments that allow us to achieve enough solidarity to effectively create sustainable alternatives to the neoliberal order."[20] Hardt, Negri, and Day offer much to understand emerging forms of activism, particularly in their emphasis on movements as networks where new activist capacities are developing. In Hardt and Negri's case, *Multitude* emerged as a more significant contribution than *Empire*, largely because of the latter's esoteric prose and its lack of substantive comment on existing activism. In *Multitude*, the authors make a serious attempt to engage the practices of today's activists with larger theoretical insights into war, democracy, and the fabric of global resistance. Hardt and Negri's conception of "the multitude" as an inclusive protest network is shared by me and by others; it is an explanation that fits an era where activists hold global ambitions, but have significant reservations about established Left groups. In a similar vein, *Multitude's* preference for grassroots activism is also widely acknowledged, and the implications this holds for existing top-down Left groups are surely important. One notes a similar appreciation in Day's extensive comments on modern activism, even though he prefers to situate this work in a localized, affinity-based context.

Still, any serious analysis into Hardt, Negri, and Day must question the problems posed by over-emphasizing the potentials of today's activists and misrepresenting the nature of obstacles they face. First, on the terrain of political economy, claims alleging the dominance of "immaterial labour" do not square with empirical realities. Indeed, while Hardt and Negri re-emphasize this point often, it is never accompanied by economic research, or even a gesture toward quantitative proof. If they did such work, it would likely discover important shifts in labour markets: the dominant role of finance capital, the rapid dissemination of global money, and the proliferation of precarious, temporary, low-wage service-sector work. But these trends, as I discussed in Chapter 3, have hardly erased the existence of a global working class, the dominance of an elite ruling class, and the enduring significance of resource, extraction, and manufacturing industries. Claims around "immaterial labour" are overblown in Hardt and Negri, even if trends in labour markets pose new challenges for activist resistance.

Secondly, the emphasis Hardt, Negri, and Day place on radical politics "outside capitalism" — be it through the "exodus" of the multitude or the growth of "post-anarchist" affinity-based activism — misses, in many respects, the main contribution of today's protest movements as a beacon for mass support. In recent years, what has been remarkable about progressive activism is not its isolation "outside" conventional politics, but its widespread hearing in mainstream society, on a scale most thought impossible. It would be wishful thinking to call Occupy Wall Street or Idle No More "counter-hegemonic" forces, but it is also false to insist they are more radical once submerged from view and cut off from wider support. On the contrary, as I explain in this book, activists have made their most significant gains through broad, spirited appeals to others frustrated with the diminishing returns of mainstream movements. The notion that activism is most effective "on the margins" is in fact a throwback to earlier, pessimistic thinking on the Left, which is likely why Day offers this dim assessment of human nature in "modernist revolution":

*The sudden collapse of the neoliberal order would indeed create the conditions for a modernist revolution, which many of us would find quite heartening. But, as has happened so many times before, very few people would be ready to accept a life of non-domination and non-exploitation — most would seek new masters, and a few would try to accommodate them.[21]*

As this book explains, such a view hardly fits today's mood. The sense of retreat felt widely on the Left during the 1980s and 1990s has now changed with a new generation of idealists. What's more, the movements these idealists are building have inspired those frustrated by a world of war, poverty, ecological ruin, and frustrated hopes. So, in trying to understand activism, we must move beyond abstractions and analyses aimed at the margins. While retaining some of the existing literature, this is the task we turn to next.

## THE PLACE, IDEAS, AND ORGANIZATION OF PROGRESSIVE ACTIVISM

*Progressive social movements do not simply produce statistics and narratives of oppression; rather, the best ones do what great poetry always does: transport us to another place, compel us to relive horrors and, more importantly, enable us to imagine a new society.*

*We must remember that the conditions and very existence of social movements enable participants to imagine something different, to realize that things need not always be this way. It is that imagination, that effort to see the future in the present, that I shall call "poetry" or "poetic knowledge" . . .*

*In the poetics of struggle and lived experience, in the utterances of ordinary folk, in the cultural products of social movements, in the reflections of activists, we discover the many different cognitive maps of the future, of the world not yet born.*

— *Robin D.G. Kelley*[22]

Robin Kelley, among the most articulate of writers on social movements, wrote these words to encourage scholarship that grasps the substance of modern dissent. His call to embrace "poetic knowledge" is an invitation to look at progressive activists in a more genuine way — as generators of knowledge, as authors of their own story, and dreamers of a better world. That is quite different approach from the one taken by Social Movement Theory and some movement thinkers, who frequently understand emerging forms of progressive activism from inside their own preconceptions. With our eyes closed, we can imagine social scientists and intellectuals in white lab coats, dissecting bits of protest phenomena to suit a preconceived hypothesis. With our eyes (and minds) open, we understand activism on a far deeper level, one that grasps the reality of what social movements truly offer, and their importance in shifting our social and political assumptions.

This is an approach others have called "movement-relevant theory," and it is one with a great deal of promise. It refers to writers seeking to understand progressive activism on its own terms. Initially, this involves recognizing that movements themselves engage in theory-making, and that accessing those contributions requires engagement with activists on the ground. With that point of departure, movement-relevant theorists help stimulate critical thought and activist experimentation, ideally with one's political commitments made explicit.

This is a radical departure from the academic distance common to most social science, but necessarily so; the purpose is to recognize activists as equals in the process of theory-making, and to then produce work that puts the "needs of movements at its heart." Chris Dixon and Dennis Bevington, two activist-academics, were among the first to articulate this approach:

> *To produce movement-relevant theory, it is not enough simply*
> *to identify with a movement or study a movement. Instead,*
> *there is a distinct process that involves dynamic engagement*
> *with movements in the formulation, production, refinement,*
> *and application of the research.*
>
> *Moreover, the researcher need not and in fact should*
> *not have a detached relation to the movement. Rather, the*
> *researcher's connection to the movement provides important*
> *incentives to produce more accurate information, regardless of*
> *whether the researcher is studying a favored movement or its*
> *opponents.*
>
> *And while movement-relevant theory is not entirely new,*
> *the present moment offers distinct opportunities for it to play*
> *a more prominent role in social movement scholarship.*[23]

My own contribution to movement-relevant theory studies certain key features of activism, the first of which concerns its *place.* In the early years of the Industrial Revolution (in the eighteenth and nineteenth, or, in some contexts, early twentieth centuries), this was often the workplace with its abysmal conditions. For other political traditions — anarchist, social democratic, or feminist — the place of activism was perceived to be elsewhere: wherever the battle was joined for protecting certain communities, for capturing the helm of political parties, or against the forced definition of gender roles. In today's protest movements, "place" is a concept that, on the surface, at least, appears both perplexing and controversial. Activism appears to be happening on a number of levels at once — local, regional, national and global — and disagreement prevails over the relative importance of certain of these levels.

Some, like Hardt and Negri, think today's movements are mostly "transnational," regardless of where a specific episode of protest originates. Others have argued that while it may be transnational in spirit, the place of struggle for today's activists is grounded in national jurisdictions, or nation-states, which remain central players in today's world economy. Global capitalism itself, however capable of transferring wealth internationally, is the creation of nation-states, and multinational corporations waste no time seeking protection or legislation from states to suits their interest. Sam Gindin is an advocate of this view, but he offers the following argument to bridge national-transnational perspectives:

> *A focus on the national state is not a diversion from the international struggle; rather, it represents a nationally-based internationalism. Successful national struggles depend on others elsewhere also being in struggle: as inspirations, as experiments we need to critically study and learn from, and to create enough international turmoil to limit the isolation of any particular struggle.*
>
> *This is true for us, and it is true for Third World countries (e.g. the current struggles in Latin America). They will only be able to win there when we expand their space for struggle through resistance here.*
>
> *As for the global redistribution of wealth and economic potential that is so fundamental to any notion of justice, we must first actually take national state power to carry out such concrete solidarity.[24]*

Gindin's "nationally-based internationalism" is a thoughtful contribution, but it hardly ends controversies about seeking state power (which takes us to the thorny issue of elections, and whether they are a useful space for progressive activism). Still, Gindin helps us understand how global issues can be a defining force for local and regional campaigns, a trend that certainly fits the international resonance of the Arab Spring, Occupy Wall Street, Idle No More, climate justice movements, and cascading protests against trade deals and military invasions. Indeed, some forms of transnational agency also challenge traditional definitions of local/regional/national protest, particularly given today's communications technologies and frequent lack of interest (often among youth) in the flavour of politics at home. The movements I discuss in this book demonstrate such complexity around issues of place in emerging forms of activism.

*Ideas* are the second feature worth studying in today's protest movements, a subject no less controversial than discussions of place. At issue here are the visions activists offer toward winning support and proposing alternatives. In earlier protest eras, in a context where industrial workers suffered continuous, back-breaking work for meagre wages, socialists and syndicalists articulated ideas about workers' control of production, and a society planned on the basis of human need. Many social democratic and anti-colonial thinkers, in contrast, evoked patriotic ideas of a better nation given the right priorities; often facing off against the revolutionaries in their midst, they argued against radical shifts and urged a more moderate set of priorities at the national level. Some anarchist and feminist thinkers, choosing a different course, posited ideas about freedom from all reactionary views, with a steadfast insistence on the inalienable rights of individuals. In each of these cases, we see examples of thinkers and activists drawing on alternative conceptions of society and communicating their ideas in the effort to win support.

Today a common accusation is that activists are inclined to ideas that espouse "anti-politics," with no (or few) detailed alternatives to propose. Some attribute this to a wider refusal of mainstream politics by many of today's activists, a sentiment that dovetails with the public's contempt for most politicians and conventional political institutions. A common reaction — evidenced in declining rates of voter participation in most places — has been to reject formal politics entirely, a result certainly welcomed by strategists in mainstream political parties.

And yet, as this book makes plain, thinking about protesters' ideas today in purely negative terms is mistaken. A dimension of today's protest movements is profoundly affirmative, and — while rejecting the political status quo — posits an idea (countless ideas) of a more just world. This is the dimension of activism amplified in recent mobilizations, and its optimism, while diverse and decentralized, is infectious. Over a decade ago, Naomi Klein documented this process in the emergence of Zapatismo, and its impact on demonstrations elsewhere:

> *What often are reported as menacing confrontations are often joyous events, as much experiments in alternative ways of organizing societies as criticisms of existing models.*
>
> *The first time I participated in one of these counter-summits, I remember having the distinct feeling that some sort of political portal was opening up — a gateway, a window, "a crack in history," to use Subcomandante Marcos's beautiful phrase.*
>
> *This opening had little to do with the broken window at the local McDonald's, the image so favoured by television cameras; it was something else: a sense of possibility, a blast of fresh air, oxygen rushing to the brain. These protests — which are actually week-long marathons of intense education on global politics, late-night strategy sessions in six-way simultaneous translation, festivals of music and street theatre — are like stepping into a parallel universe.*
>
> *Overnight, the place is transformed into a kind of alternative global city where urgency replaces resignation, corporate logos need armed guards, people usurp cars, art is everywhere, strangers talk to each other, and the prospect of radical change in political course does not seem like an odd and anachronistic idea but the most logical thought in the world.*[25]

With these words, Klein raises an important theme long identified by those seeking to understand activism: that dissent is a learning process in itself. Very quickly, the domain of negative or cynical anti-politics can broaden in moments where activists gain a sense of their power. This was a process Émile Durkheim, the famous (and often misunderstood) sociologist, once described as "collective effervescence," where fears and prejudices are diminished through the energy generated by shared ideas and practices.[26] Rosa Luxemburg, a Polish socialist, remarked on a similar process in her famous assessment of labour strikes; broad participation in mass campaigns, she insisted, was the "life-giving spark" that would make socialism possible.[27]

But most notably, over the past years, as activists have mobilized against neoliberalism and war, the tendency toward what some call anti-systemic movements has been conspicuous. Protesters initially drawn into struggle for particular causes soon found themselves making the leap to more ambitious and far-reaching perspectives. As activists charted a course for future organizing, arguments for reforms to trade deals or multilateral institutions won less support than arguments against commodification itself, against the interests that profit from war, and for a deeper understanding of today's neoliberal conditions. Amidst the tear gas and riot police in Seattle, the huge marches against war in 2003, and the rise of the Arab Spring, Occupy, Climate Justice, and indigenous rights movements, few cries were heard for "corporate responsibility" or "peacekeeping." The most popular slogans were ambitious claims: "This is what democracy looks like", "Our world is not for sale", "A better world is possible", "No blood for oil", "We are the 99 per cent", "Closed for climate justice", "Idle No More".

These slogans reveal a vibrant culture of learning in today's protest movements, and ideas abundant with alternatives. Susan George has explained this by juxtaposing a new acronym to Margaret Thatcher's oft-repeated doctrine of "TINA" (there is no alternative): "To TINA, say TATA — there are thousands of alternatives."[28] Greg Albo agrees, and flatly denies that today's activists are purely reactive:

*The problem is not one of ideas to oppose neoliberalism: the Left has never had more blueprints of alternative social orders, imaginative policies and experiences to draw upon, and feminism, anti-racism and ecology have hugely enriched our conception of the tasks ahead. The prospects of Left renewal pivot around rebuilding an active democracy and exploring new organizational forms of political unity.*[29]

Albo directs our attention to the *organizations* activists create, the third (and last) key feature of today's protest movements that deserve our attention. As long as there have been campaigns for social justice, activists have built organizations to accomplish their work. In the early twentieth century, for example, workers engaged in "red unionism" believed it was necessary to develop radical trade unions outside the divisive realm of organized labour; doing so, they felt, allowed them to project an inclusive and democratic vision where "one big union" could build a mass movement of workers. In other periods, socialists and anarchists created illegal groups committed to insurrectionary tactics; they believed their tight-knit organizations could deal crippling blows to ruling powers at the right moment. Many social democratic and anti-colonial leaders, in similar terms, believed in the necessity of organized rules and procedures within activist organizations, but often with the aim of seeking state power for elites, and rarely for the grassroots who supported their cause. Feminist, anti-racist, and gay rights movements, in different periods, have built organizations where those persecuted could seek support and develop the capacities necessary to seek social change. In these organizations, we see evidence of activists equipping themselves with strategies to meet demands posed by their historical conditions.

If there is a notable characteristic of today's protest movements in this longer history, it is a reluctance to establish formal organizations, elaborate manifestos, or permanent alliances with large progressive groups such as unions, political parties, foundations, and faith communities. That caution is often mirrored by established progressive groups who, despite frequent support of grassroots activism, often perceive such movements as a threat to their own coherence. An "organizational gap" then emerges; established progressive groups frequently miss out on the energy of the new activists, while protest movements suffer when the urgency that created them subsides. This book, however, is concerned with the exceptions to that rule: It documents moments where grassroots activism has made an impact on established progressive groups, creating new moments for collaboration. These examples hold lessons to inform new strategies for progressive organizing, and clues about how to challenge the neoliberal establishment that remains dominant today.

And yet, understood against the backdrop of progressive history, the reluctance today's activists often have to engage with established groups is understandable. No one wants to languish in bureaucratic talk shops or surrender to cults of personality. In this context, one can appreciate why protest movements have been hesitant to work within Left groups visible to public scrutiny and open to wider participation. Nonetheless, as Jo Freeman famously remarked in her feminist classic "The Tyranny of Structurelessness," there is no such thing as an unstructured group; today's activists have developed organizations with built-in contradictions, despite any well-meaning words otherwise.[30]

As the examples in this book reveal, a movement's approach to organization reflects its political priorities and its capacity to facilitate crucial discussions: how to organize most democratically and effectively; how to assess (and work within) existing progressive institutions; how to understand the relationship between war and capitalism; how to interact with the nation-state; how to assess (and draw the connections between) social problems of alienation, exploitation, and oppression on the level of gender, race, sexuality, ability, and others. The ways in which these debates unfold, and the manner in which activists engage with each other in the process, are shaped by the organizations activists build and the conversations they facilitate. These organizations, and their interaction with established politics, determine how protest movements develop and the impact they will have.

So, to sum up: *Place, ideas* and *organization* — these are the features of activism worth further study, each of which offers lessons about progressive organizing in tough times. This is my view as an academic, and as an activist who believes the future belongs to grassroots organizing, to efforts empowering everyday people to change themselves, their community, and their society. Those goals, I think, we are more likely to achieve if we can come to a better understanding of progressive activism and what inspires today's protest movements.

# 6

# THE FUTURE OF GRASSROOTS ACTIVISM:
## KEY THEMES TO KEEP IN MIND

*People can change anything they want to. And that means everything in the world. People are running about following their little tracks — I am one of them.*

*But we've all got to stop just following our own little mouse trail. People can do anything — this is something that I'm beginning to learn.*

*People are out there doing bad things to each other. That's because they've been dehumanized. It's time to take the humanity back into the centre of the ring, and follow that for a time.*

*Greed, it ain't going anywhere. They should have that in a big billboard across Times Square. Without people you're nothing. That's my spiel.*

*— Joe Strummer*[1]

Joe Strummer, the legendary, kinetic frontman for The Clash, once spoke these words to inspire collective action for social justice and reject, where possible, the lonely "mouse trails" of daily life under capitalism. These were ideas he came by honestly. Strummer came from a family of white, well-salaried privilege; his father was a clerical officer in the British Foreign Office (often living overseas), while Joe and his brother were sent to private boarding school. Strummer, bright and capable, could have easily followed his father's path to a comfortable life, but he tossed that "mouse trail" aside — first for a jaunt through art school, and later for a memorable rise in the punk rock scene.

Strummer was also a political activist who fought the rise of white supremacist groups and challenged neoliberalism at home and abroad. His call for personal sacrifice and political commitment is shared by today's protesters who reject the neoliberal consensus of modern politics and consumption-obsessed uniformity of our contemporary culture. The movements they form aim to take back public spaces from corporate control and bring politics down to a grassroots level. They encourage bottom-up activist capacities that can challenge (and even shift) larger forces.

That is the narrative I have explored in this book, one that offers the best hope for progressive politics in generations. In chapter one, I traced the origins, scope, and influence of emerging forms of activism, and their significance in historical terms. With that established, chapters two through four took a closer look at grassroots activism in social movements, working-class politics, and Left political parties. In each of these realms there was evidence to suggest a rethinking in the place, ideas, and organization of progressive activism — one inspired by people taking politics back from an elite mould and doing it themselves.

In many respects, today's protest movements, like others before them, have redefined the scope and meaning of activism. In doing so, they have more in common with the activism of previous eras than most are willing to admit. Much like the movements of the nineteenth and early twentieth century, today's activists have struggled to locate the best place for progressive organizing. But while earlier movements launched campaigns to reinvent local or regional politics, many of today's activists have espoused a "nationally-based internationalism," where grassroots solidarity reaches across borders to embolden local campaigns. Often, this has involved a blurring in the place of dissent, as local, national, and global realms are perceived as part of a joint effort. Indeed, today's international solidarity campaigns have given new meaning to the expression "think globally, act locally." Today's activists think globally, act locally, and network themselves at both levels.

In similar terms, amidst the tired infrastructure of industrial relations, the involvement of unions in grassroots activism has ushered new energy into labour movements. Like earlier activists who sought to develop labour's potential, unions inspired by protest movements have emerged as prominent voices for community needs, global peace, sustainable economics, and genuine democracy. Activists engaged in Left political parties have offered similar contributions, viewing elections as moments where they can tap into the energy of the grassroots. Significant problems remain, and activists will certainly face pressure to hollow out their ideas or seek alliances with sources of elite power. Still, Left parties and unions can gain energy and purpose from protest movements. Alternatively, they could also follow the "mouse trail" of neoliberalism, and lament its diminishing returns.

Lastly, we should acknowledge that the ideas of today's activists are neither unique nor unprecedented. Those with longer memories may recall others claiming that "a better world is possible." The will to posit bold ideas has long been a hallmark of progressive activism, whether it aimed at an end to male domination, colonial oppression, wage slavery, or uncritical frameworks of higher education. To grasp the ideas of today's activists, however, one needs to appreciate the "politics" of "anti-politics." There is no ideology that unites these militants, and no political organization capable of capturing the diverse fabric of dissent.

There is instead a shared commitment to ask ambitious questions, to do politics yourself, and to challenge the onward march of neoliberal capitalism. Today's activists will not blindly follow those who don't share these commitments; they are quiet no more, and determined to stay that way. That mood has created new opportunities, where new experiments in activism can be explored.

And yet, while noting these promises of grassroots activism, one must appreciate the challenges it faces. Currently, Western governments remain open to tar sands expansion, yet activists and scientists have proven this undermines efforts to tackle climate change. Despite the hard work of human rights campaigners, polls suggest most Israelis think discrimination against Arabs in Israel and Israeli-occupied Palestine is justified on national security grounds, a view that goes unchallenged by Israel's Western supporters. Despite the inroads made by Québec Solidaire, the Parti Québécois was the choice for most progressive voters in recent elections. Idle No More represents an important, defiant challenge for indigenous rights to date, but settler communities remain deeply divided on (and at times hostile to) interruptions caused by protest actions. Western unions, despite holding considerable power, offer little of the chutzpah seen in their corporate opponents, and this after years of neoliberal reforms. In the Middle East, which has seen upstart mass movements and new links of solidarity with the West, activists are often divided along sectarian lines, divisions often fostered by the presence and patronage of imperial powers.

As these circumstances make plain, activists and movements face a world of contradictions. But as a mentor of mine once said, there are two general choices one has when faced with that reality. One can pursue "bad social science," and either ignore contradictions or assume they aren't important. That, unfortunately, is the analytical approach most scholars bring to progressive activism; they accept, uncritically or fitfully, the posture of "academic distance," or the limits of their own assumptions. US voters are dismissed as conservative, or excused for being misled. NGOs are heralded as builders of "global civil society," or ridiculed as "agents of imperialism." Unions are pardoned for their defeatist posture, or lampooned as bureaucratic dues-collection agencies. Activists in the global South are ignored by Western movements, or uncritically lauded as signposts of revolution. These postures evade difficult realities activists must address, and a serious evaluation of the world in which we live.

"Good social science," my mentor explained, starts from a different premise. It is curious enough, and brave enough, to grapple with contradictions — for doing so leads to genuine insight that creates new knowledge. As Bertolt Brecht, the great activist-playwright, once said, "in the contradiction lies the hope" — the hope for activism that brings "poetic knowledge,"[2] for insights into the world we want, and ideas about how we can build it despite the calamities all around us. When we take this point of departure, the potentials for protest movements are easier to locate, even if dispiriting options loom. As was the case for those before them, today's activists have choices, many of them tough choices, if their aim is to move beyond the position of a committed global minority. This book ends by identifying two choices activists should consider as building blocks for a new global Left. First, on the terrain of ideas, I urge activists to champion the anti-systemic spirit of modern dissent — the politics of contemporary "anti-politics" — and make opposition to neoliberalism a meeting point between those of differing views. In making this case, I review the examples of US filmmaker Michael Moore's approach to the Democratic Party, and Antonio Negri's support of the European Union constitution, as unfortunate cases moving in different directions.

Secondly, in surveying forms of activist organization, I make a strong endorsement of what I call participatory radicalism — bold, broad, inclusive activism targeted for a mass audience — to guide future work in progressive organizing. I contrast that to the "autonomism" and "pedagogical space activism" that have been more popular in recent years. Both of the latter perspectives, despite raising valuable questions, fall short as vehicles to spread grassroots activism beyond a committed minority. I end by urging readers to consider participatory radicalism in their own activist work; such an approach, I firmly believe, presents the best conditions to renew the Left and deepen the imprint of today's upstart protest movements.

## THE ART OF BEING UNREASONABLE (BEWARE THE LESSER EVIL)

*Be realistic. Demand the impossible.*

*— Situationist movement (France, 1960s)*

Among many other slogans, these were the defiant words that inspired progressives in an earlier era, and they fit nicely with the rebellious spirit of today's activists. While some suggest today's activism is just about saying "no," this book has drawn attention to the affirmative politics behind today's "anti-politics," and the depth of insight in activist ideas. Whether one studies anarchist-inspired thinkers like David Graeber, social democratic thinkers like Susan George and George Monbiot, or proposals for global boycott campaigns in the writing of Arundhati Roy, a host of alternative frameworks compete for the attention of activists. All of them take inspiration from the anti-systemic mood in today's protest movements. And yet, while this mood has remained influential, some movement thinkers have taken another path, often in response to setbacks or lulls in activist efforts. These actors are often fierce critics of neoliberalism, but then, paradoxically, have gone on to suggest "progressive alliances" with others on the global Right. Often, these alliances are framed as realistic choices for activists in challenging conditions, as acts of pragmatism. Michael Moore, the activist filmmaker, and the popular movement philosopher Antonio Negri offer two notable cases in point.

As many have pointed out, Moore is one of the most popular communicators of progressive ideas alive today. Since producing his widely acclaimed *Roger and Me* in 1989, which chronicled the corporate destruction of his hometown of Flint, Michigan, Moore has gone on to win acclaim unheard of for most Left public figures. His books have broken sales records. On its own, *Stupid White Men* spent fifty-nine weeks on the *New York Times* bestseller list, and sold over four million copies worldwide. In 2002, Moore's *Bowling for Columbine* earned the most money ever for a documentary, over $21 million, and an Academy Award for best documentary film. Fittingly, Moore used the occasion of his award speech to lambaste the current Bush administration soon after the invasion of Iraq began: "We live in fictitious times," he intoned from the stage, "… where we have fictitious election results that elect a fictitious president. We live in a time where we have a man sending us to war for fictitious reasons."[3]

Moore's popularity increased when his explosive film *Fahrenheit 9/11* took direct aim at the Bush administration only months before the 2004 US presidential elections. As Republican hawks squirmed under the heat of Moore's exposure, *Fahrenheit 9/11* won awards and played to packed audiences around the world. Rush Limbaugh, a bellicose voice of the American Right, dismissed *Fahrenheit 9/11* "as a pack of lies"[4]; Christopher Hitchens, a progressive turned advocate of the US "War on Terror," declared the film a "sinister exercise in moral frivolity."[5] While Moore's work was not without its own flaws, his populist approach drew the ire of American Empire and its defenders unlike any other critic.

At the same time, Moore's ideas had undergone considerable change by the time *Fahrenheit 9/11* was released, most notably in abandoning his previous criticism of "lesser evilism" in American politics. In 2000, Moore channelled his energy and reputation into backing Ralph Nader's independent bid for US president, and faced howls of anger from Democrats as a consequence. In that election, he challenged the notion that US voters should choose between two pro-business political parties. Moore urged Americans to vote for something they believed in: "We are at the place we are at now because we have settled for so less, for so long. If we keep settling it is only going to get worse. [With] the lesser of two evils, you still wind up with evil. We are being asked to choose the second worst candidate."[6]

By the time *Bowling for Columbine* and *Fahrenheit 9/11* appeared in theatres, however, Moore's approach had changed. At this point, he stressed the urgency of defeating George W. Bush at all costs, and also — joining many other former Nader supporters — cast aspersions on those supporting Nader's bid for US president in 2004. At first, as Democrats voted for their leadership candidates, Moore threw his support to General Wesley Clark, the military leader of the 1999 US-led bombing campaign in the former Yugoslavia. Moore had stridently opposed that war, likening it to the militaristic gun culture he pilloried in *Bowling for Columbine*. Nonetheless, in an open letter, he urged Clark to join the Democratic leadership race, and his reasoning for doing so was revealing:

> *Right now, for the sake and survival of our very country, we need someone who is going to get The Job done, period. And that job, no matter who I speak to across America — be they leftie Green or conservative Democrat, and even many disgusted Republicans — EVERYONE is of one mind as to what that job is:*
>
> *Bush Must Go.*
>
> *This is war, General, and it's Bush & Co.'s war on us. It's their war on the middle class, the poor, the environment, their war on women and their war against anyone around the world who doesn't accept total American domination. Yes, it's a war — and we, the people, need a general to beat back those who have abused our Constitution and our basic sense of decency.[7]*

In the aftermath of war in Iraq, and with mounting demoralization on the US Left, Moore urged his supporters to put aside differences with

Democrats. Suddenly, defeating George W. Bush was more important than challenging the limited framework of US politics. After Clark lost the Democratic presidential nomination to John Kerry, Moore stumped for Kerry with a fervour that left little room for debate. After hearing one of Moore's pro-Kerry appeals, one student activist wrote about its implications:

> *Like everything else, his scathing attacks against the Right are dulled by an endorsement for the Democrat. Moore forgets what he once knew about the American political system. The Right is organized and without our own independent organized resistance, we will continue to lose ground.*
>
> *When the right-wing wants to ban gay marriage this is what they do: they get Republicans to push for a constitutional amendment banning gay marriage. Democrats exclaim "No! We can't write bigotry into the constitution! Let states decide." And then the Democrats, as Kerry is doing, lead the charge to ban gay marriage one state at a time. The right-wing gets their way thanks to Kerry not in spite of him. This is the ill logic of lesser evilism …*
>
> *Moore attacked the Republicans for scaring us into voting for Bush. Yet Moore scares us into voting for Kerry. Without trumpeting Kerry's conservative positions, Moore is left reminding us how bloodcurdling Bush is.[8]*

As many observers have pointed out, Kerry was almost indistinguishable from Bush on a host of issues beyond gay rights. Most notable among these was the Iraq War, where Kerry's views were clear: "I do not fault George Bush for doing too much in the war on terror; in fact I believe he has done too little."[9] This hawkish reality, however, was sideswiped by the greater urgency to oust Republicans from power, as progressives played a risky game they ultimately lost. The assertion of independence from neoliberalism, so ardently championed among today's activists, was exchanged for alliance with a "lesser evil."

Antonio Negri, among the most celebrated Left intellectuals, found himself enmeshed in similar circumstances. In *Empire*, Negri had described the world as a seamless entity of deeply woven transnational capitalism. And yet, in the run-up to France's May 29, 2005, national vote on the proposed European Union (EU) constitution, Negri lent his support to the "Yes" side of this contest, clearly favouring an empowered Europe as a progressive option to American imperialism. Indeed, Negri appeared on a speaking platform with Julien Dray (leader of the neoliberal French Socialist Party), and Daniel Cohn-Bendit (former 60s radical and French member of the EU parliament) insisting that French voters eschew "medieval mindsets" and "narrow-minded nationalism," and vote "Yes" for a more unified Europe.[10]

To many of his admirers, Negri's actions were perplexing. The EU constitution was widely recognized as a neoliberal instrument encouraging dramatic cuts to public programs codified by stringent legal safeguards. Why would Negri, who argued that states didn't matter, make such an intervention? The answer he offered to French journalists began by explaining he was a "revolutionary realist," and continued with the following rationalization:

*The constitution is a means of fighting Empire, this new globalized capitalist society. Europe has the chance of being a barrier against the pensée unique of economic unilateralism: capitalist, conservative, reactionary. But Europe can also construct a counter-power against American unilateralism, its imperial domination, its crusade in Iraq to dominate petrol. The United States has understood this well, and has, since the 1950s, fought like a madman against European construction.[11]*

In an odd twist of position, Negri declared the EU as a potential platform for his envisioned "multitude" of resistance movements, albeit within a regional, "federalist" framework. The inclusion of the term "federalist" was important, for it allowed Negri to counterpose a cosmopolitan "Yes" side to a "nationalist" constituency behind the "No" campaign. Those opting against a united Europe, he reasoned, were returning to the French nation-state as a bulwark against Empire, an option Negri disparaged as "bound to disappear."[12] For activists to move forward, he claimed, they must transcend the trappings of national politics and assert themselves on a broader and more ambitious continental stage.

Salvatore Cannavò, the deputy editor of *Liberazione,* a popular Italian socialist paper, claimed Negri's ideas were entirely predictable. How could the analysis of a seamless Empire, Cannavò argued, explain the aggressive actions of the American state in Iraq? The Iraq War had polarized the EU politically and created tense divisions between Europe and the United States. This was hardly the picture of a uniform Empire; Negri's analysis needed to change if it was to have some basis in reality. Accordingly, then, Negri switched to arguing for transnational resistance within Europe, and disparaged those pointing in a different direction. If the "Yes" side won, he claimed, a more progressive form of capitalism would be posed against "American unilateralism."[13]

Negri's ideas here were quite similar to Moore's. By holding up "American unilateralism" as the primary problem, Negri urged his followers toward the "lesser evil" of European capitalism. As Moore drove Americans toward Kerry by lambasting Republicans, Negri urged French voters to reject the isolated "bunker of backward nationalism."[14] Ultimately, as with Moore, French voters rejected Negri's advice. In a vote where over 70 per cent of the electorate participated, 55 per cent cast ballots against the neoliberal EU constitution.

In this context, Negri's claim that "No" voters were reactionary was deeply flawed, and accurate for only a small minority. The French far Right did indeed campaign for a "No" given its racist hostility to Turkey's proposed membership in the EU, but this did not figure as a prominent argument for most "No" voters. At issue, instead, was the neoliberal framework in which the constitution was conceived. France had mobilized sizable anti-neoliberal movements since the 1995 protests against its government's right-wing reforms. In 2002, as most mainstream observers remarked on the surprising performance of fascist Jean-Marie Le Pen, millions nonetheless cast ballots for presidential candidates of the radical Left. An anti-neoliberal mood was evident once again in 2005, and France joined the Netherlands in rejecting the EU constitution. In the run-up to the vote, mass meetings sprang up across France rejecting the lesser-evilist logic of "Yes" campaigners, and *altermondialistes* ("other globalization" activists) emerged at the heart of these efforts. Against Negri and others who urged compromise with neoliberal politicians, activists said a "No" vote meant "a better world is possible."

The crucial point here, of course, is not to target Moore and Negri, who themselves are important figures in global activism. Such an exercise in finger-wagging misses a more significant absence in today's protest movements: the lack of any unifying "meeting point," on the terrain of *ideas*, that draws activists together. In previous times, the ideologies of revolutionary socialism, syndicalism, or anarchism had played such a role, but the unfortunate results (and historical interpretation) associated with these movements have made life for today's activists more complex. If anything, today's activists are predisposed to ideas positing an undefined and inclusive approach, even if rhetoric, at times, does not match reality. But herein lies a challenging question: How can activists avoid the pitfalls of earlier movements, while also positing ideas that embrace what I call participatory radicalism, an activist approach both inclusive and progressive? That requires an analysis not only of economic questions (neoliberalism), but also of racist, sexist, and homophobic prejudices (among other things). Today's activists do not privilege economic analysis over these other crucial concerns.

As many have explained, any success in the economic field has required attention to these other concerns. The need to combat racism, sexism, homophobia, and any other form of human suffering has always been indispensable in uniting progressive movements, and creating the alliances required to change the world. In North America, at the turn of the twentieth century, this meant fighting for workers' unity when immigrants were used as a low-paid reserve to divide emerging industrial unions — a trend that continues today with the recruiting of "temporary foreign workers." During the heady days of 1968 and later, it meant urging united action between workers and students. Today, it often means resisting state-sponsored campaigns of Islamophobic racism in the aftermath of the US-led "War on Terror," and being loud advocates of due process and human rights for "terrorist" detainees. Neglecting such work hollows out the content of progressive ideas and allows neoliberal apologists to divide and rule their opponents. This was a point Karl Marx observed in his remarks on Irish workers under British capitalism:

> *Every industrial and commercial centre in England possesses a working class divided into two hostile camps, English proletarians and Irish proletarians. The ordinary English worker hates the Irish worker as a competitor who lowers his standard of life.*
>
> *In relation to the Irish worker he feels himself a member of the ruling nation and so turns himself into a tool of the aristocrats and capitalists of his country against Ireland, this strengthening their domination over himself. He cherishes religious, social and national prejudices against the Irish worker. His attitude is much the same as that of the "poor whites" to the [blacks] in the former slave states of the USA.*
>
> *The Irishman pays him back with interest in his own money. He sees in the English worker at once the accomplice and stupid tool of the English rule in Ireland. This*

*antagonism is artificially kept alive and intensified by the press, the pulpit, the comic papers, in short by all the means at the disposal of the ruling classes.*

*This antagonism is the secret of the impotence of the English working class, despite its organization. It is the secret by which the capitalist maintains its power. And that class is fully aware of it.[15]*

Today's activists have provided a new context where this kind of analysis can happen — where movements create moments when artificial barriers separating natural allies are broken, if only temporarily. One of the major achievements of dissent in recent years — beyond its success in bringing millions into political action — has been to refute an unnecessary division between identity-based and economically based activism (or, as the philosopher Nancy Fraser puts it, between "recognition-based" and "redistribution-based" concerns[16]). The now common sight of organizing among different kinds of activists offers an opportunity to seek out the debates that are needed to get past the regionalism, parochialism, and debilitating pessimism that made the activist Left a subculture for decades.

The anti-systemic ideas of today's activists have also influenced the *places* they have chosen for their work. In chapter five, Gindin's "nationally-based internationalism" was identified as the best term available to describe international solidarity work, for it captures the local roots and global ambitions of today's activists. The International Solidarity Movement's work in Palestine is a fitting case; while its most recognized efforts are the campaigns it carries out in Palestine itself, an equally important task involves speaking tours of ISM internationals to raise awareness in their home countries. Successive ISM campaigns have led to a profound rethinking of domestic campaigns in the West that can assist solidarity work in Palestine, drawing the connections that make human rights advocacy both participative and meaningful.

Climate justice activists, through 350.org and other networks, are also building forms of grassroots solidarity to foment a green uprising. As I was writing these words, a seventy-eight-year old grandmother in Arkansas had chained herself to machinery to protest the construction of tar sands pipelines; students held a mock funeral outside the offices of TransCanada Corp., decrying the firm's mortgaging of their future; and Aboriginal elders pledged, during a press conference in Ottawa, to block construction of tar sands pipelines. When Québec Solidaire activists exclaim that "a better Quebec is possible," and Egyptian activists name their anti-war mobilizations "another Hyde Park" (a reference to British anti-war demonstrations at their height in 2003), we see glimpses of "nationally-based internationalism" where dissent unites across borders to hold domestic regimes accountable.

## BEYOND ACTIVIST SUBCULTURES: EXITING THE MARGINS, APPEALING TO BILLIONS

*Imagination is more important than knowledge. For knowledge is limited, whereas imagination embraces the entire world, stimulating progress, giving birth to evolution.*

*— Albert Einstein*[17]

As this book has shown, what drives activism, more than anything else, is the power of imagination. Tim DeChristopher's imagination, for example, gave rise to his intervention in a rigged land auction — a choice that ultimately saved the land from natural gas drillers. That act, in turn, inspired the creation of Peaceful Uprising, among the most respected climate justice groups in North America. And as many activists acknowledge today, Peaceful Uprising's embrace of civil disobedience has radicalized the climate justice movement in general, recalling past movements against environmental racism in indigenous, black, and brown communities. All of this has facilitated new alliances and breakthroughs against fossil fuels industries.

In similar terms, Karen Lewis's imagination, and her refusal to accept the concession-based strategy of her union leadership, also sparked an exciting process of renewal in the Chicago Teachers Union. She and others then created the Caucus of Rank and File Educators, a small group that built bridges with Chicago's black and brown communities fighting against school discrimination. That tapped into a wave of anger, which soon found its voice in a successful bid to lead the union itself. And when CORE leaders assumed office, they didn't stop imagining how the union could improve — they transformed it into a more open, authentic, member-driven, and community-oriented organization. That made it tough for their employer to demonize them, and trickier to undermine their union with the usual divide and conquer strategies.

The imagination of Nina Wilson, Sheelah McLean, Sylvia McAdam, and Jessica Gordon inspired the first Idle No More conference in November 2012, a move that later united indigenous movements in a defiant call for respect and justice. Aboriginal women and youth — rarely seen as actors in mainstream politics — were authors of their own stories, and what they said moved others to action. We were challenged, as Clayton Thomas-Muller explains, to "decolonize our minds," to recognize the injustices perpetrated against First Nations, and think about how we can help restore nation-to-nation treaty rights.

During Operation Cast Lead, when white phosphorus bombs (among other weapons) rained on the people of Gaza, it was imagination that drove solidarity activists to help undermine Israel's propaganda machine. Despite mighty adversaries, they have challenged Israel's grip on mainstream opinion, raised considerable sums, and offered support to long-suffering Palestinians. In doing so, they showcased what Palestinians suffer on a daily basis, and often put their own lives at risk. They created a platform where the stories of Palestinians could be shared, and their humanity potentially restored. Throughout 2012 and 2013, Palestinian prisoners, most of whom are detained by Israel without due process, did likewise through brave hunger strikes. As David

Heap, a leading Gaza flotilla activist, told me, these efforts are inspiring larger forces to intervene on the side of the Palestinian people and to realize that fundamental rights like freedom of movement matter to everyone. But without the imagination of activists, these breakthroughs cannot happen. We use our activist imagination — what Robin Kelley calls "poetic knowledge" — to get there.

Debates about *organization* are crucial for today's activists. As this book makes plain, emerging forms of dissent have made considerable inroads by experimenting with new methods, and have enlivened political debate in doing so. We have even seen moments where these experiments have inspired breakthroughs in social movements, unions, and political parties, suggesting new potentials for resistance in cynical times.

Still, it is one thing to note the inroads made by protest movements, and quite another to address more complicated questions around activist organization. In both theory and practice, an understandable breadth of opinion exists about *how* activists seek to change the world. Here, in the last pages of this book, I review three influential views on activist organization: autonomism (a variant of anarchism), "pedagogical space" activism (in the World Social Forum movement), and what I call participatory radicalism (a term meant to capture recurring practices in many protest movements). Of these three, I end with an endorsement of participatory radicalism, but I stress that we need to evaluate all our choices with open minds and tuned ears.

Autonomism is a perspective on organization associated with anarchist currents. At the core of this perspective is an insistence on the autonomy of each activist and his or her ideas, and the necessity for movements to create spaces outside of formal politics. Marina Sitrin, an intellectual deeply rooted in the Occupy movement, has used the Spanish conception of *horizontalidad* ("horizontalism")[18]; activists build intentional (typically, temporary) communities without resorting to hierarchical decision-making structures or detailed policy manifestos. Autonomist forms of organization build communities where activists participate as they see fit. You can think of it as a setting a large table, and inviting contributions to an activist buffet.

As we saw in chapter one, the April 20–22, 2001, anti-FTAA demonstrations in Quebec City demonstrated autonomism in practice. There, protest organizers announced a "diversity of tactics" for demonstrations. Red, yellow, and green zones were designed to suit different protest tactics, with red being the most confrontational. Activists coming to Quebec City committed to not criticize each other's tactics in the mainstream press, and organized themselves in affinity groups of like-minded people committed to similar strategies.

However, problems emerged when police were unwilling to respect the agreements activists had arranged in advance. In Quebec City, brutal repression was meted out to protesters in all three zones, creating fierce debate between activists. Things were different in Seattle. An act of radical spontaneity by thousands of trade unionists caught security forces off guard. It was one thing to repress young people with nose piercings and lemon-soaked bandanas, engaged in direct action; such violence by the state, sadly, was expected and tolerable to mainstream opinion. The sight of longshoreworkers, steelworkers, and teamsters filling the streets in solidarity made matters more difficult; the Democratic Party elite was unwilling to repress the entire group. In this respect, the diversity of protest actors and strength in numbers formed a counterweight to the repressive objectives of the US state. Such solidarity in activist organization was the key to success in Seattle, but it has rarely been sought by advocates of autonomism since. Instead, they have emphasized "autonomy" for all groups (and not accountability of activists to the larger movement), and affinity-based organizing among those who already agree on finer points of principle. Such a framework places little importance on creating groups accessible to wider participation, and therefore isolates activists from others who may sympathize with them.

Occupy was a step in a more helpful direction, where encampments became living examples of direct democracy, activists sought alliances with organized labour and other social justice groups, and spirited debate helped shape the movement's next steps. It was a shining moment of autonomist horizontalism that inspired the ranks of the existing Left and raised important debates in wider society. But the intensity of Occupy activism, and the demands of life in the encampments, meant that most could not participate meaningfully unless they were unemployed or students. The movement's relative isolation meant it could eventually be policed, repressed, and dismantled by the state.

A related problem has been apparent for organizers of the World Social Forum (WSF) process who, like autonomists, have been averse to formal organizations for activist work. The Porto Alegre Charter — a founding document of the WSF events — explicitly forbids "political party representations" in conference proceedings, a position that has been defended on the grounds that it prevents the WSF being made into a "deliberative body." To date, as William Fisher and Thomas Ponniah make plain, the WSF has been presented instead as a "pedagogical space" for activists to learn from each other:

> Many activists talk about the World Social Forum as if it were a new political agent. It is not an agent, but is instead a pedagogical space and political space that enables learning, networking, and political organizing.
>
> The organizers of the World Social Forum have discouraged any interpretation of it as a deliberative body. They have focussed instead on the Forum as a pedagogical space for activists to learn what alternatives are being proposed and enacted around the world.[19]

On the surface, the case for "pedagogical spaces" seems to describe an inclusive practice, but it has encountered problems as the WSF process has unfolded. It is one thing to insist activists learn from each other, but quite another to duck questions of organization entirely. The WSF process itself is led by influential intellectuals from Brazil and France who belong to groups inclined to social democratic ideas. As a consequence, the WSF leadership promotes a certain political direction on the one hand, while urging against recognition of political parties on the other. So it was that the January 2005 WSF could be marked by three major events: first, a speech given by Brazilian President Lula da Silva to over a hundred and twenty thousand people about his ruling party's "war on poverty" (as it expelled party critics and satisfied the demands of the International Monetary Fund); second, an address by Venezuelan President Hugo Chávez to a comparably sized audience where (clad in a red Che Guevara T-shirt) he denounced US imperialism and neoliberal economics; and third, a concluding "Assembly of Social Movements" that called for global protests against war in Iraq for March 19, 2005. All of these events indicate the breadth of opinion around questions of ideas and organization. Still, befitting the philosophy of "pedagogical space" activism, time for large-scale, genuine debate was sparse. The WSF process must address this concern or risk sacrificing the inroads it has made in fostering solidarity among social movements. A good start would be to revise the ban on "party representations" in WSF events, which has not been respected in practice. Once this is done, debates around activist organization can begin, either on the basis of networked campaigns or of global demonstrations. This shift involves recognizing that the global minority tuned in to the WSF process must organize itself seriously, and communicate its ideas to people beyond the activist core.

Without question, the popularity of autonomism and "pedagogical space" activism has created both opportunities and challenges. Above all, progressives need to seek wider participation in their work if they hope to be successful. They need, to paraphrase Québec Solidaire's Françoise David, to exit the margins and appeal to billions. On this point, socialist movements of the early twentieth century offer important lessons, for they raise the necessity for activists to be both inclusive and organized in their appeals for support. In 1918, Antonio Gramsci made this point to the Italian Communist Party. His remarks are worth remembering for those keen on building effective organizations today:

> *Participation of the masses in the activity and internal life of the party ... has been seen as a danger to the unity and centralism of the party. The party has not been seen as a result of a dialectical process in which the spontaneous movement of the revolutionary masses and the organizing and directing will of the centre converge.*
>
> *It has been seen merely as something suspended in the air; something with is own autonomous and self-generated development; something which the masses will join when the situation is right and the crest of the revolutionary wave is at its highest point or when the party centre decides to initiate an offensive and stoops to the level of the masses in order to arouse them and lead them into action.*[20]

Here is the Gramsci most have not discovered. Against those who preached top-down leadership by the vanguard, Gramsci maintained that progressive organizations required an engaged and politicized membership base. Rosa Luxemburg made a similar argument in her debates with socialists inclined to public speaking over grassroots organizing. At the core of both visions was the need for participatory radicalism, where activists broaden the appeal of their activism through a democratic organization. With this foundation in place, activists would then search out progressive alliances required for transformative change, and inspire others to join them.

The key question, and it remains open to substantial interpretation, is whether participatory radicalism is possible, and what steps must be taken to move forward on this historic task. With all that we know from the activist events, movements, and thinkers of the past two centuries, can we expect progressives to participate in larger movements with open minds? Or are egos more likely to dominate with narrow agendas? Can a diversity of progressives come to work together, even if their differences on some subjects remain significant?

Some will say those who ask these questions are bound to fail. A reading of history, however, suggests the search for participatory radicalism is a time-honoured tradition that has brought tangible gains many take for granted today. In their rejection of neoliberalism and embrace of the grassroots, today's activists remind others that hope for a better future is not a naive fantasy. It starts with welcoming newcomers into movement work and urging them to take on leadership roles. It continues by searching out the alliances capable of presenting a challenge to our rulers, and researching the contributions of those who built activist projects in earlier eras. It requires making the energy of grassroots activism more than a zeal shared by a committed minority, and appealing for broad participation.

In all of these things, it means building the capacities of activists to create the world we deserve. And, despite persistent rumours otherwise, there are signs that suggest the path that can take us there. We must pay attention to those signs. And so, on that note, I offer this book's final words to someone else — Arundhati Roy, the talented Indian writer and activist who has said much the same thing:

> Our strategy should be not only to confront empire, but to lay siege to it.
>
> To deprive it of oxygen. To shame it. To mock it. With our art, our music, our literature, our stubbornness, our joy, our brilliance, our sheer relentlessness — and our ability to tell our own stories. Stories that are different from the ones we're being brainwashed to believe.
>
> The corporate revolution will collapse if we refuse to buy what they are selling — their ideas, their version of history,

*their wars, their weapons, their notion of inevitability.*

    *Remember this: We be many and they be few. They need us more than we need them.*

    *Another world is not only possible, she is on her way. On a quiet day, I can hear her breathing.*[21]

# ACKNOWLEDGEMENTS

This book was inspired by activists engaged in projects of social transformation. So many people have shaped its contents, but there are some I want to name as a tribute to their contributions. First, I want to thank Bethany Smith and James Burmeister for helping me continue on my activist path, and for being brave voices of peace in the face of intolerance. I also want to thank Rachel Corrie (may she rest in peace), Tim DeChristopher, Michael Moore, Cornel West, Carne Ross, Arundhati Roy, Jack Layton, Malalai Joya, Naomi Klein, and Amy Goodman, whose work inspired me to write, even in weary moments.

I was fortunate to get comments on this manuscript from Govind Rao, Andrea Harden, Adam Davidson-Harden, Alan Zuege, Barb Byers, Svend Robinson, David Heap, and Maureen O'Reilly. I was very lucky to interview an array of activists who helped shape this project's narrative: Maude Barlow, Jaggi Singh, Clayton Thomas-Mueller, Vandana Shiva, Penny McCall Howard, Lee Sustar, Joshua Brown, Jonathon Hodge, Brigitte DePape, Ritch Whyman, Starhawk, Alex Hanna, Martin Lukacs, Benoît Renaud, and Sid Lacombe. The wonderful photographic skills of Sima Sahar Zerehi , Mathieu Breton, and Marty Two Bulls give life to the book by revealing the movements it celebrates.

Strong thanks are also due to Cy Strom, my editor, for his thoughtful comments and hard work on this manuscript as it came together; I extend a similar gratitude to Jim Lorimer, my publisher, for supporting this project. But, above all, I end here with heartfelt thanks to Clare Roscoe, my life partner, for her love and support as these words were written. Any errors that remain in the book, of course, are mine alone.

# ENDNOTES

## PREFACE:

1    Quoted in Maria Popova, "Why I Write: George Orwell on an Author's Four Main Motives," *The Atlantic* (June 25, 2012), www.atlantic.com.

2    Jessica Strawser, "Alice Walker Offers Advice on Writing", *Readers Digest* (August 31, 2010), www.writersdigest.com.

## INTRODUCTION

1    Carne Ross, *The Leaderless Revolution: How Ordinary People Will Take Power and Change Politics in the 21st Century* (London: Blue Rider Press, 2011), xvi-xvii.

2    "Neoliberalism" and "global capitalism" are terms that may be foreign to some readers. Both appear to be academic jargon, but they are important as a way to grasp the aims and characteristics of adversaries of progressive movements, and what emerging forms of political activism are attempting to transform.

"Neoliberalism" (a Latin term that can be directly translated as "new liberalism") is a right-wing philosophy that espouses the primacy of individual choice, and a minimal role for government in our society. Neoliberalism was first devised by thinkers like Ayn Rand (1964), Milton Friedman (1962), and Friedrich Hayek (1944) in the decades after the Second World War, at a time when traditional liberalism was more dominant — notably in the work of British economist John Maynard Keynes.

The traditional liberalism Keynes represents was informed by the Great Depression and protest movements of the 1930s, and it laid the intellectual foundations for public health care, unemployment insurance, and other income security programs. Neoliberalism, in contrast, has called for removal of these and other related programs, believing they thwart private-sector innovation and individual entrepreneurship. In my own work, I often refer to neoliberalism as "the fend for yourself" doctrine for those unaware of this history. Since the late 1970s, neoliberalism has eclipsed Keynesianism as the philosophy that informs corporate and government decision-makers.

"Global capitalism" is the socio-economic system that has steadily grown worldwide since the Industrial Revolution of the late eighteenth and nineteenth centuries. It has several key features: the dominance of wage-based employment (something foreign to earlier agricultural societies), the accumulation of financial surplus by owners who employ workers, and the investment of this surplus to facilitate never-ending production (often leading to crises of overproduction). Readers keen on learning more about the evolution of global capitalism (and its current neoliberal phase) are encouraged to read Leo Panitch and Sam Gindin (2012), Jim Stanford (2008), Naomi Klein (2007), and David Harvey (2005).

3    I explore the contributions of Social Movement Theory and other movement thinkers in chapter five.

## CHAPTER 1

1    Quoted in Eduardo Galleano, "Guerilla Chronicle," in Tom Hayden (ed.), *The Zapatista Reader* (New York: Nation Books, 2002).

2    Naomi Klein, *Fences and Windows: Dispatches from the Front Lines of the Globalization Debate* (Toronto: Vintage Canada, 2002), 216.

3    Quoted in Paul Kingsnorth, *One No, Many Yeses: A Journey into the Heart of the Global Resistance Movement* (London: Free Press, 2003), 30.

4    Quoted in Notes from Nowhere (eds.), *We Are Everywhere: The Irresistible Rise of Global Anti-Capitalism* (London: Verso, 2004), 23–24.

5    Kingsnorth, *One No, Many Yeses,* 30.

6    Ibid., 24.

7    Maude Barlow, "The MAI and the Threat to Canadian Sovereignty," public lecture (Vancouver, BC, January 28, 1998).

8    Quoted in Naomi Klein, *No Logo: Taking Aim at the Brand Bullies* (Toronto: Vintage, 2000), 443.

9    Notes from Nowhere, *We Are Everywhere,* 92.

10   Jeffrey St. Clair and Allan Sekula (eds.), *Five Days that Shook the World: Seattle and Beyond* (London: Verso, 2000), 28.

11   John Charlton, "Talking Seattle," *International Socialism* 2:86 (Spring 2000), 9.

12   Charlie Kimber, "Taking on the Rule of Money," *Socialist Worker* (UK Version, December 11, 1999).

13   Sam Gindin, "Anti-Capitalism and the Terrain of Social Justice," *Monthly Review* 53:9 (February 2002).

14   "The Case for Globalization," *The Economist* (September 21, 2000).

15   Canadian Security Intelligence Service (CSIS), "Anti-Globalization: A Spreading Phenomenon" (August 22, 2000), www.csis-scrs.gc.ca.

16   Naomi Klein, "Farewell to the End of History: Organization and Vision in Anti-Corporate Movements," *A World of Contradictions: Socialist Register 2002* (London: Merlin Press, 2001).

17   Susan George, "What Now?" *International Socialism* 2:91 (Summer 2001), 12.

18   Chalmers Johnson, *Blowback: The Costs and Consequences of American Empire* (New York: Henry Holt Publishers, 2000), 9.

19   Quoted in Autumn Leonard et al., "Organizing After September 11," *Dollars and Sense* (April 2002), www.thirdworldtraveller.com.

20   Quoted in Teofilo Reyes, "Will the Drive to War Kill International Solidarity?" *Labour Notes* (October 2001).

21   Oxfam, "Rigged Rules and Double Standards: Trade, Globalization, and the Fight Against Poverty" (August 2002), 8, www.cbnrm.net/pdf/oxfam_001_tradesummary.pdf.

22   Ibid., 12.

23   Quoted in "On Campus and Off: Anti-war Movements See New Vigor," *Los Angeles Times* (October 28, 2001).

24   Starhawk, interview with the author (Calgary, June 25, 2002).

25   Sid Lacombe, interview with the author (Toronto, June 21, 2005).

26   Quoted in Mark LeVine, "Egypt: The Revolution That Shame Built," *Al-Jazeera* (January 25, 2012).

27   Quoted in Amy Goodman, "From Tahrir to Wall Street: Egyptian Revolutionary Asmaa Mahfouz Speaks at Occupy Wall Street," *Democracy Now!* (October 25, 2011), www.democracynow.org.

28   See Doug Singsen and Sarah Pomar, "What Bloombergville Achieved," *Socialist Worker* (July 25, 2011), www.socialistworker.org; and New York City Educator, "Welcome to Bloombergville" (June 18, 2011), http://nyceducator.com/2011/06/welcome-to-bloombergville.html.

29   Judy Rebick, *Occupy This!* (Toronto: Penguin, 2012).

30   Quoted in Amy Goodman, "Something Has Started: Michael Moore on the Occupy Wall Street Protests." *Democracy Now!* (September 28, 2011), www.democracynow.org.

31   Quoted in Goodman, "From Tahrir to Wall Street."

32   Quoted in Adele Pham, "Occupy the Hood, Occupy Wall Street," *MR Zine* (October 10, 2011), www.mrzine.monthyreview.org.

# CHAPTER 2

1   Jonathan Swift, *Gulliver's Travels* (London: Jones and Company, 1826), 5.

2   A. A. Milne, *The House at Pooh Corner* (London: Dramatic Publishing Company, 1966), 51.

3   Quoted in Amy Goodman, "Now Is Our Time to Take a Stand: Tim DeChristopher's Message to Youth Climate Activists at Power Shift 2011" (April 22, 2011), www.democracynow.org.

4   Bill McKibben, "Global Warming's Terrifying New Math," *Rolling Stone* (July 19, 2012), www.rollingstone.com.

5   Greenpeace International, "Copenhagen a Cop-out: A Shameful Failure to Save Us from the Effects of Climate Change" (December 19, 2009), www.greenpeace.org.

6   Cameron Fenton and Amara Possian, "Shift Disturbers: Youth-Led Strategies for Climate Justice Victory," *Our Schools, Our Selves* 21:107 (Spring 2012), 115–16.

7   Quoted in Goodman, "Now Is Our Time to Take a Stand."

8   Quoted in "Trumka Says Labour Wants Keystone Built, Believes Green Issues Can Be Resolved," *The Hill* (May 6, 2012), www.thehill.com.

9   Quoted in Indigenous Environmental Network (IEN), "IEN Responds to Draft Keystone XL Supplemental EIS" (March 6, 2013), www.ienearth.org.

10   Marie Adam, "Statement for 'Stop the Tar Sands' Campaign," *Greenpeace,* May 7, 2009, www.greenpeace.org.

11   Jackie Thomas, "Speech to the 'Forward on Climate' March," Washington, DC, (February 18, 2013), www.rabble.ca.

12   Sylvia McAdam, "Idle No More Is Not about 'Us' Versus 'Them'" (January 22, 2013), www.facebook.com/sheelah.mclean/posts/526317674065756.

13   Dru Oja Jay, "What If Natives Stop Subsidizing Canada?" *The Dominion* (January 8, 2013), www.dominionpaper.ca.

14   Government of Canada, "Hope or Heartbreak: Aboriginal Youth and Canada's Future," *Horizons: Policy Research Initiative* 10:1 (March 2008).

15   Pam Palmater, "Idle No More: What Do We Want and Where Are We Headed?" (January 4, 2013), www.rabble.ca.

16   Quoted in Suzanne Fournier, "Idle No More's Energizers," *The Tyee* (January 12, 2013), www.thetyee.ca.

17   Kirsten Scansen, "Indigenous Sovereignty and Human Rights: Idle No More as a Decolonizing Force," *Decolonization: Indigeneity, Education and Society* (December 12, 2012), www.decolonization.wordpress.com.

18   Ibid.

19   Devon Meekis, "Face and Leaders of Idle No More Are the Grassroots People" (January 3, 2013), www.idlenomore.ca.

20   Quoted in Palmater, "Idle No More: What Do We Want and Where Are We Headed?"

21   Bill McKibben, "Idle No More — Think Occupy, but with Deep, Deep Roots," (January 10, 2013), www.huffingtonpost.com.

22   Quoted in "PM Harper Believes Idle No More Movement Creating a 'Negative Public Reaction', Say Confidential Notes," *APTN News* (January 25, 2013), www.aptn.ca.

23   Ibid.

24   Ibid.

25   Quoted in Jesse Staniforth, "The Struggle for Unity: The First Nations Summit with Prime Minister Harper Sparks a Painful Debate Between Native Leaders and an Energized Grassroots Movement," *Nation* (January 25, 2013), www.nationnews.ca.

26   Quoted in Joel Davison Harden, "When Crisis Becomes Opportunity: Progressive Organizing after Bill C-377," *Rabble* (February 1, 2013), www.rabble.ca.

27   Ibid.

28   Emad Burnat, Remarks prior to screening of *Five Broken Cameras*, directed by Emad Burnat and Guy Davidi (Ottawa, November 9, 2012).

29   Rachel Corrie, "Rachel's Emails from Palestine," *Rachel Corrie Foundation for Peace and Justice* (September 28, 2003), www.rachelcorriefoundation.org.

30   Palestinian Red Crescent Society, "Table of Figures: Poverty" (July 7, 2002), www.palestinercs.org.

31   Desmond Tutu, "Apartheid in the Holy Land," *The Guardian*, (April 29, 2002), www.theguardian.co.uk.

32   Quoted in Canadian Union of Public Employees (British Columbia), "The Wall Must Fall: End the Occupation and Violence in Israel/Palestine" (Burnaby, BC: CUPE, June 2005).

33   Quoted in "Israel Holds Veteran French Activist José Bové," *BBC* (April 2, 2002).

34   International Solidarity Movement, "About ISM" (December 5, 2004), www.palsolidarity. org.

35   ISM-Canada, "Joining a Future Campaign: Going for the Right Reasons" (June 2005), www.ismcanada.org.

36   Samir Nasrallah, "Message from Dr. Samir Nasrallah," *International Solidarity Movement* (March 25, 2003), www.palsolidarity.org.

37   Quoted in Josie Sandercock et al., *Peace Under Fire: Israel, Palestine, and the International Solidarity Movement* (London: Verso, 2004).

38   Penny McCall-Howard, interview with the author (October 2, 2002).

39   Joshua Brown, interview with the author (October 3, 2002).

40   Quoted in Sandercock, *Peace Under Fire*, xv.

41   Quoted in Nada Elia, "The Brain of the Monster," in Audrea Lim, ed., *The Case for Sanctions Against Israel* (New York: Verso, 2012), 10.

42   Quoted in International Solidarity Movement, "Free Gaza Movement: Free Gaza Boats Arrive in Gaza," *International Solidarity Movement* (August 23, 2008).

43   Quoted by David Heap, interview with the author (February 12, 2013).

# CHAPTER 3

1    Quoted in Edith Fowke and Joe Glazer, eds., *Songs of Work and Protest* (New York: Dover Publications, 1973), 8.

2    Ibid., 9.

3    Stewart Bird, Dan Georgakas, and Deborah Shaffer, eds., *Solidarity Forever: An Oral History of the IWW* (Chicago: Lake View Press, 1985).

4    Quoted in John Allemang, "The Sorry State of Our Unions," *Globe and Mail*, May 2, 2012, www.theglobeandmail.com.

5    Ben Stein, "In Class Warfare, Guess Which Class Is Winning?," *New York Times*, November 26, 2006, www.nytimes.com.

6    Arun Gupta, "The Case Against the Middle Class," *The Indypendent* 163 (April 5, 2011),

www.indypendent.org.

7    André Gorz, *Reclaiming Work: Beyond the Wage-Based Society* (London: Polity Press, 1999), 56.

8    Kim Moody, "Does Size Matter? Strategy and Quality of Leadership Are More Important," *Labour Notes* (February 2003), www.labornotes.org.

9    Dan Clawson, *The Next Upsurge: Labour and New Social Movements* (Ithaca, NY: Cornell University Press, 2003), 46.

10    Sam Gindin, "Globalization and Labour: Defining the 'Problem,'" Address given at Brandeis University, Waltham, MA (April 24, 2004).

11    Clawson, *The Next Upsurge*, 198–99.

12    Talking Heads, "Once in a Lifetime," *The Best of the Talking Heads* (London: Atlantic Records/ATG, 2004).

13    Barb Byers, *Presentation to CLC Pension Activism Town Hall* (Ottawa, October 12, 2009).

14    Len Wallace, "Oral remarks made to the Department of Finance, Government of Canada, on 'Federal Regulation of Private Pension Plans'" (Ottawa, April 16, 2009).

15    Art Kube, "Oral remarks made to the Department of Finance, Government of Canada, on 'Federal Regulation of Private Pension Plans'" (Vancouver, April 12, 2009).

16    Jacquie McNish et al. "Beyond the Illusion of Security," *Globe and Mail*, (October 16, 2009), www.theglobeandmail.com.

17    Stephen Chase, "Parties Square Off on Federal Pension Reform: Liberals Vow They Would Take a More Activist Role and Expand CPP, Tories Warn of Spiraling Costs," *Globe and Mail*, (October 27, 2009), www.theglobeandmail.com.

18    Bob Baldwin, *Research Study on the Canadian Retirement Income System, prepared for the Ministry of Finance, Government of Ontario* (October 2009), 76–78, www.fin.gov.on.ca/en/consultations/pension/dec09report.html.

19    Quoted in Heather Scoffield, "Cut Standard of Living Now for Comfortable Pension Later: Dodge," *Canadian Press*, (November 17, 2010).

20    Quoted in Bill Curry, "Flaherty Pushes for Expanded CPP," *Globe and Mail*, (June 13, 2010), www.theglobeandmail.com.

21    Quoted in Heather Scoffield, "PRPP: Ottawa Launches New Pooled Registered Pension Plans to Boost Retirement Savings," *Canadian Press*, (November 17, 2010).

22    Joel Davison Harden, "Unions Learn From Defeat of Anti-Scab Bill", *Relay 17* (May/June 2008).

23    Quoted in Jody Sokolower, "Lessons in Social Justice Unionism: An Interview with Chicago Teachers Union President Karen Lewis," *Rethinking Schools* 27:2 (Winter 2012–13), www.rethinkingschools.org.

24    Jackson Potter, Remarks to "Lessons from the Chicago Teachers Strike," organized by Solidarity: A Socialist, Feminist, Anti-racist Organization (Chicago, October 4, 2012), www.solidarity-us.org.

25    Ibid.

26    Jen Johnson, Remarks to "Lessons from the Chicago Teachers Strike," organized by Solidarity: A Socialist, Feminist, Anti-racist Organization (Chicago, October 4, 2012), www.solidarity-us.org.

27    Quoted in Lee Sustar, "A New Day in the Chicago Teachers Union," *Socialist Worker*, (June 14, 2010), www.socialistworker.org.

28    Ibid.

29    Estelle Amaron, written Submission to the "My Favourite Librarian" Appeal, Toronto Public Library Workers Union (CUPE 4948) (September, 2011), www.ourpubliclibrary.to.

30    Sue-Ann Levy, "Ford Moves to Contract Out Trash Collection," *Toronto Sun*, (February 6, 2011), www.torontosun.com.

31    Stephen Kupferman, "How the Urban Affairs Library Got Shut Down," *Torontoist*, (March 4, 2011), www.torontoist.com.

32    Maureen O'Reilly, interview with the author (February 20, 2013).

33    John Bonnar, "Workers Protest Planned Closure of Urban Affairs Library," *Rabble* (February 24, 2011), www.rabble.ca.

34    John Michael McGrath, "Recent Fact-Checking Spree Reveals No, Etobicoke Doesn't Have More Libraries Than Timmies, Contra Doug Ford," *Toronto Life* (July 21, 2011), www.torontolife.com.

35    Paul Maloney, "Doughnuts vs Books? In Ford's Etobicoke, It's 3-1," *Toronto Star*, (July 20, 2011), www.thestar.com.

36    David Rider, "Margaret Atwood Fights Library Cuts, Crashes Petition Server," *Toronto Star*, (July 22, 2011), www.thestar.com.

37    O'Reilly, interview with the author.

38    Daniel Dale and David Rider, "Ford Unswayed by 22 Hours of Talk, Teen's Tears," *Toronto Star*, (July 30, 2011), www.thestar.com.

39    O'Reilly, interview with the author.

40    Elizabeth Church and Patrick White, "Report Proposes $17 Million in Cuts for Libraries," *Globe and Mail*, (October 13, 2011), www.theglobeandmail.com.

41    O'Reilly, interview with the author.

42    Natalie Samson, "Toronto Public Library Board Balks at 10 Per Cent Budget Cut," *Quill and Quire* (December 13, 2011).

43    O'Reilly, interview with the author.

44    Marci McDonald, "The Wierdest Mayoralty Ever: The Inside Story of Rob Ford's City Hall," *Toronto Life* (May 15, 2012), www.torontolife.com.

45    Jonathan Hodge, interview with the author (Ottawa, February 22, 2013).

46    Jamie Bradburn, "Rally Round the Library Workers," *Torontoist*, (March 14, 2012), www.torontoist.com.

47    Ibid.

48    Hodge, interview with the author.

# CHAPTER 4

1    Kurt Nimmo, "Emma Goldman for President," *Counterpunch* (March 22, 2004), www.counterpunch.org.

2    Quoted by Maude Barlow, interview with the author (June 13, 2003).

3    Jane Doe, "Jack of Our Hearts," in *Hope Is Better Than Fear: Paying Jack Layton Forward* (Toronto: Random House, 2013).

4    Quoted in James L. Turk and Chris Wahl, *Love, Hope, Optimism: An Informal Portrait of Jack Layton by Those Who Knew Him* (Toronto: Lorimer, 2012), 232.

5    Quoted in Michel Lessard, "In Quebec City, Important Speech by Malalai Joya, Afghan MP" (September 26, 2006), www.archives-2001-2012.cmaq.net.

6    Brian Topp, *How We Almost Gave the Tories the Boot: The Inside Story Behind the Coalition* (Toronto: Lorimer, 2010), 213.

7    Mike DeSouza, "Video: NDP Deputy Leader Faces Backlash over Israel Comments," *National Post*, (June 14, 2010), www.nationalpost.com.

8    Ibid.

9    Quoted in ibid.

10   Jack Layton, "Re: Show Harper the Door," e-mail message to the author (January 1, 2011).

11   Murray Cooke and Dennis Pilon, "Left Turn in Canada? The NDP Breakthrough and the Future of Canadian Politics" (New York: Rosa Luxemburg Stiftung, October 2012). www.rosalux-nyc.org.

12   Amir Khadir, "Quebec and Québec Solidaire: Linking Sovereignty, Equality, and anti-Neoliberalism," Phyllis Clarke Memorial Lecture (Ryerson University, Toronto, March 29, 2013), www.northstar.info.

13   Omar Aktouf et al., "Manifeste pour un Québec Solidaire" (November 1, 2005), www.pourunquébecsolidaire.org.

14   François Saillant and Francois Cyr, "Compte Rendu de la Deuxième Rencontre de Négociations entre l'UFP et Option Citoyenne" (January 20, 2005), www.optioncitoyenne.ca.

15   Union des Forces Progressistes and Option Citoyenne, "Statement of Principles" (February 3, 2005), www.canadiandimension.mb.ca.

16   "Twinkling" is a form of silent applause that has become quite popular in activist meetings and events. It involves raising one's hands and fluttering the fingers to indicate support for an intervention; it is less disruptive than clapping hands and is inclusive of those with hearing impairments.

17   Ahmir Khadir, interview with the author (Montreal, February 4, 2006).

18   Quoted in Norman Delisle, "Québec Solidaire Sort de la Marginalité," La Presse (February 5, 2006), www.cyberpresse.ca.

19   Ibid.

20   Quoted in Benoît Renaud, interview with the author (March 10, 2013).

21   Quoted in Jean-Herman Guay, "Débat des Chefs : La Gauche A un Nouveau Visage," La Presse (August 20, 2012), www.lapresse.ca.

22   Barack Hussein Obama, "Concession Speech" (New Hampshire, January 8, 2008), www.nytimes.com.

23   Quoted in Serge Kovaleski, "Obama's Organizing Years, Guiding Others and Finding Himself," New York Times (July 7, 2008), www.nytimes.com.

24   Barack Hussein Obama, Dreams from My Father: A Story of Race and Inheritance (New York: Times Books, 1995).

25   Ibid., 74.

26   National Public Radio, "Transcript: Obama's Speech Against the Iraq War" (January 20, 2009), www.npr.org.

27   Barack Hussein Obama, "Keynote Speech to the 2004 Democratic National Convention" (Boston, July 27, 2004), www.washingtonpost.com.

28   Susan (surname withheld), Remarks During "Camp Obama" Training Session (Burbank, CA, August 10–12, 2007), http://campobama.blogspot.ca.

29   Virginia (surname withheld), Remarks During Camp Obama Training Session (Burbank, CA, August 10–12, 2007), http://campobama.blogspot.ca.

30   Obama, "Concession Speech."

31   Peter Dreier, "Will Obama Inspire a New Generation of Organizers?" Dissent (July 3, 2007), www.dissentmagazine.org.

32   Marshall Ganz, "Organizing Obama: Campaign, Organizing, Movement," Presentation to the American Sociological Association Annual Meeting (San Francisco, August 2009), http://marshallganz.usmblogs.com/files/2012/08/Organizing-Obama-Final.pdf.

33   Barack Hussein Obama, *The Audacity of Hope: Thoughts on Reclaiming the American Dream* (New York: Random House, 2006), 52.

34   Marshall Ganz, "How Obama Lost His Voice, and How He Can Get It Back," *Los Angeles Times* (November 3, 2010), www.latimes.com.

35   Van Jones, *Rebuild the Dream* (New York: Nation Books, 2012), 47.

36   Quoted in Matt Schneider, "Wild Shoutfest Between Al Sharpton and Cornel West on Obama and Race" (April 11, 2011), www.mediaite.com.

37   Quoted in ibid.

38   Quoted in Hal Draper, *The Two Souls of Socialism* (London: Bookmarks, 1996), 24.

39   Rolling Stones, "Salt of the Earth," *Beggars Banquet* (London: ABKCO, 1968).

# CHAPTER 5

1   Frederick Douglass, *Two Speeches by Frederick Douglass* (Ithaca: Cornell University Library, 1857), 12.

2   David Graeber, "The New Anarchists," *New Left Review* 13 (January/February 2002), www.newleftreview.org.

3   Margaret Keck and Kathryn Sikkink, *Activists Beyond Borders: Advocacy Networks in International Politics* (Ithaca, NY: Cornell University Press, 1998), 30.

4   Ibid., 214.

5   Sidney Tarrow, *The New Transnational Activism* (Cambridge, MA: Cambridge University Press, 2005), 30.

6   Ibid., 25.

7   Sidney Tarrow, *Strangers at the Gates: Movements and States in Contentious Politics* (Cambridge, MA: Cambridge University Press, 2012), 2.

8   Ibid., 3.

9   Dennis Bevington and Chris Dixon, "Movement-Relevant Theory: Rethinking Social Movement Scholarship and Activism," *Social Movement Studies* 4:3 (December 2005).

10   Janet M. Conway, *Identity, Place, Knowledge: Social Movements Contesting Globalization* (Black Point, NS: Fernwood Publishing, 2004), 11–12.

11   Michael Hardt and Antonio Negri, *Multitude: War and Democracy in the Age of Empire* (New York: Penguin Press, 2004), xiii–xiv, 355.

12   Ibid., 357.

13   Ibid., 335.

14   Ibid., xvi.

15   Ibid.

16   Richard J.F. Day, *Gramsci Is Dead: Anarchist Currents in the Newest Social Movements* (Toronto: Between the Lines Press, 2005), 13–16.

17   Ibid., 65–69.

18   Ibid., 19.

19   Ibid., 4.

20   Ibid., 186.

21   Ibid., 33–34.

22   Robin D.G. Kelley, *Freedom Dreams: The Black Radical Imagination* (Boston: Beacon Press, 2002), 11–12.

23   Bevington and Dixon, "Movement-Relevant Theory," 190.

24   Sam Gindin, "Anti-Capitalism and the Terrain of Social Justice," *Monthly Review* 53:9 (February 2002), www.monthlyreview.org.

25   Naomi Klein, *Fences and Windows: Dispatches from the Front Lines of the Globalization Debate* (Toronto: Vintage Canada, 2002), xxv.

26   Émile Durkheim, *The Elementary Forms of Religious Life*, trans. Joseph Ward Swain (New York: Free Press, 1971), 217.

27   Rosa Luxemburg, *The Mass Strike* (London: Bookmarks, 1989).

28   Katherine Ainger, "Trade Wars: The Battle in Seattle," *Red Pepper* (December 1999).

29   Greg Albo, "Neoliberalism, the State and the Left," *Canadian Dimension* 36:2 (March/April 2002), www.canadiandimension.com.

30   Jo Freeman, "The Tyranny of Structurelessness," in Yves Frémion (ed.), *An Anarcha-Feminist Reader* (Los Angeles: AK Press, 2002).

# CHAPTER 6

1   Quoted in Julian Temple, *Joe Strummer: The Future is Unwritten, directed by Julian Temple* (London: Parallel Film Productions, 2007).

2   In the previous chapter, I cited Robin Kelley's use of the term "poetic knowledge", a term he uses to describe the new knowledge and practices that arrive with emerging forms of political activism. It is worth noting, however, that Kelley's use of this term borrows from the writings of Aimé Césaire. Readers are strongly encouraged to delve into Kelley's *Freedom Dreams: The Black Radical Imagination* (2002) for insights on this subject and others.

3   Quoted in "Moore Fires Oscar Anti-war Salvo," *BBC News* (March 24, 2003), www.news.bbc.co.uk.

4   Quoted in Irwin Silber, "Fahrenheit 9/11 and Michael Moore," *Zmag* 19:9 (September 2004).

5   Christopher Hitchens, "Unfahrenheit 9/11: The Lies of Michael Moore," *Slate* (June 21, 2004), http://slate.msn.com.

6   Christopher Dols, "Bombing Madison: Michael Moore's Fright Show," *Counterpunch* (October 20, 2004), www.counterpunch.org.

7   Michael Moore, "Michael Moore to Wesley Clark: Run!" (September 12, 2003), www.michaelmoore.com.

8   Christopher Dols, "Bombing Madison."

9   Quoted in John Laughland, "Man of the Moment: John Kerry," *Sanders Research* (March 8, 2004), www.sandersresearch.com.

10   Quoted in Alex Callinicos, "The No's Have It," *Socialist Review* 298 (July 2005).

11   Quoted in Vittorio de Filippis and Christian Losson, "Oui, Pour Faire Disparaître Cette Merde d'Etat-Nation," *Libération* (May 13, 2005), www.liberation.fr.

12   Quoted in ibid.

13   Quoted in ibid.

14   Quoted in ibid.

15   Quoted in Abbie Bakan, "Marxism, Oppression and Liberation," *Marxism: A Better World is Necessary* 1 (Toronto: Resistance Press, 2003), 19.

16   Nancy Fraser and Axel Honneth, *Redistribution or Recognition: A Political-Philosophical Exchange* (London: Verso, 2003).

17   Albert Einstein, *Cosmic Religion: With Other Opinions and Aphorisms*, rev. ed. (London: Dover Publications, 2009), 52.

18   Marina Sitrin, "Horizontalism and the Occupy Movements," *Dissent* (Spring 2012).

19   William F. Fisher and Thomas Ponniah (eds.), *Another World Is Possible: Popular Alternatives to Globalization at the World Social Forum* (London: Zed Books, 2003), 30.

20   Antonio Gramsci, *Political Writings* 1919–1926, ed. and trans. Quintin Hoare (London: Lawrence and Wishart, 1978), 176.

21   Arundhati Roy, "Confronting Empire," *Znet* (January 28, 2003), www.zcommunications.org.

# BIBLIOGRAPHY

350.org. "What is 350?" March 2013. www.350.org.

Aboriginal Affairs and Northern Development Canada. *People to People, Nation to Nation: Report of the Royal Commission on Aboriginal Peoples.* Ottawa: Government of Canada, 1996.

Adam, Marie. "Statement for Stop the Tar Sands Campaign." *Greenpeace* (May 7, 2009). www.greenpeace.org.

Ainger, Katherine. "Trade Wars: The Battle in Seattle." *Red Pepper* (December 1999).

Aktouf, Omar et al. "Manifeste pour un Québec Solidaire." November 1, 2005. www.pourunquébecsolidaire.org.

Albo, Greg. "Neoliberalism, the State and the Left." *Canadian Dimension* 36:2 (March/April 2002).

Alinksy, Saul. *Rules for Radicals: A Pragmatic Primer for Realistic Radicals.* New York: Vintage Books, 1971.

Allemang, John. "The Sorry State of Our Unions." *Globe and Mail,* May 2, 2012. www.theglobeandmail.com.

Amaron, Estelle. Written Submission to the "My Favourite Librarian" Appeal, Toronto Public Library Workers Union (CUPE 4948). September 2011. www.ourpubliclibrary.to/favourite-librarians.

Bakan, Abbie. "Marxism, Oppression and Liberation." *Marxism: A Better World Is Necessary* 1. Toronto: Resistance Press, 2003.

Balakrishnan, Gopal, ed. *Debating Empire.* London: Verso, 2003.

Baldwin, Bob. *Research Study on the Canadian Retirement Income System.* Prepared for the Ministry of Finance, Government of Ontario. October 2009. www.fin.gov.on.ca/en/consultations/pension/dec09report.html.

"Bali Principles of Environmental Justice." August 29, 2002. www.ejnet.org/ej/bali.pdf.

Barlow, Maude. "The MAI and the Threat to Canadian Sovereignty." Public lecture, Vancouver, BC. January 28, 1998.

Bevington, Dennis, and Chris Dixon. "Movement-Relevant Theory: Rethinking Social Movement Scholarship and Activism." *Social Movement Studies* 4:3 (December 2005).

Bird, Stewart, Dan Georgakas, and Deborah Shaffer, eds. *Solidarity Forever: An Oral History of the IWW.* Chicago: Lake View Press, 1985.

Bonnar, John. "Workers Protest Planned Closure of Urban Affairs Library." *Rabble* (February 24, 2011). www.rabble.ca.

Bouchard, Lucien, et al. "Pour un Québec Lucide." October 20, 2005. www.pourunQuébeclucide.com.

Bradburn, Jamie. "Rally Round the Library Workers." *Torontoist,* March 14, 2012. www.torontoist.com.

Brogan, Peter. "How the Chicago Teachers Fought and Won." *Rabble* (September 28, 2012). www.rabble.ca.

Burnat, Emad. Remarks prior to screening of *Five Broken Cameras,* directed by Emad Burnat and Guy Davidi. Ottawa, November 9, 2012.

Byers, Barb. Presentation to CLC Pension Activism Town Hall. Ottawa, October 12, 2009.

Callinicos, Alex. "The No's Have It." *Socialist Review* 298 (July 2005).

Canadian Security Intelligence Service (CSIS). "Anti-Globalization: A Spreading Phenomenon." August 22, 2000. www.csis-scrs.gc.ca.

Canadian Union of Public Employees (British Columbia). "The Wall Must Fall: End the Occupation and Violence in Israel/Palestine." Burnaby, BC: CUPE, June 2005.

Charlton, John. "Talking Seattle." *International Socialism* 2:86 (Spring 2000).

Chase, Stephen. "Parties Square Off on Federal Pension Reform: Liberals Vow They Would Take a More Activist Role and Expand CPP, Tories Warn of Spiraling Costs." *Globe and Mail,* October 27, 2009. www.theglobeandmail.com.

Chicago Teachers Union. *The Schools Chicago's Students Deserve: Research-Based Proposals to Strengthen Elementary and Secondary Education in the Chicago Public Schools.* Chicago: CTU, 2012. www.ctunet.com.

Chicago Teachers Union. *The Black and White of Education in Chicago's Public Schools: Class, Charters, and Chaos.* Chicago: CTU, 2012. www.ctunet.com.

Church, Elizabeth, and Patrick White. "Report Proposes $17 Million in Cuts for Libraries." *Globe and Mail*, October 13, 2011. www.theglobeandmail.com.

Clawson, Dan. *The Next Upsurge: Labour and New Social Movements*. Ithaca, NY: Cornell University Press, 2003.

Conway, Janet M. *Identity, Place, Knowledge: Social Movements Contesting Globalization*. Halifax, NS: Fernwood Publishing, 2004.

Cooke, Murray, and Dennis Pilon. "Left Turn in Canada? The NDP Breakthrough and the Future of Canadian Politics." New York: Rosa Luxemburg Stiftung, October 2012. www.rosalux-nyc.org.

Corrie, Rachel. "Rachel's Emails from Palestine." *Rachel Corrie Foundation for Peace and Justice*. September 28, 2003. www.rachelcorriefoundation.org.

David, Françoise. *Bien Commun Recherché: Une Option Citoyenne*. Quebec: Écosociété, 2004.

Day, Richard J.F. *Gramsci Is Dead: Anarchist Currents in the Newest Social Movements*. Toronto: Between the Lines Press, 2005.

de Filippis, Vittorio, and Christian Losson. "Oui, Pour Faire Disparaître Cette Merde d'État-Nation." Libération, May 13, 2005. www.liberation.fr.

Delisle, Norman. "Québec Solidaire Sort de la Marginalité." *La Presse*, February 5, 2006. www.cyberpresse.ca.

DeSouza, Mike. "Video: NDP Deputy Leader Faces Backlash Over Israel Comments." *National Post*, June 14, 2010. www.nationalpost.com.

Doe, Jane. "Jack of Our Hearts." In *Hope Is Better Than Fear: Paying Jack Layton Forward*. Toronto: Random House, 2013.

Dols, Christopher. "Bombing Madison: Michael Moore's Fright Show." *Counterpunch* (October 20, 2004). www.counterpunch.org.

Douglass, Frederick. *Two Speeches by Frederick Douglass*. Ithaca: Cornell University Library, 1857.

Draper, Hal. *The Two Souls of Socialism*. London: Bookmarks 1996.

Dreier, Peter. "Will Obama Inspire a New Generation of Organizers?" *Dissent* (July 3, 2007). www.dissentmagazine.org.

Durkheim, Émile. *The Elementary Forms of Religious Life*, trans. Joseph Ward Swain. New York: Free Press, 1971.

Einstein, Albert. *Cosmic Religion: With Other Opinions and Aphorisms*, rev. ed. London: Dover Publications, 2009.

Elia, Nada. "The Brain of the Monster." In Audrea Lim, ed., *The Case for Sanctions Against Israel*. New York: Verso, 2012.

Fenton, Cameron, and Amara Possian. "Shift Disturbers: Youth-Led Strategies for Climate Justice Victory." *Our Schools, Our Selves* 21:107 (Spring 2012).

Fisher, William F., and Thomas Ponniah, eds. *Another World Is Possible: Popular Alternatives to Globalization at the World Social Forum*. London: Zed Books, 2003.

Fournier, Suzanne. "Idle No More's Energizers." *The Tyee* (January 12, 2013). www.thetyee.ca.

Fowke, Edith, and Joe Glazer, eds. *Songs of Work and Protest*. New York: Dover Publications, 1973.

Fraser, Nancy, and Axel Honneth. *Redistribution or Recognition: A Political-Philosophical Exchange*. London: Verso, 2003.

Freeman, Jo. "The Tyranny of Structurelessness." In Yves Frémion, ed., *An Anarcha-Feminist Reader*. Los Angeles: AK Press, 2002.

Friedman, Milton. *Capitalism and Freedom*, 4th ed. Chicago: University of Chicago Press, 1962.

Galleano, Eduardo. "Guerilla Chronicle." In Tom Hayden, ed., *The Zapatista Reader*. New York: Nation Books, 2002.

Ganz, Marshall. "How Obama Lost His Voice, and How He Can Get It Back." *Los Angeles Times*, November 3, 2010. www.latimes.com.

Ganz, Marshall. "Organizing Obama: Campaign, Organizing, Movement." Presentation to the American Sociological Association Annual Meeting. San Francisco, August 2009. http://marshallganz.usmblogs.com/files/2012/08/Organizing-Obama-Final.pdf.

Ganz, Marshall. "The Power of Story in Social Movements." Presentation to the American Sociological Association Annual Meeting. Anaheim, CA, August 2001. www.hks.harvard.edu/organizing/tools/Files/MG%20POWER%20OF%20STORY.pdf.

Gindin, Sam. "Anti-Capitalism and the Terrain of Social Justice." *Monthly Review* 53:9 (February 2002).

Gindin, Sam. "Globalization and Labour: Defining the 'Problem.'" Address given at Brandeis

University, Waltham, MA, April 24, 2004.

George, Susan. "What Now?" *International Socialism* 2:91 (Summer 2001).

Goodman, Amy. "Now Is Our Time to Take a Stand: Tim DeChristopher's Message to Youth Climate Activists at Power Shift 2011." April 22, 2011. www.democracynow.org.

Goodman, Amy. "Something Has Started: Michael Moore on the Occupy Wall Street Protests." *Democracy Now!* September 28, 2011. www.democracynow.org.

Goodman, Amy. "From Tahrir to Wall Street: Egyptian Revolutionary Asmaa Mahfouz Speaks at Occupy Wall Street." *Democracy Now!* October 25, 2011. www.democracynow.org.

Gorz, André. *Reclaiming Work: Beyond the Wage-Based Society.* London: Polity Press, 1999.

Government of Canada. "Hope or Heartbreak: Aboriginal Youth and Canada's Future." *Horizons: Policy Research Initiative* 10:1 (March 2008).

Graeber, David. "The New Anarchists." *New Left Review* 13 (January/February 2002). www.newleftreview.org.

Gramsci, Antonio. *Political Writings 1919–1926*, ed. and trans. Quintin Hoare. London: Lawrence and Wishart, 1978.

Greenpeace International. "Copenhagen a Cop-out: A Shameful Failure to Save Us from the Effects of Climate Change." December 19, 2009. www.greenpeace.org.

Guay, Jean-Herman. "Débat des Chefs: La Gauche A un Nouveau Visage." *La Presse*, August 20, 2012. www.lapresse.ca.

Gupta, Arun. "The Case Against the Middle Class." *The Indypendent* 163 (April 5, 2011). www.indypendent.org.

Harden, Joel Davison. "A New Kind of Independence in Quebec." *Rabble* (April 10, 2007).

Harden, Joel Davison. "Unions Learn From Defeat of Anti-Scab Bill", *Relay* (May/June 2007).

Harden, Joel Davison. "Effective Union Organizing: How It's Done." *Socialist Studies* 9:1 (Summer 2013).

Harden, Joel Davison. "Pondering Powershift 2012: What's Up with Canada's Blue-Green Alliance?" *Our Times: Canada's Independent Labour Magazine* (November 2012).

Harden, Joel Davison. "Young Radicals Challenge Veterans on the Left." *Canadian Dimension* (July/August 2001).

Harden, Joel Davison. "When Crisis Becomes Opportunity: Progressive Organizing after Bill C-377." *Rabble* (February 1, 2013).

Hardt, Michael, and Antonio Negri. *Empire.* Cambridge, MA: Harvard University Press, 2000.

Hardt, Michael, and Antonio Negri. *Multitude: War and Democracy in the Age of Empire.* New York: Penguin Press, 2004.

Harvey, David. *A Brief History of Neoliberalism.* London: Oxford University Press, 2005.

Hayek, Friedrich. *The Road to Serfdom.* London: Routledge, 1944.

Heron, Craig. *The Canadian Labour Movement: A Short History,* 3rd ed. Toronto: Lorimer, 2010.

Hitchens, Christopher. "Unfahrenheit 9/11: The Lies of Michael Moore." *Slate* (June 21, 2004). http://slate.msn.com.

Indigenous Environmental Network (IEN). "IEN Responds to Draft Keystone XL Supplemental EIS." March 6, 2013. www.ienearth.org.

International Solidarity Movement. "About ISM." December 5, 2004. www.palsolidarity.org.

International Solidarity Movement. "Free Gaza Movement: Free Gaza Boats Arrive in Gaza." August 23, 2008. www.palsolidarity.org.

ISM-Canada. "Joining a Future Campaign: Going for the Right Reasons." June 2005. www.ismcanada.org.

"Israel Holds Veteran French Activist José Bové." *BBC*, April 2, 2002.

Jay, Dru Oja. "What If Natives Stop Subsidizing Canada?" *The Dominion* (January 8, 2013). www.dominionpaper.ca.

Johnson, Chalmers. *Blowback: The Costs and Consequences of American Empire.* New York: Henry Holt Publishers, 2000.

Johnson, Jen. Remarks to "Lessons from the Chicago Teachers Strike" organized by *Solidarity: a Socialist, Feminist, Anti-racist Organization.* Chicago: October 4, 2012. www.solidarity-us.org.

Jones, Van. *Rebuild the Dream.* New York: Nation Books, 2012.

Keck, Margaret, and Kathryn Sikkink. *Activists Beyond Borders: Advocacy Networks in International Politics.* Ithaca, NY: Cornell University Press, 1998.

Kelley, Robin D.G. *Freedom Dreams: The Black Radical Imagination.* Boston: Beacon Press, 2002.

Khadir, Amir. "Quebec and Québec Solidaire: Linking Sovereignty, Equality, and anti-Neoliberalism." Phyllis Clarke Memorial Lecture. Ryerson University, Toronto, March 29, 2013. www.northstar.info.

Kimber, Charlie. "Taking On the Rule of Money." *Socialist Worker* UK Edition, December 11, 1999.

Kingsnorth, Paul. *One No, Many Yeses: A Journey into the Heart of the Global Resistance Movement.* London: Free Press, 2003.

Klein, Naomi. "Farewell to the End of History: Organization and Vision in Anti-corporate Movements." In *A World of Contradictions: Socialist Register 2002.* London: Merlin Press, 2001.

Klein, Naomi. *Fences and Windows: Dispatches from the Front Lines of the Globalization Debate.* Toronto: Vintage Canada, 2002.

Klein, Naomi. *No Logo: Taking Aim at the Brand Bullies.* Toronto: Vintage, 2000.

Klein, Naomi. *The Shock Doctrine: The Rise of Disaster Capitalism.* New York: Henry Holt and Company, 2007.

Kovaleski, Serge. "Obama's Organizing Years, Guiding Others and Finding Himself." *New York Times,* July 7, 2008. www.nytimes.com.

Kube, Art. "Oral remarks made to the Department of Finance, Government of Canada, on 'Federal Regulation of Private Pension Plans.'" Vancouver, BC, April 12, 2009.

Kupferman, Stephen. "How the Urban Affairs Library Got Shut Down." *Torontoist,* March 4, 2011. www.torontoist.com.

Laughland, John. "Man of the Moment: John Kerry." *Sanders Research.* March 8, 2004. www.sandersresearch.com.

Leonard, Autumn, et al. "Organizing After September 11." *Dollars and Sense* (April 2002). www.thirdworldtraveller.com/dissent.

Lessard, Michael. "In Quebec City, Important Speech by Malalai Joya, Afghan MP." September 26, 2006. www.archives-2001-2012.cmaq.net.

LeVine, Mark. "Egypt: The Revolution That Shame Built." *Al-Jazeera,* January 25, 2012. www.aljazeera.com.

Levy, Sue-Ann. "Ford Moves to Contract Out Trash Collection." *Toronto Sun.* February 6, 2011. www.torontosun.com.

Luxemburg, Rosa. *The Mass Strike.* London: Bookmarks, 1989.

Maloney, Paul. "Doughnuts vs Books? In Ford's Etobicoke, it's 3-1." *Toronto Star,* July 20, 2011. www.thestar.com.

McAdam, Sylvia. "Idle No More Is Not about 'Us' Versus 'Them.'" January 22, 2013. www.facebook.com/sheelah.mclean/posts/526317674065756.

McDonald, Marci. "The Wierdest Mayoralty Ever: The Inside Story of Rob Ford's City Hall." *Toronto Life* (May 15, 2012). www.torontolife.com.

McGrath, John Michael. "Recent Fact-Checking Spree Reveals No, Etobicoke Doesn't Have More Libraries Than Timmies, Contra Doug Ford." *Toronto Life* (July 21, 2011). www.torontolife.com.

McKibben, Bill. "Global Warming's Terrifying New Math." *Rolling Stone* (July 19, 2012). www.rollingstone.com.

McKibben, Bill. "Idle No More — Think Occupy, but with Deep, Deep Roots." January 10, 2013. www.huffingtonpost.com.

Meekis, Devon. "Face and Leaders of Idle No More Are the Grassroots People." January 3, 2013. www.idlenomore.ca.

Milne. A. A. *The House at Pooh Corner.* London: Dramatic Publishing Company, 1966.

McNally, David. *Another World is Possible: Globalization and Anti-Capitalism.* Winnipeg: Arbeiter Ring Publishing, 2006.

McNish, Jacquie, et al. "Beyond the Illusion of Security." *Globe and Mail,* October 16, 2009. www.theglobeandmail.com.

Moody, Kim. "Does Size Matter? Strategy and Quality of Leadership Are More Important." *Labour Notes* (February 2003). www.labornotes.org.

"Moore Fires Oscar Anti-war Salvo." *BBC News,* March 24, 2003. www.news.bbc.co.uk.

Moore, Michael. "Michael Moore to Wesley Clark: Run!" September 12, 2003. www.michaelmoore.com.

Nasrallah, Samir. "Message from Dr. Samir Nasrallah." *International Solidarity Movement.* March 25, 2003, www.palsolidarity.org.

National Automobile, Aerospace, Transportation and General Workers Union of Canada, (CAW-Canada) *CAW Taskforce on Working Class Politics in the Twenty-First Century*. Toronto: CAW, 2001.

National Public Radio. "Transcript: Obama's Speech Against the Iraq War." January 20, 2009. www.npr.org.

"New Left-Wing Party Starts in Quebec." February 5, 2006. www.cbc.ca.

New York City Educator. "Welcome to Bloombergville." June 18, 2011. http://nyceducator .com/2011/06/welcome-to-bloombergville.html.

Nimmo, Kurt. "Emma Goldman for President." *Counterpunch* (March 22, 2004). www.counterpunch.org.

Notes from Nowhere. *We Are Everywhere: The Irresistible Rise of Global Anti-Capitalism*. London: Verso, 2004.

Obama, Barack Hussein. *The Audacity of Hope: Thoughts on Reclaiming the American Dream*. New York: Random House, 2006.

Obama, Barack Hussein. "Concession Speech." New Hampshire, January 8, 2008. www.nytimes.com.

Obama, Barack Hussein. *Dreams from My Father: A Story of Race and Inheritance*. New York: Times Books, 1995.

Obama, Barack Hussein. "Keynote Speech to the 2004 Democratic National Convention." Boston, July 27, 2004. www.washingtonpost.com.

"On Campus and Off: Anti-war Movements See New Vigor." *Los Angeles Times*, October 28, 2001.

Oxfam. "Rigged Rules and Double Standards: Trade, Globalization, and the Fight Against Poverty." August, 2002. www.cbnrm.net/pdf/oxfam_001_tradesummary.pdf.

Palmater, Pam. "Idle No More: What Do We Want and Where Are We Headed?" January 4, 2013. www.rabble.ca.

Palestinian Red Crescent Society. "Table of Figures: Poverty." July 7, 2002. www.palestinercs.org.

Panitch, Leo V. and Sam Gindin. *The Making of Global Capitalism: The Political Economy of American Empire*. London: Verso, 2012.

Pham, Adele. "Occupy the Hood, Occupy Wall Street." *MR Zine* (October 10, 2011). www.mrzine.monthyreview.com.

"PM Harper Believes Idle No More Movement Creating a 'Negative Public Reaction,' Say Confidential Notes." *APTN News*, January 25, 2013. www.aptn.ca.

Popova, Maria. "Why I Write: George Orwell on an Author's Four Main Motives." *The Atlantic* (June 25, 2012). www.atlantic.com.

Potter, Jackson. Remarks to "Lessons from the Chicago Teachers Strike" organized by *Solidarity: a Socialist, Feminist, Anti-racist Organization*. Chicago, October 4, 2012. www.solidarity-us.org.

Rand, Ayn. *The Virtue of Selfishness: A New Concept of Egoism*. New York: Signet, 1964.

Rebick, Judy. *Occupy This!* Toronto: Penguin, 2012.

Renaud, Benoît. "A Chronology of Solidarity and Militancy: How the Québec Students Won." *Socialist Worker* 446 (Canadian version, April 6, 2005).

Reyes, Teofilo. "Will the Drive to War Kill International Solidarity?" *Labour Notes* (October 2001).

Rider, David. "Margaret Atwood Fights Library Cuts, Crashes Petition Server." *Toronto Star*, July 22, 2011. www.thestar.com.

Ross, Carne. *The Leaderless Revolution: How Ordinary People Will Take Power and Change Politics in the 21st Century*. London: Blue Rider Press, 2011.

Roy, Arundhati. *An Ordinary Person's Guide to Empire*. Cambridge, MA: South End Press, 2004.

Roy, Arundhati. "Confronting Empire." *Znet* (January 28, 2003). www.zcommunications.org.

Saillant, François, and Francois Cyr. "Compte Rendu de la Deuxième Rencontre de Négociations entre l'UFP et Option Citoyenne." January 20, 2005. www.optioncitoyenne.ca.

Samson, Natalie. "Toronto Public Library Board Balks at 10 Per Cent Budget Cut." *Quill and Quire* (December 13, 2011).

Sandercock, Josie, et al. *Peace under Fire: Israel, Palestine, and the International Solidarity Movement*. London: Verso, 2004.

Scansen, Kirsten. "Indigenous Sovereignty and Human Rights: Idle No More As a Decolonizing Force." *Decolonization: Indigeneity, Education and Society* (December 12, 2012).

Schneider, Matt. "Wild Shoutfest Between Al Sharpton and Cornel West on Obama and Race." April 11, 2011. www.mediaite.com.

Scoffield, Heather. "Cut Standard of Living Now for Comfortable Pension Later: Dodge." *Canadian Press*, November 17, 2010. www.capebretonpost.com.

Shiva, Vandana. Interview by Author. Washington D.C.: April 20, 2000.

Silber, Irwin. "Fahrenheit 9/11 and Michael Moore." *Zmag* 19:9 (September 2004).

Silver, Beverly. *Forces of Labour: Workers and Globalization Since 1870*. London: Cambridge University Press, 2003.

Singer, David. "Don't Be Duped Again: Why Workers Should Reject 'Anybody but Bush.'" *Gloves Off: Bare-Fisted Political Economy*. August 2004. www.glovesoff.org.

Singsen, Doug, and Sarah Pomar. "What Bloombergville Achieved." *Socialist Worker*. July 25, 2011. www.socialistworker.org.

Sitrin, Marina. "Horizontalism and the Occupy Movements." *Dissent* (Spring 2012).

Sokolower, Jody. "Lessons in Social Justice Unionism: An Interview with Chicago Teachers Union President Karen Lewis." *Rethinking Schools* 27:2 (Winter 2012–13). www.rethinkingschools.org.

St. Clair, Jeffrey, and Allan Sekula, eds. *Five Days That Shook the World: Seattle and Beyond*. London: Verso, 2000.

Staniforth, Jesse. "The Struggle for Unity: The First Nations Summit with Prime Minister Harper Sparks a Painful Debate Between Native Leaders and an Energized Grassroots Movement." *Nation* (January 25, 2013). www.nationnews.ca.

Stanford, Jim. *Economics for Everyone: A Short Guide to the Economics of Capitalism* (Pluto Press: 2008).

Stein, Ben. "In Class Warfare, Guess Which Class Is Winning?" *New York Times*, November 26, 2006. www.nytimes.com.

Strawser, Jessica. "Alice Walker Offers Advice on Writing." *Readers Digest* (August 31, 2010). www.writersdigest.com.

Sustar, Lee. "A New Day in the Chicago Teachers Union." *Socialist Worker*, June 14, 2010. www.socialistworker.org.

Swift, Jonathan. *Gulliver's Travels*. London: Jones and Company, 1826.

Tarrow, Sidney. *Strangers at the Gates: Movements and States in Contentious Politics*. Cambridge, MA: Cambridge University Press, 2012.

Tarrow, Sidney. *The New Transnational Activism*. Cambridge, MA: Cambridge University Press, 2005.

"The Case for Globalization." *The Economist* (September 21, 2000). www.economist.com.

Thomas, Jackie. "Speech to the 'Forward on Climate' March," Washington, DC, February 18, 2013. www.rabble.ca.

Topp, Brian. *How We Almost Gave the Tories the Boot: The Inside Story Behind the Coalition*. Toronto: Lorimer, 2010.

Touraine, Alain. *The Voice and the Eye: An Analysis of Social Movements*. Cambridge: Cambridge University Press, 1981.

"Trumka says Labour Wants Keystone Built, Believes Green Issues Can Be Resolved." *The Hill* (May 6, 2012). www.thehill.com.

Turk, James L., and Charis Wahl. *Love, Hope, Optimism: An Informal Portrait of Jack Layton by Those Who Knew Him*. Toronto: Lorimer, 2012.

Tutu, Desmond. "Apartheid in the Holy Land." *The Guardian*, April 29, 2002.

Union des Forces Progressistes and Option Citoyenne. "Statement of Principles." February 3, 2005. www.canadiandimension.mb.ca.

Wallace, Len. "Oral remarks made to the Department of Finance, Government of Canada, on 'Federal Regulation of Private Pension Plans.'" Ottawa, April 16, 2009.

# INDEX